IWO JIMA

Richard F. Newcomb

This is a detailed history of the greatest amphibious assault ever launched, where, in the words of Fleet Admiral Nimitz, "uncommon valor was a common virtue." Iwo Jima was a vital step on the path to Japan in WW II and the Japanese were determined to hold out to the last man. Interwoven with the factual account of the Marine victory are individual stories and recollections, both from the words and letters of combatants of both sides. The author, a long-time newspaperman, was a war correspondent and an editor with Associated Press.

IWO JIMA

Richard F. Newcomb

This is a detailed history of the greatest amphibious assault ever launched, where, in the words of Fleet Admiral Nimitz, "uncommon valor was a common virtue." Iwo Jima was a vital step on the path to Japan in WW II and the Japanese were determined to hold out to the last man. Interwoven with the factual account of the Marine victory are individual stories and recollections, both from the words and letters of combatants of both sides. The author, a long-time newspaperman, was a war correspondent and an editor with Associated Press.

LARGE PRINT BOOKS
by Richard F. Newcomb

Abandon Ship!

Iwo Jima

Savo

IWO JIMA

RICHARD F. NEWCOMB

John Curley & Associates, Inc.

South Yarmouth, Ma.

Library of Congress Cataloging in Publication Data
Newcomb, Richard F
  Iwo Jima.

  Large print ed.
  1. Iwo Jima, Battle of, 1945. 2. Large type
books. I. Title.
[D767.99.I9N4 1980]   940.54'26   79-28470
ISBN 0-89340-257-5

Published in Large Print by arrangement with Richard F. Newcomb.

Distributed in the U.K. and Commonwealth by Magna Print Books.

Printed in Great Britain

TO THE MEN OF

THE FIFTH AMPHIBIOUS CORPS,

THE DEAD AND THE LIVING

Author's Note

As do most professions, the military has its own specialized technical language. The civilian often finds this obscure or confusing, and I have avoided such usage where possible. A few notes may be helpful in getting over the remaining hurdles.

The Marines are organized in units, ranging upward in size as follows: the squad, platoon, company, battalion, regiment, division, and corps. In general, three squads make a platoon, three platoons a company, three companies a battalion, three battalions a regiment, three regiments a division, and more than one division a corps.

In this campaign, the Marines used three divisions (minus one regiment) organized as the Fifth Amphibious Corps, abbreviated as VAC. For most of the campaign the divisions and regiments were disposed as follows:

	Fifth Division	Third Division	Fourth Division	
W e s t C o a s t	26th, 27th, and 28th Regiments	9th and 21st Regiments	23rd, 24th, and 25th Regiments	E a s t C o a s t
	Gen. Keller E. Rockey	Gen. Graves B. Erskine	Gen. Clifton B. Cates	

(N ↑ indicating North, West Coast on left, East Coast on right)

To avoid lengthy repetition in unit identification, the Marine abbreviation system is used. For example, 1/25 means 1st Battalion, 25th Regiment; 3/9 means 3rd Battalion, 9th Regiment. If division identification is important, it is written 1/25/4 and 3/9/3.

Gun sizes are used by both sides in a welter of inches, milimeters, and centimeters. As a gauge, 75 millimeters equal approximately 3 inches, 155 millimeters about 6 inches.

It will be obvious that I have had the help of a great many persons in gathering the information for this book. It would not be practical to list them all here, but I would like them to know that their friendship and assistance is appreciated. The help of a few has been so outstanding that I must mention them. Fred Saito of Tokyo, an old friend and fine author in his own right, provided invaluable assistance in locating and interviewing Japanese sources concerning Iwo Jima, and in finding many of the photographs. John H. Marley, archivist in Marine headquarters, was most efficient and gracious in helping me in the Marine records. Henry I. Shaw, Jr., senior historian of the Marines' World War II historical project, read the manuscript and made valued corrections and suggestions. To all of them, and to many others, my sincere thanks.

I am indebted to Jack Elcik for the endpapers and maps.

RICHARD F. NEWCOMB

FOREWORD

The assault on Iwo Jima has been called the classical amphibious operation of recorded history. The capture of Iwo was considered vital to the war effort in the Pacific by no less an authority than General Marshall. In view of the character of the defenses it was fortunate that less seasoned or less resolute troops were not used, said Admiral Spruance. Admiral Nimitz remarked that uncommon valor was a common virtue on Iwo.

The largest force of Marines ever committed to action captured the island after thirty-six days of bitter fighting. Although the supporting forces of all services contributed magnificently to the final victory, it was the Marine combat teams that had to close with the enemy and destroy him.

It was a high honor to command such troops.

H. SCHMIDT,
General U.S. Marine Corps, Retired

Contents

IWO JIMA

Part One

SULPHUR ISLAND

Chapter 1

General Kuribayashi was not alarmed by his first view of Iwo Jima. True, there was much barren ground, but it was June and there were fringes of green on the slopes of Suribachi.

Tuft grass and bean vines had been planted on the sandy saddle of land between Suribachi and the plateau in the north. There were some trees, and off to the east of Motoyama there was even an oak forest. Fumes from sulphur springs were heavy over the village, but nearly a hundred children stood outside the little school, waving flags to greet him.

Some pandanus and sugarcane had been planted in swales, and near the houses in the village the vegetable gardens looked green and fresh. There were patches of lemon grass, which the villagers distilled for lemon oil, and of derris elliptica, from which they made rotenone. Now and then, a bird sang, and the General was fond of both birds and children. A little north and west of the village were a small sugar refinery and vats for the recovery of sulphur. (The sulphur obtained from the island, of course, accounted for the name Iwo Jima, or Sulphur Island.)

The island was near the southern end of the Nanpo Shoto, a chain of islands hanging down from Japan like the beard of a mandarin. Iwo Jima was one of the Volcano Islands and was, in fact, made up of the twin cones of a volcano that had arisen from the sea. At the southern end of the island, the cone of Suribachi thrust nearly straight up to a height of 550 feet. The mass of rock, gray and black and brown, could be seen from many miles at sea, long before the rest of the island came in view. The volcano had been dead for many years, and a few footpaths led to the top, which was not flat, but hollowed out like a deep dish. The word suribachi was a common one in Japan, in this context meaning cone-shaped mountain.

When there was no mist around the rim, the rest of the island could be seen from the top, stretching nearly 5 miles to the north. At the base was a narrow neck of land, mostly coarse sand, black along the east beaches and yellow on the west. Along the east, the land rose steeply from the water, in a series of terraces, to about a hundred feet, but on the west beaches the slopes were gentler and the sea shallower.

The neck of land widened gradually for more than a mile north from the base of Suribachi and then flared out, mostly to the east, so that the island was about 2½ miles wide in the center and approximately 5 miles long. All this northern part of the island, forming about two-thirds of the area, was high ground, a rocky plateau nearly 300 feet above the sea. The middle of the island was fairly level, with occasional hills, the highest rising to 382 feet.

Motoyama, the largest village, stood

over the second volcano, in which the fires still burned. Sulphur bubbled to the surface here and there, giving off noxious fumes, and the ground was hot in many places. The ground fell slightly toward the coasts, then sharply to the beaches in steep cliffs a hundred feet or more in height. Altogether, the island was less than 8 square miles in area.

General Kuribayashi was not long distracted by thoughts of birds and children. He had been sent to defend the island – not to save it but to defend it, to hold it as long as it could be held, and that meant until death. Iwo Jima was part of the empire, only 660 miles from Tokyo and an actual part of the Prefecture of Tokyo. Located on a line straight north from the Marianas, almost exactly halfway between Saipan and Tokyo, it was the first part of the empire to be threatened by the enemy.

The General was aware of this even before he was called to the office of the premier, General Hideki Tojo, late in May, 1944. Kuribayashi had been in

Tokyo nearly a year, after three years in Manchuria and China. But he did not think of Iwo Jima when Tojo summoned him, because he had heard that another general was to be sent there.

Tojo had said to him: "Only you among all the generals are qualified and capable of holding this post." Kuribayashi's face remained solemn. He and Tojo had often quarreled over policy. Perhaps the rumor was true that the other general had talked himself out of the Iwo Jima assignment. At any rate, it was now to be Kuribayashi's, and Tojo said: "The entire Army and the nation will depend upon you for the defense of that key island."

Kuribayashi replied, very seriously, that he was honored to be chosen.

Kuribayashi left home on June 10. He did not take with him the sword that had been in his family for generations, nor did he take the sabre that the Emperor had given him in 1923 when he graduated from the Staff College, second in his class. He said nothing to his

7

wife and children, but he wrote to his brother, in fine, bold brush strokes:

"I may not return alive from this assignment, but let me assure you that I shall fight to the best of my ability, so that no disgrace will be brought upon our family. I will fight as a son of Kuribayashi, the Samurai, and will behave in such a manner as to deserve the name of Kuribayashi. May ancestors guide me."

He came ashore at the East Boat Landing, under the shadow of high cliffs, and strode up the dusty road into Motoyama to meet Rear Admiral Teiichi Matsunaga. The Admiral, who had arrived only a few days before to take command of all naval forces on the island, was primarily an airman. His 22nd Bomber Group had sunk the British battleships Prince of Wales and the Repulse early in the war, and he had brought with him the Hachiman Unit of pilots, named for a Japanese war god. The Admiral's thoughts were on the skies, and on his stomach, which was already troubled by the bad drinking water on the island.

Kuribayashi was soon appalled by the state of the island's defenses. There seemed to be no plan nor even any firm command. Captain Tsunezo Wachi of the Navy had been island commander since February, and Colonel Kanehiko Atsuchi commanded the Army forces. But there was little cooperation among these groups. The airmen considered themselves elite and kept apart, the Navy ground forces were unhappy at being assigned to what was essentially Army duty, and the Army was traditionally sullen at being under naval command.

When Captain Wachi had arrived on Iwo Jima, Chidori (Airfield No. 1) had been in commission nearly a year. It was built as a triangle with three runways, the longest paralleling the east beaches on the neck between Suribachi and the plateau to the north. Wachi's command included 20 patrol planes and 1,400 men, and in March, 600 more Navy men arrived.

Soon Colonel Atsuchi followed with five battalions of soldiers. The Colonel himself was fifty-six, possibly the oldest colonel in the Imperial Army. He was amiable and well liked, but he had never been to staff school, and his last previous post had been in Korea, where there was no fighting. His battalion commanders included an ancient lieutenant colonel, one major, and three captains, two of whom had not even gone to the Military Academy.

In March, 1944, Lieutenant General Eiryo Obata, Commanding General of the 31st Army, came up from Saipan. He was only a year older than the Colonel – they had been classmates at the academy. Obata was furious to find that artillery was being placed on the high ground in the north. This contradicted the doctrine that invasions must be met at the beach.

"These guns are useless," he said. "The enemy can only land on the beach. Take all the guns down there and build pill-boxes."

General Obata returned to Saipan, and the men who had pulled the guns up to high ground with the strength of their backs began to move them down again.

That was in March, and now it was nearly July. The Allies had landed in Normandy, crushing German defenses that were among the most powerful ever constructed. The American Marines and the Army were lodged on Saipan, beginning the reduction of the Marianas, Japan's strongest bastion. It was clear to Kuribayashi that no beach defenses could hold against the Americans. He ordered the artillery dragged back to the north, or hidden in the foot of Suribachi.

It was his first order, and both the Army and the Navy opposed it. They could not see, as Kuribayashi did, that the time had come to break with tradition. He could not spend all his strength at the beach if he were to hold the island for the longest possible time. He must conserve his resources in Suribachi and in the north, paying them

11

out as slowly as the enemy allowed him to.

General Kuribayashi was as strong as the rock on which he stood. He did not rescind his order.

The General was fifty-three years old, and very tall for a Japanese, nearly 5 feet 9 inches. He weighed 200 pounds and had the unmistakable potbelly of the samurai. That belly, as Tokyo Radio later blared, was "packed full of strong fighting spirit."

In service for thirty years, Kuribayashi had served all over the world. In 1928, as a thirty-seven-year-old captain, he went to Washington as deputy military attaché, and for two years traveled throughout the country. He was surprised at his friendly reception, and his weekly letters to his wife, Yoshii, were chatty and full of good humor. In each one were little drawings or cartoons for his son, Taro, who could not yet read. Kuribayashi spent some time in Buffalo and sketched a picture of his landlady for the boy: "This big, tattooed lady tidies Daddy's room. She is bigger than a sumo wrestler. She is a kind woman, and it is good for Daddy to practice English conversation with her."

When Kuribayashi left Fort Bliss after studying cavalry training, Brigadier General George V. H. Mosely gave him a portrait of himself, inscribing it: "With high regard and esteem. I shall never forget our happy association together in America. Best wishes to you and to Japan."

Kuribayashi returned to Japan for a short reunion with Yoshii, who resented the fact that Japan could not afford to send her with her husband, as other countries did. But in 1931 he was sent to Ottawa as military attaché. Again he had the opportunity to see America, and he wrote to Yoshii: "The United States is the last country in the world that Japan should fight. Its industrial potentiality is huge and fabulous, and the people are energetic and versatile. One must never underestimate the American's fighting ability."

His views had never changed, and in this summer of 1944 he began to prepare for the American attack with full appreciation of what was ahead. Imperial General Headquarters had decided that he would have the 109th Division, based then at Chichi Jima (Father Island), 140 miles north of Iwo Jima, and such other forces as might become available. These were to increase rapidly, for with the fall of Saipan all troops then preparing for the Marianas would be diverted to Iwo Jima. The first to fall to Kuribayashi was the 145th Infantry Regiment, about 2,700 men under Colonel Masuo Ikeda. The General was fortunate, for these were Kagoshima boys from Kyushu, the home of Japan's best soldiers.

The largest force was the 2nd Mixed Brigade, half of the 109th Division, about 5,000 troops. Kuribayashi ordered the brigade down from Chichi Jima, under Major General Kotau Osuga, and they began arriving in July and August. The brigade was not up to the 145th in quality, but Imperial

General Headquarters was still reluctant to withdraw its crack troops from Manchuria or China.

General Kuribayashi had missed the first U.S. carrier attack on Iwo Jima, which took place the afternoon of June 15. Rear Admiral Joseph J. Clark, with seven carriers (TG 58.1 and 58.4 of Mitscher's force), launched fighters in squally seas from 135 miles east of Iwo Jima. In a slashing attack, 10 Zekes were destroyed in the air and 7 more on the ground, against a loss of 2 American planes. It was over in minutes, but that night a Japanese soldier wrote in his diary: "Somehow my faith in our Navy air groups has been somewhat shaken."

The same day, at Chichi Jima, Clark's planes smashed 21 seaplanes and set fire to three small freighters and a hangar. The next afternoon in very bad weather, Clark sent 54 fighters back to Iwo. No Japanese planes were aloft, but the Americans claimed 63 planes on the ground. The Marines, assaulting Saipan on the fifteenth, had plenty of trouble, but not from planes from Iwo Jima or Chichi Jima. Jocko Clark had taken care of them.

A few days after Kuribayashi arrived, Clark was back at Iwo – his mission to cut off Japanese planes or ships trying to reinforce Saipan. Clark launched 51 Hellcats from south of Iwo on June 24. Halfway to the island, they met the defenders coming out and slaughter followed. Two-thirds of the Japanese pilots were students, and 29 fighter planes (Zekes, Hamps, and Judys) were destroyed. But it was only the beginning. Admiral Matsunaga, who had only been on Iwo for six days, sent off 20 torpedo bombers, and not one returned to Iwo Jima. He sent off a third wave of 41 planes, and only 24 returned. The day cost him 66 planes in all; the Hachiman unit had been cut to pieces. Two weeks later, what was left of it – 41 Zekes and 13 bombers – was sent back to Japan. The Admiral's stomach was very bad by this time, and he went into the hospital.

After the raid of June 24, a soldier wrote in his diary: "Oh, is the Empire out of ships? Out of planes?"

Kuribayashi, after watching the raid, wrote to his youngest daughter, then ten years old. Using a pencil and writing very carefully so that the little girl could read it, he said: "Your father is now having a hard task and may not return. I have indeed nothing to worry about, except about you, Takako. Let me pray that you will grow up fast and in health, so that you will help your mother...."

The raid made Kuribayashi more determined than ever. At Tokyo he had said he would need guns and ships and men "Give them to me and I will hold Iwo." Now it was clear that he would get no ships and no planes. With men and guns he could hold Iwo, but not forever. He was glad he had left his sabre at home.

Kuribayashi began at once to push forward his plan. No attempt must be made to hold the beaches. He would station only automatic weapons and infantry there, holding his main forces in the north and in Suribachi. Once the enemy landed, he would be exposed on the isthmus and could be destroyed by artillery, rockets, and mortars. If they succeeded in advancing northward, Kuribayashi would retreat slowly, exacting the highest possible toll as he withdrew. This was his assignment – to give up the island at the greatest cost to the enemy.

His plan drew instant fire. The Navy officers, particlarly Captain Samaji Inouye, second in command after Admiral Matsunaga, declared it was unthinkable to give up the beaches, and that certainly they could not lose Chidori, the largest field on the island and the only one able to accommodate bombers. After all, the Japanese had studied beach defenses for 80 years. But what about Normandy, Kuribayashi replied, and Saipan, Tinian, and Guam?

Colonel Tadashi Takaishi of the 109th Division staff agreed with Kuribayashi, but the General's chief of staff, Colonel

Shizuichi Hori, opposed the plan. He had once been an instructor at the Military Academy and had a pedant's scorn for the field commander. Inouye and Hori, a strange alliance of Navy and Army, would not be silent, and General Osuga was enlisted on their side.

One night, after a particularly violent quarrel, Kuribayashi told his aide, Major Yoshitaka Horie, that he did not believe he could stomach Hori and Osuga for long. Both sides, of course, had been reporting this battle to their superiors in Tokyo, and Major Horie volunteered to go there with a confidential appeal from Kuribayashi for a complete change in the higher echelons of command.

General Kuribayashi was very depressed. After reviewing his forces, he said to Horie: "These are no soldiers, just poor recruits who don't know anything. Their officers are either fools or superannuated scarecrows. We cannot fight the Americans with them." But for the time being he didn't accept Horie's offer.

On July 3, a naval ammunition dump near the East Boat Basin exploded with a tremendous roar. Rumors spread that an enemy agent was ashore and had set it off. A lieutenant told his men to speak softly near the coast; enemy submarines with listening devices might be lurking offshore.

The next day, planes of the U.S. Army's 28th Photo Reconnaissance Squadron made sixteen passes over the island at less than 2,000 feet. The photographs were so clear that they became the basis of all future Marine planning.

Admiral Clark also came back, to celebrate July 4, and bagged four small ships in the Bonin Islands. No planes rose from Iwo Jima to challenge him, and his destroyers shelled the island from close range. The 6-inch naval guns on Iwo were silent. Admiral Matsunaga had forbidden them to fire and thus reveal their position. By now, the sailors in his fleet were offering memberships in the "Jocko Jima Development Corporation," with deeds to "choice locations of all types in Iwo, Chichi, Haha, and Muko Jima, only 500 miles from downtown Tokyo."

One of Kuribayashi's first decisions was that the civilians must go, and as soon as shipping could be found, they were sent off to Japan. By the end of July, only servicemen and Korean laborers remained. The General decided, too, that the program of tunnel and cave development must be pressed. There were many natural caves on the island, and the ground was excellent for tunneling. The soft volcanic stone could be cut with hand tools. Cave specialists came from Japan to make measurements and ground tests and draw blueprints for fortifications. From experience in China, they knew that good ventilation could be assured if entrances and exits were built at different levels, and they knew how to lay out tunnels to neutralize blast shocks near the openings.

During the summer, the garrison was doubled by the arrival of 7,350 Army troops and 2,300 Navy men. With the latter came a new commander, Rear Admiral Toshinosuke Ichimaru. He arrived on August 4, the same day on which he was appointed. One minute he was commanding the Oi Naval Air Wing, a flight training center near Tokyo, and the next minute he was en route to Iwo Jima to relieve Admiral Matsunaga. It had not happened quite that fast, but it almost seemed so.

Admiral Ichimaru had been a cripple since 1926, when he crashed in an experimental plane. His right leg had been broken and had not healed properly. The deformity made him limp, and he bitterly resented that he was only allowed training commands. To take up his time, he wrote poetry, in both the 31-syllable and 17-syllable styles; he even tried classic Chinese style, comparable to writing in ancient Greek or Latin. His poetry was of high quality, and his calligraphy was exquisite.

When told that at last he was to have a combat assignment, he immediately set down his joy in a poem:

Grateful to His Majesty for giving me
A chance to fight on the foremost front,
I depart with buoyant heart,
Filled with joy and exultation.

In the twilight, the waters of Lake
   Hamana cool,
Sending breezes to fill my garden,
Fragrant with sweet oleanders in full
   bloom.

Let me fall like the flower petals scatter.
May enemy bombs aim at me, and
   enemy shells
Mark me as their target.

I now go and will never return.
Turning my head, I see the majestic
   mountain.
May His Majesty live as long as it.

   The Admiral bid farewell to his wife
and children, and flew immediately to
Iwo Jima, taking his good sword with

him. Matsunaga greeted him warmly; they were old friends from the same province in Kyushu and had been class- mates at the Naval Academy. Ichimaru was surprised to find Matsunaga in good health.

"I heard you were dying," he said. Matsunaga explained that he had been quite ill, probably from the water on the island, but had recovered on a diet of sake. He was embarrassed to confess this and had at first refused to stop drinking water. Finally, the medical officer had said: "Why not? Frenchmen drink only wine." Matsunaga went home to Japan, and Ichimaru took up the only task he wanted – preparing to die for the Emperor.

Water was indeed a serious problem. The island had not a single stream, and the ground was so porous it would not hold water. Around Motoyama, the civilians had dug hundreds of cisterns, carving them from the soft stone at various levels, so that when one filled, it would overflow into the next lower one.

The roofs of the buildings were also piped into the cisterns, to catch the April rains against the dry season. But the cisterns could not supply 20,000 troops, so work parties were set to digging wells and erecting storage tanks. It was an absolute rule that water could be used only for drinking. Near the end of July, a soldier wrote in his diary: "This is a queer place. We catch water when it rains, but still we cannot wash our faces or take baths. All day long it is very hot."

The only bathing allowed was in the sea, or with water carried from the sea. To supplement the drinking supply, an old Scotch marine boiler was set up near the East Boat Basin to distill seawater. A 10,000-gallon concrete tank was built to hold the water, and other tanks were set up around the island. Troops in the north and those assigned to building fortifications inside Suribachi were clever in fashioning condensers to extract water from the steaming fumaroles. These units, of all sizes, consisted basically of a funnel to catch the steam and a condensing tube to cool it into water, which dripped into buckets. There were hundreds of these, and they were to prove invaluable. Only one attempt was made to drill for water, just south of the village of Motoyama. No worse place could have been chosen. The hole was abandoned, dry, at 147 feet.

Seven hundred men of the 204th Naval Construction Battalion arrived in July, and one of the first casualties was the oak forest. Saws sang night and day as the trees came down to make bunkers and fortifications of all kinds. Then the buildings in the villages began to disappear, and one day Colonel Ikeda came to ask Captain Wachi if he might have the school-house. He needed the timbers for underground bunkers. The Captain gave approval, and in one day the building was gone. The next day, Captain Inouye stormed into Wachi's headquarters. "How could you, a Navy man, give that precious timber to the Army?" he demanded. Wachi thought a while and then said: "First, we have lived on this island many days and you have never asked me for it. Second, we are all Japanese and we all share the same burden."

Captain Wachi plainly would not last long. He had already gotten in trouble when he ordered that all food and supplies were to be shared equally. Only the Army liked that. They had been getting the lowest calorie ration. The Navy ate much better, and the airmen best of all. One thing he did insist on, until the last, was keeping the keys to the cisterns. One day a lieutenant criticized one of Captain Wachi's anti-aircraft batteries after a raid. In a fury, the Captain turned and slapped him. A short time later Wachi's telephone rang.

"This is Ichimaru," the Admiral said. "I have heard of non-commissioned officers slapping enlisted men, but this is the first time I have heard of a commanding captain slapping an admiral's adjutant." The Admiral was more sorrowful than angry. Wachi was a fine man and well liked, but the strain was too much for him. He was relieved of command in October and sent to Tokyo. There Captain Ko Nagasawa told him: "Wachi, you were not sacked. You have earned a rest. Before you lose your temper, just look at yourself." It was true; he was haggard and emaciated. After the war he became a Buddhist priest.

By midsummer, the artillery was arriving and also a new weapon, the rocket gun. The Japanese Army had been working many years to perfect these guns for use in breaking out of static situations, such as river crossings or cliff scalings. Seventy guns were ready, and they and their crews were ordered to Iwo Jima under Captain Yoshio Yokoyama. The 20-cm. (8-inch) type was fired from a barrel that could be assembled in parts. The 40-cm. (16-inch) rocket was fired from a wooden chute. In theory, the smaller rocket had a range of 2,400 yards, the larger of 3,600 yards. Actually, there was little chance of accuracy. One advantage was that the launching frames could be quickly dismantled and moved or hidden.

Six new split trail 75-mm. mountain guns arrived in July and were placed around Osaka Yama (Hill 362A) to cover the second airfield and the western beaches. The anti-tank gun units also came in, the first being the 8th Independent Battalion with Captain Hajime Shimizu commanding. He had only four 47-mm. automatic cannon. Lieutenant Goro Wakatsuki set up two of them north of the Quarry, near Airfield No. 2, and the other two at the cliff overlooking the East Boat Basin. Over the next three months, the 9th, 10th, 11th, and 12th Battalions arrived, but none of them was at full strength. The sinking of supply ships between Japan and Iwo by American planes and submarines was beginning to take a heavy toll. Many guns were lost en route, others arrived without optical sights, and most of the battalions were short of men. Captain Shimizu, for example, had 190 men, instead of 260, and the full complement never did show up.

The 26th Tank Regiment, homeward bound from North Manchuria, arrived in Yokohama in the first days of July, and the men were given ten days' leave. The commanding officer, Lieutenant Colonel Takeichi Nishi, spent several days with his family in Tokyo and then visited Imperial General Headquarters to receive new orders. He was delighted to find that he was being assigned to General Kuribayashi's command. Both cavalrymen, graduates of the elite Cavalry School, they were closely bound by their love of horses, despite differences in age, rank, and social status.

Nishi, a baron, was of an old and wealthy family. The most famous horseman in Japan, he had competed throughout Europe in 1930, creating for himself the classic image of the cavalryman – a dashing fellow, daring on the field, irresistible in the boudoir, and unquenchable at the bar. He returned from Europe 20,000 yen poorer, but with a wild horse he had bought from the

Italians for $500. Both sides considered it a bargain – the Italians had gotten rid of a horse no one could ride, and the Baron had acquired at small price a beast that thoroughly challenged him.

"If that's a really headstrong horse," he had said, "it's just the one for me, a headstrong man," and he bought Uranus, a stallion of Anglo-Norman stock.

The stories of his escapades preceded him to Japan, and when he returned, he had to face the Baroness. But she was a wise and beautiful woman, and she only smiled. She had heard such tales before, and she knew that her husband was only twenty-eight and must have his fling. In the end, he would return to her.

In 1932, Nishi took Uranus to the Olympics in Los Angeles, and again his charm and vitality conquered all, even the intense anti-Oriental feeling of the West Coast. On the afternoon of August 14, the Baron and Uranus won the gold medal for Japan in the Prix des Nations, the individual jump event. As the newspapermen crowded around him, the Baron said very simply, "We won it," meaning himself and the horse, himself and Japan.

Before his return to Japan many stories were circulated – of the Baron and Hollywood actresses, of the Baron and prodigious drinking feats, of the Baron and Americans who implored him to stay in the United States. But he went home, faced the Baroness again, and bought a motorboat named Uranus II and a 12-cylinder, gold-painted Packard, both of which he raced at high speed.

But now he was forty-three, and age and the cold winds of Manchuria had cooled his youthful ardors. The Baroness was winning her waiting game.

On his last day in Tokyo, Baron Nishi went out to the Imperial Veterinarians School in the suburb of Setagaya to say goodbye to Uranus. The horse was now twenty-five years old, and the Baron caressed him and clipped a bit of his mane to keep in his inner pocket.

"I am a man misunderstood by many all through my life," the Baron said to his aide. "This horse understood me."

The 26th Tank Regiment sailed from Yokohama on July 14, 600 men and 28 tanks in the Nisshu Maru. In other vessels of the convoy were 7,000 troops and the tank regiment's remaining 13 tanks. Three days later, as the convoy approached Chichi Jima, the submarine USS Cobia (SS245) closed on it and launched torpedoes. The Nisshu Maru was struck astern and began to sink slowly. Only two men of the 26th Tank Regiment were lost, but the vessel went down with 28 tanks – a hard blow for Iwo Jima.

When his aide told Nishi that only two men had been lost, the Baron replied: "The loss was immense to the two men and to their families."

The regiment arrived in Iwo Jima a few days later and took up position near Motoyama. Kuribayashi received Nishi as a younger brother, and they talked, when there was time, of the old cavalry days. Kuribayashi was beloved by all cavalrymen. In 1939, when he had headed the Cavalry Administration Bureau in the War Ministry, he had organized a contest to pick a cavalry song and had personally selected the winning entry. It was "Aiba Shingunka" ("The Military Horses March") by Nobuo Kuboi, an unknown poet. The song became a classic in Japan. The opening verse could have special meaning for any cavalryman, particularly Nishi:

For many a month since we left the
  homeland
We have marched across mountains and
  rivers
This beloved horse with whom I share
  life and death,
The horse and I are comrades, blooded
  through the rein.

But there was little time for sentiment. Saipan had fallen on July 9, Tinian on August 1, and Guam on August 10. The

34

Marianas were gone. General Obata had been killed on Guam, and with him had perished the doctrine of defense at the water's edge. If the Americans could not be thrown back from the beaches in the Marianas, they could not be stopped at any beach.

Late in August, reinforced in his arguments by the debacle in the Marianas, General Kuribayashi made his final proposal:

1. The Japanese forces would not open fire against enemy landing vessels.

2. No opposition to enemy troops would be made at the beaches.

3. When the enemy had penetrated 500 yards, automatic weapons near Chidori Airfield would open fire, supported by artillery in Suribachi and on the Motoyama plateau.

4. The main defense would be made from the underground installations in the north, and no attrition would be attempted at Chidori. After initial fire, all guns at Chidori would withdraw to the north.

In addition, food supplies were to be built up to a reserve of 75 days. Allowing for casualties, it was expected that this might be stretched to 150 days. Weapons and ammunition were to be conserved to the utmost. No resupply could be expected.

Tunneling was to be pressed, with the hope that all strongpoints in the north could be connected. The total would be 26 kilometers, including a tunnel from Motoyama to Suribachi.

The plan, violating all Japanese military doctrine, was not popular, but it was inevitable, and most of the officers were at last prepared to accept it. General Osuga, egged on by Colonel Hori, was not. There were other dissidents. Finally, eighteen officers were sent home, and replacements came out to Iwo Jima. Hori and Osuga did not go home. They maintained they were ill and entered the underground hospital in the north end of the island. When the landing came they were still there, and they died on Iwo Jima.

Though the final breach did not come until December, Kuribayashi replaced Osuga with Major General Sadasue Senda, an artilleryman who had fought the Russians in Manchuria and the Chinese in Canton. In place of Hori, Kuribayashi made Colonel Takaishi chief of staff of the 109th Division.

With these changes, the Iwo Jima force began to take on a semblance of unity. When Captain Wachi went home, Admiral Ichimaru moved into full command of all naval forces on the island. The Navy had not yet surrendered to the Army, but with the passing days it became clear that interservice rivalry was an insupportable luxury. The war was coming closer, and they were all Japanese first.

Chapter 2

The assault on Iwo Jima was inevitable. General Hap Arnold of the Army Air Forces realized that as early as July 14, 1944 and recommended it. The Marines were just finishing Saipan and still had Guam and Tinian ahead, but Arnold was thinking of VLR (the Very Long Range bomber program) and the B-29. He drew a line from the Marianas to Japan, and it ran right through Iwo Jima. The B-29's must have it as a fall-back, and the P-51's would need it to give them fighter escort.

The VLR bomber concept was a bold one. As early as May, 1941, Boeing Aircraft Company had been ordered to proceed, when ready, with production of the B-29 Superfortress. The order, for a plane twice the size of any then in use, was based only on a wooden mock-up

38

and several tons of blueprints. No such plane had ever flown. Late in 1941, when the first one lifted off the runway, 1,664 of the giant planes were on order. In the service they called this "the three-billion-dollar gamble."

It paid off, because the plane turned out to be the battleship of the skies, 65 tons of gleaming silver, too proud even for camouflage. The Superfortress had a range of 3,500 miles with a 4-ton bomb load, against the B-17's 2,400 miles and 2-ton bomb load. Four special Wright engines gave it a speed of 350 miles per hour, a good 50 miles per hour better than the last evolution of the B-17. In addition, it had a pressurized cabin, central fire control, and power turrets.

From the beginning it appeared that the B-29 would be too late for the European Theater (in fact, it was never used there). But by the time the Marianas campaign was in full swing, the Army had 500 B-29's with crews ready to go. It was then that General Arnold recommended Iwo Jima. It was the only island between the Marianas and Japan where airfields could be built to handle B-29's.

The Navy was not yet ready to agree. It had opposed from the first the high-production priorities given to the B-29 program. But now it was a fact, embodied in its own command, the Twentieth Air Force, operating directly under the Joint Chiefs of Staff. Thousands of Japanese still burrowed in the Marianas, sniping at the Marines, as the bulldozers began leveling the islands, building the largest aerodromes ever seen.

Early in October, 1944, Admiral Chester Nimitz flew from Pearl Harbor to San Francisco, taking with him his planning chief, Captain Forrest Sherman. Admiral Raymond A. Spruance, commander of the famed Fifth Fleet, came up from Southern California, where he had been on leave, and Fleet Admiral Ernest J. King flew in from Washington. The finest strategic brains of the United States Navy gathered around a table in the office of the Commander, Western Sea Frontier.

Captain Sherman, a brilliant planner, read a paper he had prepared under the title, "Future Operations Recommendations to CominCh." It recommended that, instead of the Formosa-China axis, the next targets be the Iwo Jima-Okinawa axis. Admiral King, tall, lean, unsmiling, listened in silence, studied the paper for a while, and then rejected it. The Joint Chiefs of Staff, on which he sat as Navy representative, had already decided on Formosa-China. Nimitz and Sherman set out to change King's mind, always a formidable task. Spruance, small and bright as a bird, sat watching. Sherman's keen mind and Nimitz' wise counsel gradually began to have an effect. Finally King turned to Spruance. "Haven't you anything to say?" he asked, "I understand Okinawa is your baby." Spruance, who could have given Coolidge lessons in brevity, replied: "I have nothing to add to Chester." King thought a little longer, then capitulated. The admirals had their answer by the next night: Proceed with Iwo Jima and Okinawa. The Joint Chiefs of Staff directive of October 3, 1944 set the course of the war to its conclusion.

Admiral Nimitz was not specifically ordered to take Iwo Jima. He was told that Formosa was no longer an objective, that an island in the Nanpo Shoto was wanted instead. It must be an island capable of supporting several airfields. There was only one such island – Iwo Jima.

Nine days later, on Columbus Day, October 12, the first B-29 winged into Isley Field on Saipan. "It was "Joltin' Josie, the Pacific Pioneer," with Brigadier General Haywood S. Hansell, Jr. at the controls. "Possum" Hansell, first commander of the 21st Bomber Command, an old man in the AAF at forty-one, was not going to delegate this honor. Throughout the island thousands of men stopped work and watched in awe as the silver bird set down on a runway that was far from ready. It was the biggest plane they had ever seen, and a thrill ran through the crowd. As they surged around it, Hansell slithered through the bomb-bay door. A new era had begun.

At Pearl Harbor, Captain Sherman and the plans staff at Nimitz' headquarters produced an outline for Iwo Jima in four days. It was called "Operation Detachment," a name later forgotten by everyone. Iwo Jima was never called anything but "Iwo Jima," an ugly name for an ugly place.

The conception was simple: Assault, reduce, and capture a rock in the sea, across a moat 700 miles wide. With the advanced state of the amphibious art, there was full confidence that it could be done. The Navy would cut off the Japanese sea and air forces, transport the troops, and put them ashore; the Marines would take the island, the Army would garrison it, and the Air Force would use it. Speed was essential. Much of the shipping would be needed for the

Okinawa invasion, scheduled right behind Iwo.

The team assigned to Iwo Jima was superb – the very men who had perfected the amphibious techniques from Guadalcanal to Guam. Nearly every problem, it was believed, had been met and mastered along the way, from the jungles of Guadalcanal up through the Solomons, and across the Central Pacific from the bloody reefs of Tarawa to the mountains of the Marianas.

Yet Iwo was different, and the difference was recognized. It had no jungles, no coral reefs, no mountains; it was nothing but a stone fortress set far out in the sea. To an astute Marine eye, it was apparent at once that the battle would mean frontal assault. If they were lucky, the Marines could close quickly and kill the defenders. It was hoped the job could be done in two weeks. It took nearly five.

The command:

1. Admiral Spruance, USN, over-all command.

2. Vice Admiral Richmond Kelly Turner, USN, Joint Expeditionary Force Commander.

3. Lieutenant General Holland M. Smith, USMC, Commanding General, Expeditionary Troops.

4. Major General Harry Schmidt, USMC, Commander Landing Force. His force, the largest Marine force ever to fight under single command, included:

    (a) Fourth Marine Division, Major General Clifton B. Cates.

    (b) Fifth Marine Division, Major General Keller E. Rockey.

    (c) In Reserve, Third Marine Division, Major General Graves B. Erskine.

Considering the size of the objective, the force assigned to capture and develop Iwo Jima was tremendous. Admiral Turner's command alone totaled 485 ships, including 4 command ships, 8 battleships, 12 aircraft carriers, 19 cruisers, 44 destroyers, 43 transports, 63 LST's, and 31 LSM's. Adding Task

Force 58 and supply and auxiliary ships, the armada came to more than 800 vessels. The Marine assault forces for Iwo Jima totaled 70,647 troops, and counting the Army garrison and Navy men assigned for duty ashore only, the entire expeditionary force aggregated 111,308 men. If the crews of Turner's ships and of Task Force 58 are added in, the entire force totaled well over a quarter of a million men.

But this array of power deceived no one, least of all the Marines. After Tarawa, the Marianas, and Peleliu, there were no illusions left. Iwo Jima would be a return to war in primitive style. Naval gunfire, planes, and artillery would be of some assistance, but there would be no room for mass or maneuver. This would be a battle of man to man, a battle of caves and tunnels, of flame and satchel charges, knives and bayonets, the rifle and the grenade.

Looking back after the battle, General Smith disclosed the fears he felt for the Marines, with whom he had served for forty years:

"I was not afraid of the outcome of the battle. I knew we would win. We always had. But contemplation of the cost in lives caused me many sleepless nights."

The General, nearing sixty-three, was going on his last campaign. This did not improve his temper, which as early as 1906 in the Philippines had earned him the nickname of "Howlin' Mad Smith." He'd been mad ever since, as fiercely partisan for the Marines as Admiral Turner was for the Navy. The operation now developing would do nothing to soothe the feelings between them.

On October 9, 1944, General Smith received Admiral Nimitz' order to prepare for Iwo Jima, and immediately set down a general outline of the campaign in a letter of two small pages. Two days later this was given to General Schmidt, commander of the Fifth Amphibious Corps (VAC), who would actually command the troops on Iwo Jima.

Harry Schmidt, then on Guam, flew

to Pearl Harbor with his staff, and planning for the assault began on October 13. General Schmidt, fifty-eight, a Nebraskan with nearly thirty-six years' service in the Corps, had commanded the Fourth Marine Division in the capture of Roi-Namur in the Marshall Islands, and of Saipan in the Marianas. Near the close of that campaign, he had been promoted to command the Fifth Amphibious Corps for the capture of Tinian. That engagement had featured the famous "back door landing," in which the Marines went in over a small beach behind the logical landing beaches and took the island with small losses. Iwo Jima had no back door.

Planning conditions for Iwo Jima were good. Both assault divisions were in the Hawaiian Islands: the Fourth Division at its permanent camp on the island of Maui, and the Fifth Division at Camp Tarawa on the island of Hawaii. The Third Division was on Guam, reforming after the bloody battle for that island. The replacements were training "live," hunting Japanese still in hiding, and in October alone bagged 617 of them.

The Fourth Division, getting ready for its fourth campaign within a year, had a leader who knew what combat was. Cliff Cates had quit the University of Tennessee law school in the middle of his bar examinations to accept a Marine commission in World War I. From the time his pants were torn off by shrapnel at Aisne-Marne in 1918, courage and stoic humor had been his hallmarks. Wounded at Soissons for about the third time, he remarked: "Better to be lucky than good-looking." In all, he had been wounded ten times and gassed and had once sent from the front a message that is now a classic in the Corps: "I have no one on my left and only a few on my right. I will hold." General Cates' Assistant Division Commander for Iwo Jima was Brigadier General Franklin A. Hart, who had made the Dieppe raid as an observer with Lord Mountbatten and had commanded the 24th Regiment at Roi-Namur, Saipan, and Tinian.

The Fifth Division had never been in combat as a unit, but 40 percent of its men had. The division formed up early in 1944 at Camp Pendleton, California, with General Rockey in his first combat command of World War II. He, too, had been through the hell in France at Chateau-Thierry in 1918, when the Marines fought as land soldiers to stem the German offensive. His Assistant Division Commander for Iwo Jima was Brigadier General Leo D. Hermle, former chief of staff of the Second Division.

General Erskine, who had gone to the Mexican Border as a boy trumpeter, now commanded the Third Division. He had fought at Soissons with Cliff Cates and had been hospitalized nine months with blast concussion. The Third, veterans of Bougainville and Guam, passed to Erskine's command after he had spent two years as Howlin' Mad's chief of staff. At forty-seven, Erskine was one of the youngest generals in the Corps, and one of the toughest.

Planning presented few problems. With material now pouring out, and with the experience of previous campaigns, it was mostly a matter of ordering men, supplies, and ships "off the shelf." Harry Schmidt was able to announce his troops assignments within six days after planning began, and all units were ordered to be ready for combat by December 15. They were to land on Iwo Jima's eastern beaches. Water was shallower on the western beaches, but prevailing north and north-west winds piled the surf higher there. The ground rose more gently on the western coast, and General Cates at one point did propose a landing there. The eastern beaches, with Suribachi jutting out at the bottom and sharp cliffs rising at the top would give the Japanese excellent fire straight up and down the beaches. Cates thought a landing just south of the high ground on the west coast might provide an entry to the central plateau at less cost. The terraces on the eastern beaches were sure to be a costly barrier, but the Navy did not like the water conditions on the west. The eastern beaches were chosen, with alternate plans for the western beaches if necessary.

The eastern beaches, forming a narrow, black berm backed by a series of terraces, ran 3,500 yards from Suribachi to the East Boat Basin. The planners split them into 500-yard segments, numbered left to right: Green, Red 1 and 2, Yellow 1 and 2, and Blue 1 and 2. The Fifth Division, landing over the three left beaches, would cut across the isthmus to the west coast, hold on the right, and turn left to capture Suribachi. The Fourth Division was to move into the center of the isthmus, while its right flank wheeled to take the high ground above the East Boat Basin. The taking of this ground and Suribachi was vital, to cut off the enemy's fire across the beaches. They must be taken quickly, if casualties were not to become insupportable. With the southern part of the island secured, both divisions would turn north, free from fire at their backs. It was decided that the Third Division should be combat-loaded and transported to the beachhead, instead of standing ready at Guam. This turned out to be one of the most vital decisions of the planning. Since speed was the essence of the campaign – the Army Air Forces were pressing for the use of Iwo Jima, and much of the shipping would be needed for the Okinawa invasion – part of the Army garrison forces would be sent with the assault waves and the rest would arrive soon afterwards. The attack plan was Marine doctrine – land as many troops as possible, as fast as possible, and move, move, move – never allow the enemy to recover, regroup, or counter-attack.

One serious difference arose in the planning. On October 24, Harry Schmidt asked the Navy for ten days of bombardment by a cruiser division and three battleships before the landing.

Admiral Turner rejected that. He said ships would not be available, they could not be rearmed in time for D-Day, and the bombardment would result in "loss of surprise." There would be no surprise at Iwo Jima; Kuribayashi had been waiting eight months.

General Schmidt made his second request on November 8. This time he asked for nine days' bombardment. Again he was refused. Admiral Turner replied that the Navy's original plan would stand – three days of bombardment.

Howlin' Mad Smith got into the argument then. The truth was that the Navy was planning its first big offensive showpiece – an attack on the Japanese homeland by Task Force 58 – in conjunction with the Iwo Jima invasion. General Smith felt that this dramatic sortie – partly planned, no doubt, to counteract the growing glamour of the B-29 offensive – was strictly secondary.

"I could not forget," he wrote later, "the sight of Marines floating in the lagoon or lying on the beaches of Tarawa, men who died assaulting defenses which should have been taken out by naval gunfire."

On November 24, Harry Schmidt asked for just one more day of bombardment – four days instead of three. This request got as far as Admiral Spruance. He said it was not feasible, because the bombardment should be simultaneous with his carrier strikes against Japan, and they were planned to last only three days.

Snorted Howlin' Mad Smith in his memoirs: "To my way of thinking – and I am sure I was right – the operation was planned for the capture of Iwo Jima, but Spruance permitted the attack on Japan to overshadow the real objective." Colonel Robert Heinl, the Marine historian, said that canceling the fourth day of bombardment was "a costly irony and an example of a subsidiary operation overriding the primary objective."

The last straw, as far as the Marines

were concerned, was Admiral Spruance's notice that he was withdrawing two new 16-inch battleships, the Washington and the North Carolina, from the bombardment force. He was taking them with him on the run to Japan. Spruance apologized for the change in plans, adding, "but I know you and your people will get away with it."

Howlin' Mad Smith wrote: "I reflected ruefully that naval thinking had not changed in the twenty-five years since I was at the Naval War College." That was when he had found the college "bogged down in obsolescence," the lessons of World War I pointing "backward instead of forward." But the Navy bombardment plan remained at three days, and the argument will never be settled.

In the Marianas, other Superfortresses followed "Joltin' Josie" and on October 20, Brigadier General Emmett (Rosie) O'Donnell arrived to activate the 73rd Bombardment Wing. After a few practice runs against Truk, the B-29's made their first attack on Iwo Jima November 5. The Japanese sent up a dozen fighters but they did not attack, apparently overawed by the giant bombers. The B-29 bombardiers were so nervous that they dropped only a quarter of their bombs within 1,000 yards of the aiming point. Another attack three days later was even less successful.

The first strike on Tokyo, coded San Antonio I, was set for November 17. Bad weather pushed it back to November 24, but it finally got away – 111 Super-fortresses, with Rosie O'Donnell leading in Dauntless Dotty. The weather over Tokyo was so bad that the bombardiers couldn't even see the ground from 30,000 feet and the Superforts rocketed by at an incredible 445 miles per hour, pushed by a 120-knot wind. About 125 fighters came up and one B-29 fell, the first lost in combat. Another ditched on the way home. Psychologically, the results were considered good; all airmen took heart. The effect was not lost on the Navy.

Kuribayashi was nettled more by the B-24's. They went into action against Iwo Jima in August, and beginning in September were hitting the island twenty or more times per month. The Japanese decided to hit back. On November 2 they sent 9 twin-engine bombers against Saipan, but lost 3 of them for no results. Five days later 10 bombers went down and 3 were lost. Finally, on November 27, they scored. Two twin-engine bombers attacked early in the morning, as the B-29's were loading bombs for a Tokyo strike. One B-29 was smashed and 11 others were damaged in that raid; a second raid later the same day got 3 more B-29's. At a half a million dollars per plane, this was expensive. Thus far Possum Hansell had lost more B-29's to raids from Iwo Jima than he had on Tokyo missions. There was worse to come. In a combined high- and low-level attack on December 7, the Japanese smashed 3 B-29's and damaged 23 more.

The next day, in operations already planned, the United States struck back.

Twenty-eight P-38 fighters swept over Iwo Jima at 9:45 A.M., strafing ground targets. Sixty-two B-29's followed at 11 A.M. and dropped 620 tons of bombs; at noon, 102 B-24's finished up with another 194 tons of bombs. In the afternoon, Rear Admiral Allen E. Smith came by with cruiser Division 5, the "Iwo Jima Milk Run Special." For seventy minutes, six destroyers and the heavy cruisers Chester, Pensacola, **and** Salt Lake City shelled the island, with no reply from shore. The ships had made one earlier visit, on November 12, firing before dawn at lights on shore. This time they added 1,500 rounds of 8-inch fire and 5,334 5-inch shells to the air bombardment. The result: the Iwo Jima airstrips were back in service in 24 hours.

There was no secret about what was happening on Iwo Jima – it was getting stronger every day. Good reconnaissance photos had been taken regularly since the first ones, made by Jocko Clark's flyers on June 15. The island's defenses were going steadily underground. Open gun pits were dis-appearing, pillboxes and blockhouses were multiplying, the second airfield was nearing completion, and a third field was being started in the north. In spite of ship sinkings, supplies were getting through, both East and West Boat Basins were in use, and the garrison was growing. The Japanese obviously intended to fight for Iwo Jima and to make the price heavy.

In Hawaii, the Navy and the Marines studied the reconnaissance photos and worried about the beaches. The sand was obviously deep and soft, the terraces steep; getting off the beaches was vital. The Navy built wooden sleds, so that the bulldozers could pull supplies up the inclines. Somebody rounded up 2 by 4's for poles, to get communication wires off the ground. Marston matting, a punched-steel planking in 10-foot lengths, was hinged together on the long edges and rolled into bundles. The idea was to pull it out into a metal carpet over the sand. LST's and LSM's could unload directly onto the beaches; cranes and bulldozers would have to move heavy equipment inland to high ground. And this must be done under fire. Armored bulldozers were part of the answer, and they welded sheet-steel cabs for the drivers, with only slits for their eyes.

Besides the Marine divisions' own Pioneers, the Navy added three full SeaBee battalions for the assault. The 31st Battalion was to go in with the Fifth Division, the 133rd Battalion with the Fourth Division; the 62nd Battalion, airstrip specialists, was assigned to Corps. Half of the 70th SeaBee Battalion, pontoon and harbor specialists, was ordered along with twenty-five self-propelled barges and six sets of causeways. The causeways, 175 feet long and side-carried on LST's, were to be rigged perpendicular to the beaches for unloading troops, machines, and vehicles.

The main landing vehicle for the Marines was the LVT – landing vehicle, tracked, armored – and the Dukw, amphibious trucks. Each Marine division had its own Dukw company, and the Army provided three more, companies with white officers and Negro drivers.

Two hospital ships, the Samaritan and the Solace, were assigned, along with the auxiliary hospital ship Pinckney and four LST's – 929, 930, 931, and 1033 – especially fitted out to handle casualties close to the beach. One LST had a bank for refrigerated whole blood. Each Marine division had its own hospital, the Navy had another, and the Army prepared to land its 38th Field Hospital. Five thousand beds were prepared in Saipan and Guam.

It was necessary to think of everything – pencils, blood, toilet paper ("this item," said the orders, "will be stowed under tarpaulin at the rear of all landing vehicles to protect it from spray"), matches, gasoline, socks, bullets, wooden crosses (prepainted), water, welding rods, garbage cans, splints, food, spark plugs, blankets, flares, dog food, maps, holy water, smoke pots, paint, shoelaces, fingerprint ink, batteries, rockcrushers, bulbs, cigars, asphalt machines, carbon paper. The Fifth Division alone carried 100 million cigarettes and enough food to feed Columbus, Ohio, for thirty days.

Ships began loading as early as November, every parcel stenciled, weighed, sized, and stowed in a particular spot. Marked photos showed where the cemetery would be located, orders specified the exact depth of burial and space between bodies (3 feet from centerline to centerline of body, fifty bodies to a row, 3 feet between rows). The graves registration team would land on D-Day, equipped with its own bulldozers to bury the bodies exactly 6 feet deep. Then men would mound each grave with a special wooden form.

A few days after Christmas, the "Fubar Follies," Sergeant Lee Cohen master of ceremonies, gave its last performance, and the Fourth Division began its descent from Camp Maui, 1,500 feet high on the side of Haleakala, the world's largest extinct volcano. It was ready to load for its longest trip to battle – 3,791 miles from Pearl Harbor to Iwo Jima.

The Fifth Division began loading Christmas Day, first elements going aboard the transport Athene at Hilo. By January 4 the division reported "all aboard." As vessels finished loading, they became part of the Joint Expeditionary Force assembling at Oahu. By mid-January there were hundreds of transports, cargo ships, LST's, LSM's, and auxiliaries.

Final rehearsals in Hawaii were about as satisfactory as usual. Some outfits were not present, others had only part of their equipment. Dukws were not launched for fear sea spray might corrode the ammunition they carried, and LST's did not beach because of reefs. Final liberties in Honolulu were about the same – the city jammed, ten men for every girl, hamburgers sold out, and bars loaded to capacity. The USO and the YMCA did good business, too, but there was no escaping the fact that you had to go back on board.

The ships began moving out, the slower ones first. By January 27th, when the bulk of the Fifth Division sailed, they were all gone, carrying not only men but well over 100,000 tons of assault cargo. To fuel the armada, the Navy was prepared to deliver 4.1 million barrels of oil. Deep in the hold of a transport, sweat slowly ringing the armpits of his green T-shirt, a Marine corporal carefully oiled the valves of his trumpet. He wanted to be sure they worked when next he played with the "Just 4 Fun Show," which had already played the foxhole circuit on Roi, Saipan, and Tinian. Next to him, a Swede from Pennsylvania, inevitably named Swenson, silently and endlessly honed the blades of six knives. He had made them from the leaves of old auto springs, "the best kind of steel for this." As a mortar-squad leader he would be carrying 106 pounds of equipment across the beach, but he'd find a spot somewhere for his knives; he liked knives. In another ship, the enlisted men gave Jumpin' Joe a birthday party. Lieutenant Colonel Jumpin' Joe Chambers was their battalion commander, and he was thirty-seven. The only card they could find said "So Now You're 8." Somebody penciled a 3 in front of the figure, and the men added their sentiments: "Why Grandpa, what long gray hair you have!" and "Too old for combat duty." Somebody wrote "Very best wishes. Sincerely yours."

In December, the Navy made two more raids on Iwo Jima. On Christmas Eve, Admiral Smith signaled the ships of Cruiser Division 5, "Under way to deliver our Christmas presents," and shelled the island with 1,500 rounds of 8-inch. Two small ships were sunk, one in the East Boat Basin. Christmas night, the Japanese retaliated. They sent planes down from Iwo Jima and destroyed 4 B-29's on Saipan and damaged 11 more. Cruiser Division 5 returned to Iwo Jima

December 27 and sank two more ships. No more raids came from Iwo Jima.

The Navy's final raid on Iwo Jima came on the afternoon of January 25. Rear Admiral Oscar C. Badger led a force in the new battleship Indiana. Here 16-inch 45's, the biggest naval guns yet brought against the island, lobbed in 203 shells, and cruisers added 1,300 rounds of 8-inch fire. It was another annoyance to the Japanese. B-24's had not missed a day since December 8. In all, the planes had dropped nearly 7,000 tons of bombs. The Navy added 23,000 rounds of fire, from 5-inch to 16-inch. The target was not softened, it was "hardened."

By early February, the pieces of the giant puzzle began falling into place. The Third Division started loading at Guam; ships bringing the rest of the force arrived in the Marianas, singly and in groups of a dozen to a hundred. Planes brought in vital spare parts, some all the way from the United States. Welding torches burned all night, making repairs. Supply ships ran up masthead lights to help the small boats find them – three vertical green for fresh food, three vertical red for dry stores. Ships awaiting service kept spotlights on their bow numbers through the night. Small boats churned through the crowded anchorages with guard mail, maps, the latest intelligence summaries, hydrographic reports. In thousands of corners, seeking privacy, Marines wrote that last letter home. They were allowed to say they were at sea, going into combat – nothing more except that they could make "general statements about the weather." In the Eldorado, Admiral Turner's new command ship, Howlin' Mad Smith paced the deck, waiting, as were all the men, for action. The waiting is the worst.

Chapter 3

By the middle of September, the mornings and evenings were becoming quite cool at Iwo Jima. First Class Private Kazuyoshi Sonoyama of the Twenty-first Special Machine Cannon Unit spent the entire night of September 19 unloading two barges that had arrived from Chichi Jima. There was more night work now, because of the increased air raids and sinkings by submarines north of the island. Fewer ships were calling, and most of the steel, cement, and guns were coming in by barge or small, fast ships from Chichi.

Private Sonoyama did not complain of the work; it was just that he was not feeling well. The bad water taken from wells that stank of sulphides was causing diarrhea and paratyphoid. It weakened the men, as did the loss of sleep from the air raids. The raids were nearly worthless as far as knocking out the airfield was concerned, because Kuribayashi had instituted a special regime. As soon as the planes withdrew, 2,000 men and every truck on the island rushed to the task of filling the craters. Rocks were brought from the quarry, and fifty men were assigned to each bomb hole. Within five hours, ten at the most, the field was again operational. The raids actually raised morale. Private Sonoyama said after the raid of September 22, "Our spirits were raised a hundred times. We are filled with spirit to serve the country."

The last warships to visit the island were the light cruiser Tama and three destroyers, which ran in quickly on August 22 and unloaded some specialized units.

First Lieutenant Hajime Hamamura, twenty-six, commander of the 2nd Company, 12th Independent Anti-Tank Battalion, was tired of the war. He had enlisted at nineteen "to get it over with," but seven years later he was still at it. His wife and baby were in Hiroshima, and he thought often of them. He also thought of his sister, Yukiko, who lived in Honolulu as Mrs. Nobuo Takeuchi. It must be pleasant to live in Hawaii, he thought.

Ensign Toshihiko Ono received a draft of fifty-five Army men in mid-September, and a curious gun battery they made. Ono was an economics graduate of St. Paul's University in Tokyo and had never seen the Navy; no ships were left. He knew even less of artillery, and his Army draft was a sad lot. Their ages ran from thirty-one to forty-five, and most of them were debilitated from bad diet and long years in the field. But somehow they wrestled two 15-cm. guns (6-inch), taken from a heavy cruiser, over the beach and up to the cliffs in the north. Around the guns they mounted ten 13-mm. machine guns and ten 25-mm. anti-aircraft guns in a horseshoe formation and christened it Tenzan (Heavenly Mountain) Battery.

Strangely, morale began to improve.

Private First Class Shigeru Yoshida, twenty-two, a stone mason, had been building fortifications near the beach since March. The machine-cannon posts had walls of concrete 5 inches thick and a roof 6½ inches thick, reinforced with three layers of steel rods. They were carefully built, with steps leading down from the rear and a lookout tower on top pierced on the four sides for observation. Yoshida and others laid up the mortar and machine-gun positions with walls of cement and stone, with roofs of reinforced concrete 12 to 20 inches thick. Hundreds of Korean laborers toiled long hours daily on the work, and the soldiers, half-believing themselves, taunted them with stories of the barbarian invaders soon to come. The Americans, they said, cut the left forearm bone of each captive and fashioned it into a letter opener, which was sent to the collection of the Jew Roosevelt. And everyone knew, of course, the stories of the Marines who carried pliers to yank out the gold teeth of dead Japanese. Or cut off their heads, to make ash trays of the skulls. The effect was powerful, for the Orientals abhor the desecration of the dead.

The Autumn Worship of the Imperial Ancestors was celebrated on September 23 with gifts of imperial cake and a package of cigarettes, and the next day it was back to work. The tunneling was progressing well, except around Motoyama, where the volcanic fire was close to the surface. Using picks and shovels, and lines of soldiers to pass out the rock and sand in buckets, the men worked in shifts from 3 A.M. to 11 P.M. The passages had to be at least 30 feet below ground, for protection from heavy bombardment, but near the volcano the men could work only eight to ten minutes at a time. The underground temperature often rose to 160 degrees, and they wore masks against the fumes.

Within Suribachi, a 7-story gallery was undertaken. Specifications called for 35 feet of overhead cover, all caves to be at least 5 feet wide, 35 feet long, and 5 feet high. The walls were plastered, and steam, electricity, and water were piped in. Some caves were shored and cribbed with logs, driftwood, and parts of wrecked aircraft. The blast revetments were of concrete. All entrances, in the mountain and elsewhere, were angled at 90 degrees a few feet inside, to protect against flame-throwers, artillery, and demolitions charges. Drainage was good and, where necessary, the caves were cleverly vented at the top for escape of steam and sulphur fumes.

In the north, two very heavy fortifications were built – one near Motoyama for central communications and control of all artillery fire, and the other just south of Kitano Point. The latter, General Kuribayashi's headquarters, consisted of a cave system connected by 500 feet of tunnels as much as 75 feet underground. Three small concreted rooms were the personal warroom of the General, and there were other sections for the staff, coding, and communications. Niches for sleeping were cut in the passageways. The main communications blockhouse, above the surface, was 150 feet long and 70 feet wide, with walls 5 feet thick and a roof 10 feet thick. Inside, ten radio operators were always on duty.

South of Motoyama on Nidan Iwa (Hill 382), highest point on the island after Suribachi, the Japanese constructed a radio and weather station. But the main fortification here was a giant blockhouse on Tamana Yama (Turkey Knob), east and south of Nidan Iwa. General Kuribayashi called Colonel Chosaku Kaido down from Chichi Jima in October to command all artillery on the island. The Colonel, just the man to force Army-Navy cooperation, decreed that all artillery would be controlled from his headquarters in the Tamana Yama blockhouse. Like the one in the north, this one had walls of reinforced concrete and a roof thick enough to withstand the heaviest bombardment.

Osaka Yama (Hill 362A) had no less than four tunnel systems, the largest containing a thousand feet of passageways and seven entrances on three sides of the hill. Inside was a natural cavern 68 feet underground, with a main chamber 20 by 80 feet and numerous alcoves. Another system had 340 feet of tunnels serving anti-aircraft guns on top of the hill. It was possible to enter at several places on the back of the cliff and pass up ammunition to the guns through four shafts.

In the east, where Major General Senda was building his headquarters, and in several places in the north, there were equally elaborate systems.

By early October, Private Sonoyama's foot was swollen and discharging pus. He wrote in his diary that he was losing weight, and that his foot was sore from "much running." The bombers were coming more often, and Sonoyama "got terribly scared" when the bombs fell near him. When he was able, he was put on water-fetching detail, or collecting firewood, or taking lunch and tea down to the workers at the piers. There he heard, as early as October 20, that Iwo Jima would soon be invaded.

The last water in the cisterns gave out on October 26, and every day the men looked for rain, but none came.

Colonel Nishi strode around the island in his cavalry boots, super-intending his men in burying their tanks, or dismounting the turrets and hiding them in the rocks so that not even the barrels showed. This narrowed the field of fire, but the guns were aimed right – straight down the island, from where the enemy would have to come to capture the high ground.

It was thought, at first, that Nishi's tanks might rove the island as sort of a "ranger battalion," but this quickly proved to be unfeasible because of the terrain. The tanks went into the ground.

Occasionally, the Colonel could be seen riding horseback, a strange sight on the island. He urged Kuribayashi to ride too, but the General would not. He preferred to walk, or to ride in a motorcycle sidecar. The Colonel finally gave up riding, too, after one horse was killed by bomb fragments. He still carried the whip he had used on Uranus at the Olympics, and in the pocket over his heart were the wisps from the horse's mane.

There was one surprise left for Nishi. In October he was sent to Tokyo to see if he could get more tanks and other weapons. He finally returned in December with twenty-two tanks, but he had a sore trial at home. He was suffering from "Iwo sickness," as were most of the men, and it was intimated to him that he did not have to return to the island if he did not wish to.

"I cannot do that," he said. "My men are waiting for me." He said good-bye to the Baroness once more and patted the children on the head as they crowded around him. He knew what they were thinking, and he said: "A serviceman is not always required to die. Your father will not die meaninglessly. I will try as tenaciously as possible to live." He refused his eldest son, Yasunori, permission to go to the airport with him. The Baroness watched the Army car carry him away. They had been married more than twenty years and had lived together less than seven.

For Kuribayashi, November 20 was a special day, the twentieth birthday of his son, Taro, and the General wrote to him:

"I, your father, stand on Iwo Jima, the island which will soon be attacked by the American forces. In other words, this island is the gateway to Japan. My heart is as strong as that of General M. Kusunoki, who gave his life for Japan 650 years ago at the Minato River." He referred to the Japanese national hero, Masashige Kusunoki.

"As he could not, neither can I expect to return to Japan alive, but I am proud and feel honored to fight until death comes," the General wrote. "Today is your birthday, and you are now twenty. Now you will be called on to make many decisions on your own, and to arrive at the best solution you will have to do much self-examination.

"That is the first step to become a man of culture. Strong will is essential for a man – a weak-willed man can accomplish nothing. Many murderers are weak willed, as are many who commit other serious crimes," he wrote. Drawing upon the years of success in his own profession, the General said:

"Willpower is the essence of manhood – a man's success is determined by the strength of his will. You have not yet developed your will and, in your present state, you cannot head my household successfully. I am praying to God on this, your birthday, that you will train your will and that you will develop into a trustworthy man for Japan. Particularly, you must become the foundation of our home after my death.

Take it easy, Taro
Very truly yours,
Your Father."

The following night, the General wrote again to his wife. He spoke, as he had the week before, of the air raids on the homeland. The radio told him that the air-raid sirens were often heard now, and he said: "It won't be long before you will be experiencing the real thing. Be prepared for them."

Noting that her letters spoke of visits she was making, he said: "You had better not go visiting any more as you might get caught in the air raid." He spoke of household repairs: "Did you get the floor of the kitchen chinked?" and "If not, have it done, as those drafts may give you colds." Taro could do it, he said, with matting or roofing paper. As for their daughter, Takako, "I hope that she can attend college later, but until the war ends she may pay taxes and do her bit by working in a defense plant."

Of his own condition, he said merely: "There are still many ants, flies, and bugs troubling us, and the ants crawl over us in swarms."

As November turned into December, the real meaning of the loss of the Marianas began to come clear. The B-29's no longer bothered with Iwo, concentrating on the bigger prize, the home islands. But the B-24's were over Iwo nearly every night, and Navy carrier and cruiser forces were often around Iwo and the Bonins, to the north. On December 1, though Kuribayashi did not know it, the submarine Spearfish (SS 190) came to periscope depth quite near the east coast, soon after dawn, and took photographs of the beaches. The sub submerged once when a Betty took off from the airstrip but went back for a second look and also made recordings of the sounds on the island.

The air raids caused little real damage on Iwo, but they did disrupt life. The men were sleeping whenever they could, and those not required to do night unloading were in bed early.

The air raids against Saipan, ordered by Tokyo in an effort to smash the B-29 forays against Japan, were not popular on Iwo. They were obviously futile, and the retaliation hurt Iwo Jima. Master Sergeant Taizo Sakai, handling communications to the homeland, saw many dispatches urging that the Toki (kite) operation be canceled. It was, the dispatches said, "like pouring water on hot coals or poking a hornet's nest."

General Kuribayashi wrote to his wife that his schedule was "often upset by the enemy air raids, and it seems that we sleep much more than ten hours. As we have to seek shelter many times during the day, we must make every free moment count."

The General himself was well. He had changed into winter clothes and "I always wear my bullet-proof belt and good-luck charm. At night I remove only my hat and boots and sleep under one comforter.

"My brother officers say that I am getting fat – they may be right." But "many men have an unknown fever. My chief of staff and many other officers and men were or are in bed, some as long as forty to fifty days, but the ailment has never attacked me."

For his wife, he had this advice: "Use your waist belt and chemise and keep warm and wear my camel-hair shirt instead of your cotton one. Because you cannot get fuel enough, be sure to wear enough clothes to keep your warm.

"I was sorry to hear that winter has come to Japan, and that the cold weather is chapping your hands. You have my sympathy," he said, and added the advice of an old field soldier: "Dry your hands well, and rub them vigorously whenever you wet them.

"I was also sorry to hear that you were so short of fuel that you could heat water for only one bath every ten days," he said. "I understand that the fuel situation is much worse than last winter. I understand how the lack of a regular bath bothers you, as we are unable to bathe over here."

Then he outlined for her his own schedule:

"I arise at 5:30 A.M., but many of the

troops arise at 4 A.M. or work all night and sleep during the day. I wash, exercise with my wooden sword, eat breakfast at 6 A.M., and start inspecting the front lines at 7 A.M. I return about 11 A.M., check the staff work, eat lunch, and watch troop maneuvers from 2 P.M. to 4 P.M., eat supper at 5 P.M., sing some songs or recite poetry, and go to bed at 6 P.M. to drop immediately into a deep and fatigued sleep."

By December, most of Iwo's defenses were in place, the real ones and the dummy ones. Many false positions were built of wooden frames, covered with sand and rock, and even false "fire lanes" were laid out. The "tanks" were moved often, to confuse aerial reconnaissance, and every position, real or false, was camouflaged with great skill.

Kamikaze scarves were given out late in the year, and some units wore them to a man. This was the hachimaki, the white headband worn for centuries by samurai. Many men wore sennimbari sent from home, the cotton band of one thousand stitches. Wrapped around the belly, it warded off enemy bullets.

In the pillboxes, the men pasted up the "Courageous Battle Vow":

> Above all else we shall dedicate ourselves and our entire strength to the defense of this island.
> We shall grasp bombs, charge the enemy tanks, and destroy them.
> We shall infiltrate into the midst of the enemy and annihilate them.
> With every salvo we will, without fail, kill the enemy.
> Each man will make it his duty to kill ten of the enemy before dying.
> Until we are destroyed to the last man, we shall harass the enemy by guerrilla tactics.

In the big raid of December 8, the alarm system on the island failed. At the Tenzan Battery, Ensign Ono looked up at the black bombers and shouted to his men, "Go to the shelters." He threw himself into a trench with Seaman First Class Rikio Matsudo, and they huddled together as the ground shook. Later they found forty large craters all around them, and two of the anti-aircraft guns were smashed.

This raid was a "Pearl Harbor Day" present for the Iwo garrison. Twenty-eight P-38's came over first, bombing and strafing, and were followed by 62 B-29's and 102 B-24's, dropping over 800 tons of bombs, Cruiser Division 5 finished up in the afternoon with seventy minutes of shelling. Private Sonoyama was not impressed. He noted in his diary only that: "Today was the third anniversary of the war. We had a ceremony of bowing to the Emperor." Nevertheless, from this day on not a single day passed that B-24's were not over the island at least once.

Colonel Kaido formally inspected his artillery in mid-December, and he was not satisfied. Junior officers had reported to him, praising each others' work, but he was used to this and not a bit taken in by it. He reported to Kuribayashi that combat training was not tough enough and the bad aim of his gunners worried him.

"Ammunition is short," the Colonel said, "and there is no hope of replenishment. It is vital that direct hits be scored by all fire."

Too much wiring was exposed, and camouflage and gun protection were not always good. Some crews were poorly trained, made errors in calculation, and ordered wrong corrections. Communications by signal, telephone, and radio were imprecise and often wrong in terminology; there was too much unnecessary chatter on the circuits. He ordered training redoubled.

Toward the end of December, work troops were set to tearing down the last houses in Motoyama village. It was hardly recognizable any more, with the school and all public offices gone.

"It was best when the civilians were here," one soldier wrote wistfully in his diary. Then, he recalled, the main street in the village was known as "the Ginza of Iwo Jima."

"Day after day and night after night the enemy comes over," another man wrote. "At night I only sleep about two hours, so during the day I daydream, thinking about the times when I used to work in Japan. I want to return to Japan quickly to see all the familiar faces of my family. I imagine the children have all grown considerably. When I will return to Japan is really uncertain."

The news from home was not encouraging. Letters said that black beans and fish roe were scarce and there would be fewer rice patties for the New Year than last year.

Iron was being taken from everywhere, and containers were so scarce that the soldiers on Iwo were being urged to send their empties home, in order that relatives might send them gifts. The cotton contribution required of each family was 4 pounds, and some families took the cotton from their own cushions to meet the levy.

Lieutenant Noboru Ito got a letter from his children saying, "Fight hard, Father. Work hard."

Tadataka Miura's wife wrote him: "When the time comes, I shall wield your sword, rush into the enemy ranks and die gallantly with our children."

No pens or razors were for sale, and there was no firewood or kerosene. Genza Tokigoe wrote to her husband, Sumio, that he should not worry because there was plenty of hard coal and the house was warm.

Matozo Ueda's wife wrote that her heart was broken. She was in Chosen and had taken months to gather a comfort bag for her husband, but at the post office they told her, "No more parcels may be sent from here."

Twice more, as the year waned, Kuribayashi wrote to his wife. His concern now was mainly for her and the children. "I have learned that the enemy has started their bombing offensive against the Japanese homeland," he wrote. "It seems that their targets are now military facilities and industries, but no one can foretell where or when they'll bomb. I am sorry for the widows and children who will be frightened terribly by the bombings."

He gave explicit instructions as to how Taro should strengthen the air-raid shelter, how to remove incendiary bombs, and how to keep warm in the shelter.

As to his own situation: "We were attacked continuously throughout December 8, both with naval gunfire and airplanes. They kept it up all night as well, and since have hit us seven or eight times every night. The casualties from the bombing have not been great, but we have been unable to get any rest, nor can we get much work done as we must run to the shelters so often."

Even under the enemy pounding, he could not forget that he was a father. "I read Yoko's letter," he wrote, "and was disappointed at her penmanship and grammar."

His last letter of the year, dated December 22, was almost entirely concerned with his family. The only mention of his own trouble was this: "On Iwo Jima we dare not show a light at night, so we go to bed in the shelters at nightfall, thus getting some sleep."

This letter was a long one, and it was all about home.

"I surely sympathize with you now that Tokyo is being bombed around the clock," he began. "It won't be long before they start bombing the fortified and residence areas as well, and I am afraid that they will use incendiaries and that shell splinters from our anti-aircraft guns will drop on our house.

"I have heard that the Tokyo city management has volunteered to secure civilian valuables. I believe that it would be a good plan to turn our stocks and bonds and other valuables over to them. Make a list of them, and give each of the children a copy."

His admonitions were:

"Eat earlier than usual because it is bad to be raided during a meal. Go to bed early, and get as much sleep as possible.

"Save your canned foods for use during the air raids.

"Consider your footwear carefully. Bear in mind that our home may be destroyed and that you may have to walk 8 or 10 miles to find shelter. I believe that my short boots will be best for you, that sport shoes will be best for Taro and Yoko. The Army shoes might fit Taro, they are in the wooden box in the upstairs reception room."

He did not forget Mr. Maoka, who had been his orderly with the Tokyo Division. Mr. Maoka had become ill on Chichi Jima and had been sent home. Mrs. Kuribayashi proposed to send him some cigarettes, but the General counseled her: "I think that because he could not join me here such a gift would make him feel worse." With rueful irony he appended, "It is this war which makes such problems of small matters."

Among the garrison, there was never any mystery as to what was to come. As early as December 26, an enlisted man wrote in his diary: "I think we should be especially cautious around January. It is said that thirty transports and three Marine divisions and the fleet have been assembled."

Others chose the year-end to sum up. One soldier wrote that he had now been away from Japan ten months. "During this time," he said, "I have been sick, and many of my comrades have died as the result of enemy bombing. They have all scarificed their lives for us." Looking ahead, he wrote: "We all welcome the New Year. We are determined to advance and annihilate the Americans and the British. They must pay for those of us who have died in battle."

Another said that the naval raid of December 27 had set fire to some ammunition before it could be unloaded. "It is regrettable beyond words," he said. Private Sonoyama told his father: "I keep working without even rest when I have a stomach ache. I have to be thankful."

On New Year's Day, the 19th year of Showa, there was a little sake for every man. "They must be eating rice cake at home now," Sonoyama wrote. "We have had something to celebrate with, and we ate rice cake of remembrance. We had many good dishes for the New Year."

On January 5, Admiral Ichimaru called the naval officers to his command post. In a pedantic voice, as if addressing students, he told of the destruction of the Japanese fleet at Leyte, and of the loss of the Philippines.

"It is now very logical to assume that the next American landing will be made here at Iwo, Formosa, or the Kurile Islands in the north," he said. "The possibility of the Iwo operation is quite high.

"There are three basic formulas to counter an enemy landing attempt. One is to engage the enemy fleet on the ocean before the enemy starts landing. Two is to intercept the enemy right at the beach line when the landing starts. Three is to attack the enemy after he has landed. Now we have to discard the first two methods; we do not have sufficient surface strength to engage an enemy fleet on the sea, nor do we have any adequate firearms to match the enemy's guns at the beach.

"I expect every one of you will here-after orient your troops for the third formula of fighting. Conserve water and provisions. Our objective will be to pin the enemy on the island, exact continued toll, and keep the enemy fleet around this island for as many days as possible."

The officers returned and spoke with their men. There was nothing to do but dig and wait.

The raids were very bad now, and the men could not get their sleep. "Because of the previous day's fatigue, I fell asleep in the ammunition warehouse," one said. "When I awoke the enemy warships had gone. I am amazed at the enemy's daring."

Another said: "I woke up at 5 A.M. With ten air raids nightly I am not able to get my sleep. You can see by my eyes that my body is exhausted."

In the midst of final preparations, Kuribayashi wrote a last letter to "My dear Taro and Yoko" on January 18. He spoke only as a father to his children.

"The other day I sent one of your letters back to you with your errors noted," he said. "Later, I found that I had made two errors in those corrections. Check your dictionary and correct the letters. Yoko, you make errors in spelling and grammar, and you do not write legibly. You should improve your penmanship and write without errors. In Japan, others will not respect you if you make errors in letters.

"I wish I knew how long the war will last. They can completely destroy Tokyo with their bombers. They have already ruined much of London and Berlin. No one can foretell the future of Japan, but we must have courage and do our best for our country.

"If your mother moves to the country, you should go with her, Yoko. But you, Taro, should stay in Tokyo and continue your studies. I know that it will be hard for you to be separated from your mother and your sister, but you must train your will. If you can become a two-year student at Waseda University, you will probably have to work at an Army depot. As the depot will be an enemy bombing target, be careful not to get hurt.

Very truly yours,
Yours Father."

There was much work for the garrison, repairing damage from the raids. Private Sonoyama said "It was war all day" on January 5, when both planes and ships came against the island. He spent the next three days clearing the wreckage of barracks and offices destroyed in the shelling. He found some radishes in a garden: "It's really delicious to eat them a little at a time."

But he was very sick, and there were many funerals. On January 24, they buried Shogazaka Kiyoichi, killed in the raid the night before, and the next day it was Oishi Tsunemori. Sonoyama's feet were always numb and his head was heavy, but he felt guilty that he could not work. "I feel bad about taking rest. I have lost weight, but I should do my best until the end."

The end was known to be not far away. The officers told their men: "It is possible that the enemy will land on the 30th of January, President Roosevelt's birthday, or on February 23 [sic], Washington's Birthday." The men were also told that if they had to leave water containers behind, they should destroy them or put hydrocyanic acid in them.

In late January, Kuribayashi wrote his wife a very straight letter (he never knew which one would be his last):

"The war will not end soon and the enemy gets stronger all the time. At Saipan alone, some 150 B-29's are based; by April they will have 230, and by the end of the year, 500. So you can see, the bombing of Japan will get steadily worse.

"And when Iwo Jima falls, many bombers will be released for bombing Japan. The Americans will probably invade Japan at Chiba and Kanagawa Prefectures (just south and east of Tokyo), then advance toward Tokyo. Listen to the radio and read the newspapers so that you will be able to judge the situation and plan accordingly.

"The war in the Philippines is going against us and I am sure that the enemy can invade Iwo Jima at any time. No one here expects to return alive, but we are determined to do our best. Do not plan for my return. Do not be surprised when you hear that I have died.

"Do not let others, particularly reporters, read my letters, as they would publish the information.

"I hope that you can buy a plot for my burial in Tokyo, but if not there, any plot is all right. I am sure that my ashes will not be sent home, but my soul will remain with you and with the children.

"Take care of your health and live as long as possible so that you can care for the children.

Very truly yours,
Tadamichi."

Like every wife with a husband at the front, Mrs. Kuribayashi had hoped for a miracle. But the General tried once again to prepare her.

"It is odd that you dreamed about my transfer," he wrote. "It cannot happen. We will be invaded at any time and no one can then get off of the island. A commander-in-chief is never transferred before a battle. Please stop hoping that I can return alive, that you will ever see me again. All officers and men overseas, except those in China and

Manchukuo, will be killed too."

He tried to tell her that he would not be the only one. "Lt. Gen. Baba was recently appointed as an Army commander of the Southern Area and he will share the same fate, as will Lt. Gen. Sato, Watanabe, and Kitamura. That date – death – will be unavoidable."

There was a short letter on February 3. He had not heard from his wife in twenty-three days, and he feared that she was sick.

"Are you still in Tokyo? Believe me, the bombings will get steadily worse so I wish that you'd go to a safe place. You probably won't be killed directly by a bomb, but you could easily be burned or be hit by a bomb fragment. The enemy uses incendiaries here, which cause fires even though there is nothing to burn. They also drop drums of jellied gasoline which explode and make seas of fire.

"In spite of the heavy air raids, I am, fortunately, healthy. We are getting a few vegetables from our small gardens, and while taking an unexpected bath the other day, I found that I was getting fat.

"Most of the command has been sick, but I've been fortunate.

"Maj. Omoto, 1st Adjutant General, is leaving for the Imperial Headquarters today. He will take this letter to you. Don't ask him to send me anything.

"Take care of yourself and get a massage occasionally to help you overcome your fatigue.

"Tell Taro to behave himself.

Very truly yours,
Tadamichi."

Two days later, his radiomen reported to Kuribayashi that all United States aircraft had changed code signs. The meaning of this was clear.

February 11 was the last good day. It was Emperor Meiji's birthday, the 2,605th anniversary of the founding of the nation, and a holiday in Japan and in the islands. For this special occasion, the "Song of Iwo Defense" was released to the public and caused a sensation in Japan. On Iwo Jima, all units assembled in the open near their posts and listened to broadcasts of this song, written especially for them. In a great wave of patriotism and reverence, they all performed the ceremony of Distant Worship for the Emperor. Rice cake was given out, and red bean rice, and some of the men drank their last beer or sake. The enemy sent over twenty-two heavy bombers, and that night there were ten alarms.

"Everybody is tired from anti-aircraft battle day and night," Private Sonoyama said, "but we are proud that we are going to fight to the end."

Two days later he made the last entry in his diary. "It rained all day. Listened to records in the afternoon – it's been a long time. Listened again at night."

He never returned to Izumo, in Honshu.

The sailing of the convoys from Saipan was known immediately. A naval patrol plane reported on February 13 that 170 ships were moving northwest from Saipan. All troops in the Bonins and on Iwo Jima were put on alert. Major Mitsuaki Hara marched the 1st Battalion, 145th Regiment south from Kita Village, into positions around Airfield No. 1. He placed the 1st Company on the west side, and the 3rd Company on the east side, directly behind the beach. With the 2nd Company, he set up battalion headquarters in the crook between the runways at the north end of the field.

Probationary Officer Yutaka Sugawara, who had arrived that very day from Chichi Jima, took over the last mobile radar unit of the 109th Division. He found it set up with four trucks on Higashi Yama, in operation only four days. Superior Private Yoshiji Urazaki was too late. His radar unit had already been destroyed by naval gunfire. He retired to a cave, not sure what to do.

"At home, news of the convoys leaving Saipan caused a wild reaction.

Uniformed schoolboys stormed into Perry Park at Kurihama, near Yokohama, the site where Commodore Perry had come ashore nearly a century before to reopen Japan to the Western world. The boys, rallying under the banner of the Imperial Rule Assistance Youth Corps, rushed the granite shaft and in a frenzy of patriotism toppled it to the ground and spat upon it.

When the shelling began on Friday morning, February 16, the Iwo garrison stayed underground. Sugawara watched in frustration as the naval gunfire destroyed his radar unit on Higashi, smashing telephones, radio, and all other equipment. He and his men were left only with rifles. A well on the east coast near Higashi was destroyed, and Fujio Hanozono of the 5th Anti-Aircraft Unit, wrote: "The number of near-hits is horrible."

As he looked out at the fleet offshore, one man wrote: "My heart sank.

"Kiba and I agreed this was our final day, and resolved to die happily together, for, no matter how we looked at it, it was a hopeless situation."

Chapter 4

Task Force 58, the most powerful carrier force ever to put to sea, sailed from Ulithi February 10 to attack the Japanese homeland. For every sailor, from Admiral Nimitz down, it was a rare moment.

In the armada were 116 warships, nearly every one new since Pearl Harbor and all capable of better than 30 knots. In the heart of it were the carriers, 16 of them in all, mounting 1,200 planes. Around them were 8 new battleships, 15 cruisers, and 77 destroyers – a fleet stretching far beyond the horizon. In the ships were nearly 100,000 sailors and airmen, not one of them prouder than Pete Mitscher.

Vice Admiral Marc. A. Mitscher, a wizened Texan of fifty-seven, had launched the Doolittle raiders against

Japan from the old Hornet in 1942. That was already ancient history in the new art of naval air power. As Task Force 58 rode out of the anchorage, Mitscher watched from the bridge of the Bunker Hill. He was sitting on a high stool, as usual, one arm crooked over the splinter shield and his long-billed baseball cap pulled down hard over his eyes. He was, of course, riding backward ("I'm an old man now; I spent my youth looking forward"), and he was scowling. The Admiral's radio call was "Mohawk," and they were heading for "Indian country." His hatred for the Japanese was legend in the fleet. Many men still with him recalled the incident at Truk. A Japanese plane had been shot down, and one of Mitscher's destroyers signaled that it had picked up the pilot. The Admiral's signal lamp snapped back one word, "Why?"

The task force passed east of the Marianas and refueled at sea on February 14, Admiral Spruance joined the force in his flagship Indianapolis, leaving the Iwo Jima operation in Admiral Turner's hands. This was a great prestige operation for the Navy, and Spruance did not intend to miss it. He was aware that Howlin' Mad Smith and the Marines thought he was weakening the main thrust against Iwo Jima. He was aware, too, that the Army Air Forces were watching to see what carrier planes could do against Japan. He read with satisfaction Mitscher's final instructions to his pilots and his prediction, "the greatest air victory of the war for carrier aviation."

On the morning of the fifteenth, the destroyers were topped off for the last time, taking fuel from the larger ships. The weather began to worsen, the sea growing colder as the fleet neared Japan. The high-speed run-in began at 7 P.M., and tension rose among the men. Huddled around the plotting board in Mitscher's staff room on the Bunker Hill, his senior officers made final preparations for the next morning's strikes.

Younger men listened respectfully as Commodore Arleigh A. Burke made "suggestions." This was "31-knot Burke," famous in the fleet for his destroyer exploits in the Solomons. One of the youngest there was Lieutenant Byron R. White, better known as "Whizzer" White, All-American halfback at the University of Colorado. Earlier in the war he had been in PT boats in the Solomons with another young lieutenant, John F. Kennedy. They had met in London, when White was a Rhodes Scholar and Kennedy was helping his father, Ambassador Joseph P. Kennedy. They would meet again, years later, when Lieutenant Kennedy became President of the United States and named "Whizzer" White to the Supreme Court.

At 9 P.M., Captain George A. Seitz, commanding the Bunker Hill, spoke to his men over the public address system.

"You have the best of ships and the best equipment in the world, and you have had the best training," he said. "The

111

outcome of tomorrow's task is up to you. I know you will do your best."

The Protestant chaplain read to the men from the Bible:

"Finally, my brethren, be strong in the Lord, and in the power of His might. Put on the whole armor of God, that ye may be able to stand against the wiles of the Devil."

In the wardroom, the young ensigns stopped playing roulette for a few minutes.

"By dawn on Friday, February 16, the carriers were in launching position, only 60 miles off the Japanese mainland. There was snow in the air and the clouds were low, but Pete Mitscher ordered the attack without hesitation. The first planes were away promptly at 6 A.M.

The moment the word came to Guam, Admiral Nimitz personally scrawled out in longhand Communique No. 259:

"Vice Admiral Marc. A. Mitscher is in command of a powerful task force of the Pacific Fleet, which is now attacking enemy aircraft, air bases, and other military targets in and around Tokyo.

"This operation has long been planned, and the opportunity to accomplish it fulfills the deeply cherished desire of every officer and man in the Pacific Fleet." It did indeed.

To indicate that this was not an isolated action, Nimitz added:

"Surface units of the Pacific Fleet are bombarding Iwo Jima. Aircraft of the Strategic Air Force, Pacific Ocean Areas, are bombing Iwo Jima and nearby positions in the Bonins. The fleet forces are under the tactical command of Admiral R. A. Spruance, Commander Fifth Fleet."

Top target for Task Force 58 was the Nakajima Aircraft Company plant at Ota, 40 miles northwest of Tokyo. The B-29's had attacked it only six days before, with poor results – only eleven of the thirty-seven buildings were damaged. The carrier planes nearly obliterated the plant.

The next day, the carrier planes were back, this time attacking Nakajima's engine plants at Musashino-Tama, less than 10 miles from the Imperial Palace in Tokyo. The B-29's had had three cracks at this target, about the only damage being the plant hospital, burned to the ground with fire bombs. Despite bad weather, the Navy pilots attacked, doing more damage than any single B-29 attack. Mitscher was elated, but that night he had to admit defeat. The weather was so bad he canceled the third day of the strikes, and Task Force 58 turned back for Iwo Jima.

In the Bunker Hill's briefing room, Lieutenant Herbert Wiley, twenty-six, heard that the Springfield, Ohio, Chamber of Commerce had offered $1,000 to the first Springfield man to bomb Japan. "If the offer still stands," he said, "the chamber can consider this my claim for it." When the clippings came back from the Springfield papers, Carrier Air Group 84 wrote a song, "Thousand-Dollar Herb." Only the last line is now remembered: "Did he do it for his country? Hell no, he wants a thousand dollars."

The Navy could hardly wait to announce the results: 332 Japanese planes shot down, 177 destroyed on the ground, at least 150 probably destroyed on the first day, an escort carrier set afire, a destroyer and 9 coastal vessels sunk, many other vessels damaged and extensive damage to the aircraft plants. American losses were 30 to 40 pilots and 49 planes in combat.

It was, said Admiral Nimitz, "a victory as historic as it is decisive in the heart of the enemy's defenses." Implying more to come, he concluded: "I know that our future operations will hurt the enemy even more."

In far-off Chungking, the Chinese newspapers said the carrier raids were "an almost unimaginable epic of American might and daring."

Chapter 5

There was no final liberty at Saipan, and no grand farewell. The ships sailed in echelons, on a careful schedule, Spike Blandy's vessels leading the way on February 13. Rear Admiral W. H. P. Blandy's group included the minesweepers, the Underwater Demolition Teams in the LCI gunboats, and the bombardment ships – six battleships, five cruisers, sixteen destroyers, and a dozen carriers.

Two days later, the first of the assault ships got under way; LST's carrying Marines of the Fourth and Fifth Divisions who would be in the first landing waves, the LCS (L)'s, which were special LCI's fitted out as rocket boats, and other landing craft. The main body of transports left on February 16, carrying the bulk of the Fourth and Fifth

Divisions and supporting elements, as well as the Third Division's 21st Regiment, in LST's. Last to leave Saipan was the remainder of the Third Division in transports, sailing February 17.

When Saipan dropped from sight behind them, every man knew he was committed, the Marines most of all. The next land he would see would be alien, an island set far out in the sea. In training they had called it "Island X," or "Workman Island." For the past two weeks they had known it by its real name, Iwo Jima, and studied every feature of it on relief maps, in plaster or rubber. Now there was nothing to do but wait and prepare.

Infantrymen cleaned their weapons and recleaned them, packed and repacked ammunition, sharpened their knives and bayonets. Drivers checked their vehicles, and communications men tried out their equipment. In the USS Cecil, the Navajo teams had a final run-through. In a test over a circuit running from General Rockey's headquarters topside to a compartment below decks, four Indians beat four Marines in speed and accuracy of message transmission. In the Navajo language the Indians had an unbreakable code; no one outside the tribe had ever mastered Navajo.

In his final word to the Fourth Division, General Cates said he had no misgivings about the coming battle. "You are Marines – a word symbolic of a great fighting organization – and you will, undoubtedly, add to the brilliant record of the 'Fighting Fourth.' Good luck, and God keep you."

Inside the landing ramp of an LCVP, the last thing his men would see before the ramp dropped, a sergeant carefully painted the words, "Too Late to Worry." In an LST carrying Fifth Division artillery, Captain Remmel Dudley watched a chaplain strapping on a .45 pistol. The priest smiled and said, "Yes, prayer is good, but this thing is quicker."

Lieutenant Colonel Ralph Haas told the 1st Battalion, 23rd Regiment to have faith, fight hard, and remember the maxim "Duty is ours, consequences are God's." Four days later he was dead.

Corporal Jack M. Frazer of the 2nd Battalion, 24th Regiment, ten days short of his twenty-first birthday, was still smoking the cigars he'd gotten from the Saipan campaign. Wounded in the first wave there, he had been hospitalized. When he had written home that he couldn't get cigars, his local newspaper put on a campaign that buried him in them.

When his transport left for Iwo Jima, Frazer wrote in his diary: "I have a funny feeling things aren't going to work out so good this time." The next day, D minus 2, he wrote: "For the first time in my life I'm a little worried. We got our ammo today." But the young smoker, by then a man, lived to write: "Mar. 18 – Iwo Jima is secured. Twenty-seven days of hell."

The weather grew colder each day as the convoys moved north, and the sea was flat gray. But the nights were clear and still, with a quarter moon and millions of stars. The universe seemed unlimited, and home was so far away it could no longer be imagined. The long lines of ships, their engines throbbing softly practiced on his violin, keeping in onward, never pausing, their wakes churning up plumes of phosphorescence in the half-light. No light or movement showed on the decks, but there was life inside. Lieutenant Joe Sansone, in the rocket boat Dottie (LCS 36), broke all the rules and let his men have a can of beer every night. Better to drink it now than never. In the stern ammunition locker, Ensign Bill Starr softly practiced on his violin, keeping in trim for the Kansas City Philharmonic. Lieutenant (j.g.) Johnny Kraus practiced star sights, and the navigator taunted him. "Have we passed the Cape of Good Hope yet, Magellan?"

Far up ahead, the battle for Iwo Jima was already opening. Promptly at 6 A.M. on February 16, the same hour at which Mitscher was launching planes against Tokyo, Blandy's bombardment fleet appeared off Suribachi. Kuribay-ashi had been up nearly an hour, waiting for them. The night before, his radioman, Master Sergeant Taizo Sakai, had sent off a dispatch to Tokyo, coded gungokuhi (very secret). The General said that the entire United States Pacific Fleet was approaching Iwo Jima, and now was the time for the Imperial Japanese Fleet to come out. The reply was prompt: Now was not the time to come out, but on April 1, the Imperial Navy would set forth gloriously and push the Americans back to the mainland. Sakai had been in the Army six years, and it was the kind of reply he had expected from the Navy.

Sunrise was at 6:44 A.M. There was no sun, but the ships could be seen plainly. "What a spectacle," said Corporal Kofuku Yamakage. "I have never seen so many ships in my life."

Historically, he was seeing one of the last appearances of the "Old BB's," the old battleships. Three of them had started life as coal burners, and three of them were up from the mud of Pearl Harbor. The Arkansas, built in 1912 and the oldest battleship still afloat, had smashed the gun positions at Pointe du Hoc in Normandy. The Texas and the Nevada had also been at Normandy. The New York was making its first invasion since North Africa, and the Idaho and the Tennessee completed the force of "old ladies." Among them they mounted seventy-four guns, from 12- to 16-inch.

There were no illusions about the job ahead. Reconnaissance studies in the last four months showed how the island's defenses had grown:

	October, 1944	February 1, 1945
6-inch coast defense guns	8	6
Dual anti-aircraft	37	41
Automatic anti-aircraft	189	203
Blockhouses	2	37
Pillboxes	37	316
Covered artillery	4	70
Open artillery	22	8
Covered structure	6	15
Total targets	305	696

The increase in the number of block-houses, pillboxes, and covered artillery was amazing. Constant air and surface attacks had had an ironic reverse effect; instead of weakening the island's defenses they had strengthened them.

The bombardment plan embodied all the lessons learned from North Africa to Normandy, from Tarawa to the Marianas. The island had been laid out in numbered squares, each square assigned to a specific ship. Every known target was numbered. A master card index was kept in Blandy's ship, the Estes – each card to be checked when the target had been destroyed.

Lieutenant Colonel Donald M. Weller was in the Estes, heading the Marine gunfire team, and Marine teams were in every bombardment ship. Carrier pilots especially trained as gunfire spotters were flying from the carrier Wake Island, and the radio network tying the gunfire teams together was the most elaborate ever used. Area bombardment – haphazard plastering of the target – had been found wasteful and inefficient in previous campaigns. Iwo Jima was to be a carefully directed and controlled smashing of each known target. At least, as many as possible.

Priorities were assigned as follows:

1. Artillery emplacements, coast defense, and anti-aircraft positions that might threaten the ships, aircraft, and beach-clearing operations of the bombardment fleet.

2. Blockhouses, covered artillery, pillboxes, machine-gun pits, and command posts that might threaten the Marines in their assault on the beach.

3. Caves, fuel and ammunition dumps, and bivouac areas, targets lending support to the enemy forces.

In poor visibility, with low clouds scudding over the island, the minesweepers started in at one minute after sunrise. The sweepers went in to three miles from the beach, feeling out the enemy. There was no fire from shore.

The battleships lay several miles off, and at 7:07 A.M. Admiral Blandy gave the order "Commence firing." But ten minutes later the order was modified. Many targets could not be seen and it was nearly impossible for the planes to spot the fall of the shells. When the planes came in closer the ground gunners drove them off with heavy fire, keeping them above 3,000 feet.

Eight carrier planes made a rocket and strafing run over Airfield No. 1, and forty-two B-24's came in from the Marianas. The overcast was so thick that Blandy ordered them home with their bombs still aboard. Commander Leonard F. Freiburghouse took a couple of minesweepers up the west coast, and the Japanese did not fire on them. There were a few tense moments when "overs" from the bombardment fleet raised giant waterspouts around the little sweepers, but none were hit.

In the afternoon, the Pensacola's spotting plane, a slow Kingfisher, made a remarkable bag. The pilot, Lieutenant (j.g.) Douglas W. Gandy, radioed that a Zero was on his tail. It made a pass, missed, and roared by. Gandy pumped bullets into the Zero's tail, and it crashed into the cliffs at the north end of the beach. "I got him, I got him," Gandy called out over his radio.

In late afternoon, the Barr steamed in to within 2 miles of Higashi Rock, a mile and a half off the eastern beaches. Three officers and ten men of UDT 13 continued in small boats to the rock, where they put an acetylene lamp, set to flash white to seaward as a marker for the assault forces. As they withdrew, the Japanese opened fire, but the only casualty was Ensign C. F. Hamman, who cut himself on the rock. The light could be seen clearly from the sea, flashing thirty-five times per minute.

At 6 P.M. the bombardment fleet withdrew to sea for the night. The first of the three precious days the Navy had granted the Marines had resulted in exactly seventeen targets destroyed. Nearly seven hundred were still left.

While the first day's bombardment was under way, Admiral Turner strode into the wardroom of the Eldorado for his final press conference. More than seventy correspondents representing news media from all over the world were crowded into the room. The Admiral peered at them over his steel-rimmed spectacles; his beetling black brows and thinning gray hair gave him the appearance of a stern grandfather.

"Terrible Turner" had come a long way from the shores of Guadalcanal, where a ragtag fleet of old ships had dumped the Marines ashore and fled before the might of the Japanese Navy. The Admiral now commanded a powerful and majestic fleet that then had only been a dream. And a new policy had been announced from Washington:

"It is the express desire of the Navy Department that a more aggressive policy be pursued with regard to press, magazine, radio, and photographic coverage of military activities in the Pacific Ocean Areas."

The Admiral had always been uneasy with the press, but he was willing to give it another try. Into the room with him came his old adversary, Howlin' Mad Smith, eyes glinting behind gold-rimmed glasses, a handful of staff officers, and a surprise guest, Secretary of the Navy James V. Forrestal. His presence in the fleet had been rumored; his appearance confirmed that Iwo Jima was a "big operation."

Admiral Turner, whose duties also included censorship, began on a negative note:

"We feel that photographers are not evil," he said. "Correspondents we also have the highest regard for; they take the same chances we do. We expect facts in stories to be verified. The opinions correspondents express are their own; that's between them and the American people. Censorship will be liberal, except for highly secret, technical information."

This included, he went on, absolutely no mention of suicide planes, napalm, underwater demolition teams, or unusual weapons, American or Jap-

128

anese. There would also be no references to units or persons involved, or to Task Force 58. Within that scope, Turner said, every effort would be made to expedite the movement of press copy. For the first time, news stories could be sent direct to Guam by radioteletype – a minimum of 5,000 words on D-Day and an average of 10,000 words daily thereafter.

As to the target, Admiral Turner said:

"The defenses are thick. The number of defenders there is considerable and well suited to the size of the island. It is, I believe, as well defended a fixed position, particularly an island position, as exists in the world today.

"We expect losses. We expect losses of ships and we expect losses of troops, and we believe they will be considerable. We are taking steps, as far as our knowledge and skill and intent is concerned, to reduce these losses as far as we can, to as low figures as we can. But, we are going to have losses. However, we expect to take the position."

General Harry Schmidt's chief of staff, Brigadier General William W. Rogers, outlined the plan of attack on a wall map.

"We are to meet a strong initial defense at the beach," he said. "In that way he [the enemy] will try to do his utmost to keep us from establishing a landing and consolidating our beach-head. If he fails in that, then he has five infantry battalions at least that he can use for a coordinated counterattack any time after darkness of D-Day, preferably just before sunrise on D-plus-1 morning."

It was not yet known that the Japanese had abandoned the policy of banzai charges. They could no longer afford this waste; the policy was "ten lives for one."

Colonel Edward A. Craig, Schmidt's operations officer, said: "We expect to have 8,000 men ashore in the first hour and by nightfall we hope to have in excess of 30,000 men on the beach." American amphibious power had grown so great that this figure caused no comment.

Next to arise was Howlin' Mad Smith. Great patches of sweat showed under his armpits. His emotions were barely under control at the thought of his last campaign and of Marines about to die.

"It's a tough proposition," he started. "That's the reason we [Marines] are here.

"The Japanese, in my opinion, will have a mechanized defense," the General said. "Every man, every cook, baker, and candlestick maker will be down on that beach somewhere with some kind of weapon." The General was as mistaken in his prediction as everyone else.

"It is my considered opinion that a counterattack will be launched as soon as it can be launched," he went on. "We welcome a counterattack. That is generally when we break their backs." For the first time, the Marines were not to be granted that boon.

"We are of the considered opinion

that the correct and proper way to take this island is to do it quickly."

Kuribayashi had decided that it should be slowly and painfully.

"We may have to take high casualties on the beaches, maybe 40 percent of the assault troops. We have taken such losses before and, if we have to, we can do it again.

"Are there any questions?" asked General Smith.

"Yes," said one correspondent. "When's the next boat back to Pearl?"

General Harry Schmidt had never been good at speeches. Looking more solid and craggy than usual, he kept it short. "We are not sending any boys to do a man's job. We are going to get after them and get after them quick and get it over as quickly as we can." (His private estimate was ten days.)

"General Smith has always said 'Get on their tails and keep on their tails.' What we're going to do is take their tails away." He sat down.

When he arose to speak, Secretary Forrestal seemed almost shy, but he spoke with feeling.

"It has been said here this morning that you are honored to have me present on this operation. Quite the reverse is true. It is a high privilege for me to see in action the quality of leadership America has produced."

He said he was impressed with the material might which he saw about him, but that he was not for a moment misled.

"In the last and final analysis, it is the guy with the rifle and the machine gun who wins the wars and pays the penalty to preserve our liberty.

"My hat is off to the Marines. I think my feeling about them is best expressed by Major General Julian Smith. In a letter to his wife after Tarawa he said: 'I can never again see a United States Marine without experiencing a feeling of reverence.' Thank you Admiral," said Forrestal.

The press conference was over, except for Admiral Turner's final word to the newsmen: "I hope you get many good stories, and I hope that you don't get many sensational ones."

Chapter 6

Saturday broke clear at Iwo Jima, and the minesweepers started in at 8 A.M. This time, a dozen little wooden sweepers, YMS's of Sweep Units Five and Six, went to within 750 yards of shore, probing for mines, reefs, shoals, and obstructions.

Rifles and light machine guns fired on them from Suribachi but they kept on with their work. The Skirmish, a steel-hulled sweeper of the 185-foot class, drew 40-mm. fire but escaped hits. No mines were found and no shallows; the water was deep and cold, with heavy surf on the beaches.

The Idaho, Tennessee, and Nevada opened fire at 9 A.M. from a mile and a half out, almost point-blank range for their heavy guns. The Pensacola came close in under the cliffs to put fire

over the minesweepers, and the tempta-
tion for the Japanese proved too much.

Corporal Yamakage jumped up and
down, shouting, "Let us fire the 15-
centimeter now. We're itching for the
trigger."

"All right," Ensign Ono replied, "but
let the ship come as close as possible."

"Set the range at 1,500 meters," he
said. "Hold it, hold it . . . . . . fire!"

The first round was 50 yards short,
and the cruiser had begun to turn – but
not soon enough. In three minutes the
Pensacola was hit six times. The combat
information center was smashed, her
plane caught fire on its catapult, and
ready ammunition boxes were set off.
The ship ran for cover, her crew fighting
the fires and plugging holes near the
waterline.

"Keep firing, keep firing," shouted
Ensign Ono, with the cruiser still in easy
range.

But the gun fell silent. "The base gave
way," the corporal said, and it had. The
barrel now pointed toward the sky, and

Ono cursed in rage. "We could have sunk her. We could have sunk her."

The Pensacola soon controlled her fires and flooding, but 17 men had been killed and 120 wounded. The executive officer, Commander Austin C. Behan, had been killed instantly in CIC. At 10:25 A.M. all ships were ordered away from the beaches; it was time for the frogmen.

Underwater demolition, a vital part of amphibious operations, was still so secret it could not be mentioned in news stories. Commander Draper L. Kauffman had opened the first school in 1943 at Fort Pierce, Florida, for Navy volunteers who were "half fish and half nuts." At Saipan, in daylight and under heavy fire, the swimmers had blasted a channel 250 yards long through a coral reef to enable the Marines to land. There were no reefs at Iwo Jima, but there might be sharpened bamboo spikes just under the water at the beaches, or steel rails imbedded in the sand, or concrete blocks wrapped in barbed wire, or mines. One rumor said the Japanese had set out drums of gasoline, wired for ignition just as the Marines reached shore.

At 10:30 A.M., destroyers formed a line 2,500 yards offshore, and the LCI gunboats waddled through them, heading for a line 1,000 yards from the beaches. Quiet fell over the sea as the bombarding stopped; a gentle breeze sprang up and the sun burned off the February chill. Mist still encircled the top of Suribachi, and a seaman croaked in a strained voice. "This would be a good time for the goddam thing to blow and we could all go home."

The gunboats came on slowly, a line of seven, one for each numbered landing beach. Three more gunboats followed in a second line, then, two, and finally one, in an inverted pyramid.

The swimmers, five pairs for each beach, launched their small boats (LCPR's) from the destroyers and passed through the gunboats en route to the beach. They would leave them 500 yards out and swim to the beach if they could. They were to chart the bottom, mark the 3- and 1-fathom lines, destroy obstructions, and bring back samples of the sand from the beach.

The little gunboats, slow and ugly, somehow managed to look gallant, their flags snapping from the mastheads. In the command ship, Commander Michael J. Malanaphy's LCI (G) 627, the supply officer shut himself up in the radio shack and listened to the last-minute traffic: "Passion Fruit" calling "Fisherette," "Real Beer" talking to "Idle Swain" and "Saint Pete." In the accents of Alabama, Oregon, and Maine it all sounded unreal, but it was all too real.

Kuribayashi was watching. It could be a feint, but he knew that LCI's were assault vessels. Those coming in now could have 2,400 troops aboard. At 10:35 A.M. he made his only mistake of the campaign; he ordered, "Commence firing."

The forward line of gunboats was slow

to realize what was happening. Lieutenant Jerome J. O'Dowd in LCI (G) 457, close up under the cliffs at the East Boat Basin, told his radio officer to tell the destroyers and cruisers to cease firing or lift their aim. Splashes were rising all around him.

At the other end of the line, Lieutenant (j.g.) Wallace G. Brady in LCI (G) 450 thought it was Guam all over again – short fire from his own ships. But the swimmers came on, passed the gunboats, and swam for the beach. The gunboats let go with rocket salvos, 700 rockets at a clip, and the shore replied with small-arms fire and mortars.

Suddenly, about 11 A.M. the island defenders had had enough. Heavy artillery, hidden in the north and case-mated into the foot of Suribachi, opened fire on the gunboats. A shell wiped the 40-mm. gun platform off the bow of LCI (G) 449, killing the five men manning it. Thirty seconds later, a shell at the base of the conning tower killed twelve more men. A third shell hit the bridge, blowing out the starboard side. Lieutenant (j.g.) Rufus G. Herring, bleeding from three wounds, called the engine room with orders to back off. Then he staggered to the wheelhouse and took the wheel. No one around him was alive.

Directly under Suribachi, 473 drew the full fire of heavy and light guns and soon was on fire with 189 holes in the hull. It was Brady's turn at 11:12, and the 450 took hits on two 40-mm. gun mounts, fires broke out in several places, and one shot cut the cable on the bow anchor, sending it plunging to the bottom.

Later, the 450 claimed it was the first American ship to drop anchor in the Nanpo Shoto since Commodore Perry had in 1853. This was brought up, naturally, by Brady's engineering officer, Ensign Charles King, Jr., of Wilton, Connecticut, a descendant of the Commodore. At the moment, King was far too busy for such reflections. As he led a firefighting party, two men disappeared in a shellburst before him. He reached for a telephone, and it was shot from his hand. A few moments later the fire hose he was manning, was clipped by another shell, two inches from the nozzle.

Within minutes, every ship in the forward line was hit; the radio traffic in the command vessels told the story:

"473 is sinking rapidly and will have to be towed off the beach."

"438. Bow gun knocked out."

"457. We are taking on water."

"469. We have had several hits. We are taking water."

"449. Request doctor as have injured aboard."

"457. We are sinking."

"469. We are taking water fast."

"441. Our engines are out."

"471. We need medical assistance in a hurry. Where do we go?"

The answers were quick and sure:

From Captain B. Hall Hanlon, Commander UDT's Pacific:

"LCPR's assist LCI's where possible."

From Malanaphy: "348 assist 457."

From Malanaphy to 469: "Relieve 449."

Hanlon to Malanaphy: "466 needs tow."

Hanlon to Blandy: "Are getting heavy fire from unknown location, apparently on right flank."

Hanlon to Malanaphy: "473 has been hit."

Hanlon to Blandy: "Urgent, desire smoker."

Hanlon to Blandy: "Urgent, please increase fire on all known targets."

Malanaphy to 471, looking for doctor: "Go to any large ship."

Hanlon to Blandy: "Do we get smokers, per my request?"

The answer to that one was yes. The Tennessee, Nevada, and Idaho laid a smoke screen over the beach area, and the Nevada moved up to fire her 14-inch guns straight at the cliffs. Destroyers increased fire, and an air strike came in against the base of Suribachi. Still the Japanese batteries fired with deliberation. And still the LCPR's bore in.

In their boats, the swimmers, clad in face masks and trunks, fins over their tennis shoes, made a last check of equipment – lead lines for soundings, knives, mine detonators. Their main concern was purely occupational: cold water. Weaving through the water spouts toward shore, Ensign Frank J. Jirkla, Jr. managed a crooked smile. "What the hell," he said, "we're getting paid for it."

Despite the Japanese shelling, nearly 100 swimmers went into the water, dropping off the sides of their speeding boats. UDT 12 dropped an extra pair of swimmers as it passed Futatsu Rock, to buoy it at the 4-foot water mark on both sides.

The sea, at least, was calm, and the swimmers dove regularly, surfacing to breathe and dodge fire. The bottom was clean and hard, but the water was deep right up to the shore – no reef problems but bad for anchoring and controlling the landing fleet. There were no obstructions and no mines, perhaps due to the deep and swift water.

By noon, recovery began. Heavy shelling was still going on but the gunboats were not retreating – more than one made emergency repairs and went back into the line. They withdrew on schedule, their mission completed. And they were a battered lot. Nearly all had dead aboard. Some were burning or had holes in the hull. Few had full power left and some were under tow. One was sinking. LCI (G) 474, Lieutenant (j.g.) Matthew J. Reichl commanding, took fourteen heavy hits (probably 6-inch shells) between 10:55 and 11:03. There were three magazine explosions and four large fires, but still she moved forward. Soon, however, she began to roll, water 6 feet deep in several compartments, and Reichl headed for the Capps. The destroyer took off her men and the 474 stayed afloat, now on her starboard side. At 12:30 P.M. Reichl went back with four volunteers, but as they drew near she turned over, bottom just out of water. The Capps sank her with 40-mm. fire. The 474 lost an ensign and three enlisted men in the battle. Two others refused to leave the engines and went down with the ship: Motor Machinist's Mate First Class Orville I. McQuiston of Emlenton, Pennsylvania and Motor Machinist's Mate Third Class Joseph I. Williams of Dallas, Texas.

When the 466 came alongside the Tennessee, John Marquand went down from the bridge to get a closer look as it bobbed alongside the battleship.

"When she reached us the sun was beating on the shambles of her deck," he wrote later. "There was blood on the main deck, making widening pools as she rolled on the sluggish sea. A dead man on the gun platform was covered by a blanket. The decks were littered with wounded. ... The commanding officer was tall, bareheaded, and blond, and he looked very young. Occasionally he gave an order and then he, also, lighted a cigarette."

It was Lieutenant James J. Horovitz, twenty-seven, of Brighton, Massachusetts. Four of his men were dead, one missing, and eighteen wounded, of a crew of ninety-two. Among the wounded was Ensign Jirkla, the swimmer from UDT 12. He had just arrived at the bridge, after being pulled from the water, when a shell cut off both his legs.

Lieutenant Herring took the 449, worst smashed of all alongside the Terror, flagship of the minefleet. Seventeen of his men were dead and 20 wounded. Herring lay at the base of the conning tower, nearly unconscious, and the decks were strewn with dead. All gun positions had been smashed. The Terror helped three more gunboats that day, slinging one of them in wire cables to keep it from sinking.

Only one swimmer was missing, Carpenter's Mate First Class Edward M. Anderson. He had last been seen swimming between Futatsu Rock and the beach, mortar fire falling around him. The morning's work cost 43 dead,

153 wounded, and one missing. Of the twelve gunboats, only four were able to make Saipan under their own power. The destroyer Leutze had also been hit; 7 men were killed and 33 wounded. Among the badly wounded was the skipper, Commander B.A. Robbins. In the afternoon the swimmers reconnoitered the west beaches, with three battleships and a cruiser covering them. Without the gunboats to make it look like a landing, the Japanese gunners left them alone. No obstructions were found on the beaches.

The battleships and cruisers resumed shelling of the island. Carrier planes strafed it and dropped napalm. Forty-two B-24's from the Marianas strewed the island with fragmentation bombs. Major Kenneth Brown of Salt Lake City, a squadron commander, said he was sure the Liberators "had 100 percent hits on the target."

Kuribayashi was not concerned. He was confident he had driven off an invasion.

Tokyo Radio reported: "On February 17 in the morning enemy troops tried to land on the island of Iwo. The Japanese garrison at once attacked these troops and repelled them into the sea." The broadcast said five warships, including a battleship, had been sunk.

Admiral Soemu Toyoda, Commander in Chief of the Combined Fleet, messaged Rear Admiral Ichimaru:

"Despite very powerful enemy bombings and shellings, your unit at Iwo coolly judged the enemy intentions and foiled the first landing attempt and serenely awaits the next one, determined to hold Iwo at any cost. I am greatly elated to know that, and I wish you to continue to maintain high morale and repulse the enemy, no matter how intense his attacks, and safeguard the outer defenses of our homeland."

The true meaning of the day was that two days of bombardment had scarcely damaged the firepower ashore. Kuribayashi, in repelling the "invasion," had disclosed unknown gun positions.

Only three of his twenty blockhouses had been smashed, and only a handful of the dozens of pillboxes. In the cliffs over the East Boat Basin, where the intelligence reports had said "four possible anti-tank guns," there were now known to be thirteen guns in concrete casements, ranging up to 6-inch. Some of the shell fragments looked very much as if they came from 8-inch guns.

It was a very tense group that met that night in Admiral Blandy's cabin on the Estes. Only one day of bombardment remained, and the beaches had not even been cleared, let alone the artillery and mortars in the northern part of the island. Lieutenant Colonel Weller, the Marine gunfire officer, suggested another day's bombardment. Spruance, away on the Tokyo raid, had given Blandy the option of an extra day's delay if the target was not ready. Admiral Turner had already voted no, fearing a bad turn in the weather. Blandy declined Weller's suggestion.

Weller, mindful that the Marines

would have to cross the beaches in thirty-six hours, then asked that all fire on the final day be directed there. As he wrote later:

"Never mind the artillery, mortars, and anti-aircraft still undestroyed; never mind the inland blockhouses and pillboxes that would bar the way later. Decision: Clear the beach defenses and the coast guns commanding the beaches."

New tactics were decided on. The New York, which had been firing on targets in the center of the island, was added to the lineup for the stretch from Suribachi to the cliffs. The New York and the Nevada would concentrate on blockhouses on the beach. The Tennessee was assigned to the cliff batteries, and the Idaho to Suribachi. Ships were given permission to expend all ammunition not allocated for D-Day.

Sunday morning visibility was only fair, with rain squalls, but the battleships opened fire at 7:45 A.M. from 2,500 yards – a mile and a quarter – at

151

sea. Working carefully and deliberately, the Nevada and New York began stripping the sand from suspicious-looking hummocks behind the beach. This was done with single shells, to blow the sand away and reveal the concrete structures beneath the ground. Then a few rounds of 2,000-pound, high-capacity shells, and another blockhouse was gone. As the Japanese scurried from their burrows, the 40-mm. gunners followed them over the terraces and cut them down.

The deadly serious gunners of the Tennessee blasted the cliffs for nearly five hours, carefully picking the coastal batteries out of the bluffs. Ensign Ono watched the giant shells walking up the cliff and cried "Everybody run!" The men piled into tunnels and caves, and around them the earth moved as much as a foot. In the shock pockets, the kerosene lamps were snuffed out, and the men trembled and waited. They counted 50 shells in twenty minutes, and when the firing moved away they went out. Their battery hung over the cliff, barrels pointing toward the water. The horseshoe of 25-mm. cannon was gone, and where there had been 5,000 shells there were now two smoking craters.

"Well, boys," said Ensign Ono, "from now on we are foot soldiers. Check your rifles and bayonets, and be ready for hand-to-hand combat."

The Idaho, concentrating on Suribachi, blasted away all day, steadily pulverizing the rock and concrete at the base of the mountain. If those guns were not silenced, Marines would die.

In late afternoon the big ships withdrew and the photo interpreters went to work. The verdict was that sixteen of the twenty blockhouses on the beach had been destroyed, and half of the pillboxes. In addition, seventeen coastal batteries had been smashed, including a four-gun battery at the foot of Suribachi. There were still hundreds of guns and mortars untouched, but they would have to wait.

Late Sunday night, Blandy messaged Admiral Turner "...I believe landing can be accomplished tomorrow. . . ."

Many a Marine would never forget that the battleships still had plenty of ammunition. They had not been able to fire even the amount allotted to them.

In the Marine transports, final church services had been held Sunday morning. Attendance was, if anything, less than normal. The 23rd Psalm was a favorite, and the men recited it and sang "What a Friend We Have in Jesus," intoning the words raggedly above a quiet sea, the water hissing steadily by, the hulls of the vast fleet moving steadily northward. In an LST, a Coast Guard correspondent, Vic Hayden, said for those around him he'd be damned if he believed "that old crap about there being no atheists in foxholes." He said he was going to start the Foxhole Atheists Society in protest. Some men laughed, and others walked away.

In a Fifth Division transport, Ira Hamilton Hayes played out his macabre joke for the last time. Looking around, his eye fell on Private First Class

Franklin Sousley. "You're gonna get it, and in case I'm not there, this is for you." Then he played taps on his harmonica. Sousley was nineteen, and this was his first time out. Hayes had been with the paramarines at Vella Lavella and Gougainville, and he didn't care much for white boys. He was a full-blooded Pima and all his life had been classed with Negroes and Mexicans.

As it turned out, Sousley was going to get it, and Hayes would not be there. The Indian would return to the United States, a hero because of a photograph, a photograph that showed Hayes and Sousley side by side, raising the American flag on Suribachi with four other men. Hayes would survive to become drunk in Chicago while Sousley died in the gorge near Kitano.

In the aircraft carrier Cabot, far off at the edge of the convoy, Ernie Pyle was seasick. He was new to the Pacific and impressed with the naval might around him. But after years in Europe, and the closeness of the foxhole and the dugout, this was a strange and impersonal warfare.

The last night was a personal travail for Howlin' Mad Smith. After forty years, he was commanding Marines for the last time. He knew that tomorrow would bring terrible casualties. He had never forgotten the lagoon at Tarawa, flowing red with blood.

More than once he had remembered Admiral Hill's boast at Tarawa: "It is not our intention to wreck this island. We do not intend to destroy it. Gentlemen, we will obliterate it!"

And Marc Mitscher's signal before Saipan: "Keep coming, Marines! They're going to run away."

Late in the evening, the General went to his cabin in the Eldorado and read from the Bible. He was a Methodist and this was his custom. Then he prayed, and finally he read from the Daily Readings of Father Joseph F. Stedman. Around the General's neck was a St. Christopher medal blessed by Pope Pius X. He closed his eyes and put out the light.

Part Two

INVASION

Chapter 1

In the morning, the island was there, rising darkly from the sea against the gray horizon. It seemed strange to find it there, after so many days on the open sea. It looked alien, in an indefinable way. To John Marquand, it was Japanese, with the "faint delicate colors of a painting on a scroll of silk." To Corporal William Gadwah, a rifleman in 3/26 and a veteran of the jungle campaigns, it looked like "either a pushover or a son of a bitch." To a young lieutenant, the island, swathed in the mists of morning, was a "God-forsaken place."

But it was not just "another island." It was Japanese, it was Iwo Jima, it was part of the enemy's homeland. No foreigner had ever set foot on it. From the sea, it appeared barren and lifeless, no trees, no growing things, no trace of human life. On the left, clouds hid the top of Suribachi, its gray sides rising steeply from the sea, and to the north, the island widened out suddenly, with high bluffs along the shore. Between the two lay the beaches, black and narrow, the terraces thrusting up sharply before the ground leveled off.

In the LST's and the transports, the men had been up since 3 A.M. The last meal, in Navy tradition, was steak, an ominous breakfast.

"Give me three days of good weather," Admiral Turner had said, and by 5 A.M. it appeared that he was to get at least one. The wind was 8 knots from the north, and the surf on the landing beaches was relatively low, only 3 feet.

At Dawn Alert, the Admiral appeared briefly on the bridge of the Eldorado in his old bathrobe. As usual, he seemed utterly alone, but he was not without his own sardonic humor. The night before, listening to a Japanese broadcast that he would never leave Iwo Jima alive, he had scribbled a note to Spruance: "Maybe you'd better come rescue me."

By 6:30 A.M., all transports were in position, and ten minutes later the bombardment began. It was awesome, the heaviest prelanding bombardment in history. Admiral Spruance, racing back from Tokyo, went in himself on the Indianapolis and returned the two new battleships he had borrowed, the North Carolina and the Washington. In all, there were seven battleships, four heavy cruisers, and three light cruisers. With the destroyers and smaller vessels they began execution of the plan, "Schedule of Fires, Dog-Day."

The plan, painstakingly printed in three colors and stamped "Top Secret," had been under study in the vessels for weeks. Every shell, every mortar barrage of the day's firing was planned. Each vessel was assigned the time of fire, number of shells, and target area. Not a foot of the island, from Suribachi to Airfield No. 2, was to be left clear of fire.

At first it was slow, deliberate shelling.

The battleships, two on the west coast and five on the east, opened with 75 rounds each in the first eighty minutes. The cruisers fired 100 rounds each in a barrage that shook the island and the sea around it. Clouds of dust began to rise from Iwo Jima, at times almost obscuring it.

The gunfire stopped a few minutes after 8 A.M., on schedule, and Mitscher sent in 120 carrier planes from north of the island. Among them was one Marine squadron of 48 planes, led by Lieutenant Colonel William A. Millington. This was one of the few times Marines saw their own planes in close support, and Millington's orders were: "Go in and scrape your bellies on the beach."

Coming in from the south in two columns, the planes worked north up the landing beaches, dropping napalm on the first run. Some of the fire bombs failed to ignite, but the others spread billows of flame along the coast, and the Marines cheered. The planes came back for rocket and strafing runs, working low over the beaches for twenty minutes. Marines in the assault waves, boated and waiting to land, shouted and pounded each other.

The Army sent 44 Liberators from the Marianas, but only 15 reached Iwo Jima, dropping a haphazard 19 tons of bombs on the island. At Spruance's insistence they came in at less than 10,000 feet. He had at first refused to have them over the beachhead at all, so worried was he by their poor aim.

The naval bombardment resumed at 8:25 A.M., all fire aimed on the beaches. For the Navy, this had to be it. The first assault wave was at the Line of Departure and would start in at 8:30. The battleships belched salvo after salvo in sheets of orange flame, the concussions shattering the sea beneath the guns and the force thrusting the big ships back in the water. Above the thunderous roar of the 16-inch guns, the sharper crack of the 5- and 8-inch guns of the destroyers and cruisers pierced the air in the mightiest H-hour cannonade the

Marines had ever experienced. More than 8,000 shells smashed into the beach area in less than thirty minutes. Deep underground, in Suribachi and in the north, the Japanese waited, stunned for the moment by the concussions.

The assault force had been forming offshore since 6:30 A.M. Admiral Turner, in perfect calm, had given the order at 6:45 A.M.: "Land the Landing Force." The sea, once so empty, was now crowded with vessels stretching nearly 10 miles from shore. In five hundred ships the plan for yet another amphibious operation began to unfold. Hatches opened, cargo booms went out, boats were put in the water, cargo nets were slung down the sides of ships. Radio circuits crackled into life, telephones rang throughout the ships, and thousands of engines, gasoline and diesel, were started.

The Line of Departure, LD, was established at 7:30 A.M., 2 miles offshore and parallel to the beach, a control vessel marking either end. Along the line, tiny vessels marked out the boat lanes, and the Assistant Division Commanders went to the line as observers, Brigadier General Hart for the Fourth and Brigadier General Hermle for the Fifth. The LST's opened their bow doors, and assault Marines launched in their LVT's, armored amphibious tanks armed with 75-mm. howitzers and three machine guns. They would climb 50 yards inland and form a ring of fire for the following waves.

Boated and circling, the first three waves were ready at the line by 8:15 A.M. From the air they looked like water bugs, trailing white-plumed wakes. The sun was stronger now, and the island was many shades of brown and yellow. In a smart breeze, tiny pennants snapped from hundreds of mastheads. It was a fine day.

The Central Control vessel dipped her pennant exactly at 8:30 A.M., releasing the first wave of assault troops, and the battle was on. Sixty-eight LVT (A)'s of the 2nd Armored Amphibian Battalion crossed the line and headed in, naval shells still whistling overhead. The LCI's moved in for the last mortar barrage of 20,000 rounds, and the second assault wave crossed the line, 1,360 Marines in LVT's. Eight more waves formed behind them, ready to land at five-minute intervals. In less than forty-five minutes there should be 9,000 men ashore.

Just as the air observer overhead called out "Leading wave 400 yards from shore," the naval shelling lifted to move inland and the last air assault came down. This was Millington's belly-scraper mission and it roared over the beaches just off the sand.

The first LVT (A)'s hit the sand on Red 1 at 8:59 A.M., one minute ahead of time, and in the next three minutes on every beach from Suribachi to the cliffs, except Blue 2. Before them, only a few feet inland and rising nearly straight up, was the first terrace, from 10 to 15 feet high and composed only of loose sand. It was quickly apparent that only tracked vehicles could make it, and not all of them. The amphtracs attacked it, and some got to the first plateau, grinding up the face in showers of sand. Some churned 50 to 75 yards inland on the center and north beaches, but down near Suribachi the cliff was impassable. The LVT (a)'s plopped back into the water, swam out and turned to fire from the sea.

For the first few minutes there was no fire from the defenders, and the leading waves of troops scrambled from their LVT's and began to climb the terrace. It was like climbing a waterfall. Loaded down with equipment, from the 51 pounds carried by a corpsman to the 122 pounds saddled onto a mortarman, the men "swam" up the sea of volcanic sand, fighting to reach the harder ground of the first plateau. There was, as yet, no fire against them. Kuribayashi's plan was holding up well; let them swarm onto the plain and then annihilate them.

The third wave, with 1,200 men, beached at 9:07 A.M., and five minutes later nearly 1,600 men came in on the fourth wave. Other waves of men were right behind, ready to fall on the shore almost as regularly as the surf. Kuribayashi's time had almost come. A desultory rattle of small-arms fire began to come from the nearest lines.

As strength ashore began to build, Colonel John R. Lanigan's 25th Regiment formed and started to move inland, turning to the right toward the Quarry. Colonel Walter Wensinger's 23rd moved straight in toward Airfield No. 1. Next to them to the south, Colonel Thomas A. Wornham's 27th Regiment drove inland to curve around west of the airfield. The 28th of Colonel Harry B. Liversedge raced straight ahead with three jobs: to cut across the narrowest part of the island, turn south to take Suribachi, and turn north to help take Airfield No. 1. The first of these jobs fell to the 28th's 1st Battalion, Lieutenant Colonel Jackson B. Butterfield, the second to the 2nd Battalion, Lieutenant Colonel Chandler W. Johnson; and the third to the 3rd Battalion, Lieutenant Colonel Charles

E. Shepard, Jr.

Nearest Suribachi, Captain Osada's 312th Independent Infantry Battalion was waiting. Major Matsushita's 10th Independent Anti-Tank Battalion lay behind Yellow 1, in front of the slope leading to the main runway of Airfield No. 1; Just north of that, behind Yellow 2, was Captain Awatsu's 300th Independent Infantry Battalion. It is no longer possible to say how many were still alive, but of Matsushita's 300 men, 6 were alive when the battle ended. The 312th and the 309th had each started out about 800 strong. Of the 1,600 men, 42 survived the battle.

One of these was Superior Private Nosaro Fuji, thirty-one, a devout Buddhist. The rolling naval barrage struck the 309th squarely, and of the 40 men in his company, only 10 men were left at the end of one minute. Fuji had been fighting since 1936, and he longed to return to his candy store in the town of Miyazaki on the island of Kyushu. He stumbled north, fleeing the barrage, and found a cave in the crook of the runways at Airfield No. 2. There he stayed for nineteen days, as the war passed over his head.

As the landing progressed, the 312th gave ground slowly toward Suribachi. They fought all day and well into the night. Nine men of the battalion, about one in a hundred, lived through the battle.

On the morning of February 19, Private Shigeru Yoshida did not go outside. There was nothing more he could do.

For nearly a year he had been working at the top of the terrace, overlooking the east beaches. Each day, as he was told, he had laid up stones to make ammunition pits and shelters in the ground. On this February morning, Private Yoshida stayed in his cave at the foot of Suribachi. Around him he spread his gas mask, ointment for mustard gas, and bleaching powder to clear gassed areas. He brewed tea near a fumarole and waited.

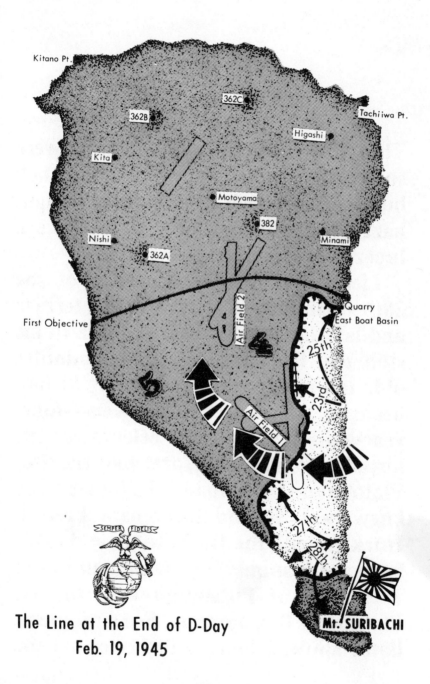

Kitano Pt.

362C

362B

Tachiiwa Pt.

Higashi

Kita

Motoyama

382

Nishi

Minami

362A

Quarry
East Boat Basin

First Objective

Air Field 2

25th

23rd

Air Field 1

27th

28th

SEMPER FIDELIS

Mt. SURIBACHI

The Line at the End of D-Day
Feb. 19, 1945

Chapter 2

The first thirty minutes ashore were surprising An occasional mortar shell burst on the beach, and there was a light haze of small-arms fire, almost like a breeze on the prairie.

Lieutenant Wesley C. Bates of the 28th scrambled to the top of the terrace and lay there, exhausted and sick to his stomach. The battle was not ten minutes old, and so far was like nothing he had been led to expect. The twenty-four-year-old Texan (he'd celebrated his birthday a month before) had the 2nd Platoon of C. Company. To his right, he knew, was Second Lieutenant Fred J. Huckler, with the 1st Platoon, and to his left was (or should be) Lieutenant Frank J. Wright of Pittsburgh with the 1st Platoon of B. Company. For a moment, Bates allowed himself to hope that the

Japanese had secretly withdrawn from the island.

Sergeant Thorborn M. Thostenson and a corporal ran to the first pillbox. They threw three or four grenades, and the corporal ran inside. He came out with his bayonet dripping blood, trotted to a second pillbox, and jumped on top of it. Fire from another pillbox killed him. Bates' dream was shattered.

Leapfrogging forward in little bunches, the men began to pass the pillboxes, blowing some and bypassing others. The sun was getting hot, and so was the mortar and small-arms fire.

Private First Class John H. Henning, twenty, of Guthrie, Oklahoma arrived out of breath. He'd been chasing his squad leader, Sergeant J. D. Dawson, twenty-five, of Odessa, Texas, across the island. When they came to a pillbox with no way around it, they went over it. ("There was nothing I could do about it," Henning said.) Private First Class Paul Adams had stuffed his field jacket in his pack – machine-gun fire chewed it off his back. Private First Class James B. Treadway, twenty-three, of Walnut Creek, California had a bump on his head where a bullet had traveled right across his skull, in one side of his helmet and out the other.

Lieutenant Wright reached the western shore about 10:30 A.M. He had started as a platoon leader with sixty men. The only men still with him were Private First Class Remo Bechelli, twenty-six, of Detroit and Private First Class Lee H. Zuck, twenty-two, of Scranton, Arkansas. On the way across, Zuck had leaped to the top of a 20-mm. gun emplacement and killed eight Japanese, one after the other, as they ran out the back door.

Bates reached the shore at nearly the same time as Wright. It had taken just ninety minutes to cross the isthmus, but only four or five men remained with him. The island could not yet be called cut in half. Turning back to look for his platoon sergeant, Lewis G. Pickens, Bates walked erect with a rifle in his left hand, unaware for the moment of any opposition.

As he came in sight of his company, some less than 150 yards in from the landing beach, Bates waved for them to come on. They waved him back, and almost instantly he knew why. A machine gun to his left opened fire, and a bullet broke his left forearm. Even as he fell he thought, "Oh, oh, Purple Heart." Then he saw a private, beating his bleeding head against his rifle butt and eating sand. A corpsman was running to help the private, and that was all Bates remembered for a while.

When his head cleared, he got up and rallied some men near him. The fire was intense now, and the noise and detonation of big shells all around was nearly suffocating. The Lieutenant was afraid for a moment that they were cut off on the western side. But men were coming through, incredible though it was.

Gunnery Sergeant Harry L. Mowery crouched in a hole near the center of the island. As men passed in either direction, he found out what they knew and passed the information on to the next party. No wire men were out yet, and everything was word of mouth.

Bates slowly learned where his men were. Pickens was wounded, and Sergeant Michael R. Kost, leader of the third squad, was dead. His runner, Private First Class Lloyd Tudor, a quiet boy, had slowly bled to death from a leg wound. But still the men came on. Platoon Sergeant Jesse J. Sutfin came in with the remnants of A Company's third squad.

Captain Dwayne E. Mears of Bakersfield, California had the idea that blockhouses could be attacked with pistols. Time after time he did it, smashing forward across the island. Just as he reached the west coast, a bullet pierced his throat and blood spurted out. He lay still, but a private began to cover him with sand. Bobo Mears cried, "Get the hell out of here! I'm all right." In the late afternoon they got him to a ship, but he died the next morning.

There was only one company commander of 1/28 left in the action. Captain Aaron G. Wilkins had held A Company near the beach until the 2nd Battalion, massing for the assault toward Suribachi, was ready. Then Wilkins started his men for the west side. Driving across in high excitement, the men sometimes watched Tony Stein. He was twenty-four and had been at Guadalcanal, Bougainville, and Vella Lavella. For this one, he had a special weapon, a "stinger." Tony had been a toolmaker in North Dayton, Ohio and had fashioned a hand machine gun from the wing gun of a wrecked Navy fighter.

He was the first man out when A Company moved, and he ran for a pillbox. Right behind him came Sergeant Merritt M. Savage, a demolitions expert, and Corporal Frederick J. Tabert. With only his stinger, Corporal Stein attacked one pillbox after another, Tabert and Savage close after him. In the first hour Stein killed at least twenty Japanese. Then he did a strange thing.

He took off his helmet and shoes and ran for the beach to get more ammunition. He made eight trips in all that day, and twice his stinger was shot from his hands, but at the end of the day he was still firing it. As his Yugoslavian mother always said, "He's a tough one, that Tony."

Taking Suribachi had been drilled into 2/28 until they thought it would mean the end of the war, and they piled ashore on Green Beach with fierce determination. It was after 9:30 A.M., and the Japanese in the mountain had now recovered. Heavy mortar fire was falling, and the gunfire came in short, purposeful bursts – no target, no fire. Some LVT's made it to the beach, others barely got through the surf line, and none could climb the terraces. The men piled out and scrambled for cover, splayed flat against the terraces, crouching in shell holes, and realizing, suddenly, that others were being hit. The beach was jammed with men, waiting, it seemed, for leadership – and then it came. Up the beach, erect and contemptuous of the fire, strode a short, fat man shouting "Okay, you bastards, let's get the hell off this beach!" It was the battalion commander, Lieutenant Colonel Chandler W. Johnson, and by the sheer force of his personality, the men were lifted off the beach and started inland for Suribachi.

Right behind Johnson ran the battalion adjutant, Second Lieutenant G. Greeley Wells, a map case bobbing at his belt. In the case, for a very good reason, was an American flag. At rehearsals, each officer stood and recited his duties, and Wells always ended with the phrase "...and I carry the flag." Johnson would growl, "Why?" and Wells would reply, "Because it says so here." It became something of a joke in the battalion. At Guam, just before the battalion transferred from the Missoula to its LST, Wells had gotten his flag from the transport's office, and he had it with him now.

Lieutenant Charles F. Suver climbed to the top of an LVT in the tank deck of LST 634. It was 5:30 A.M. and time to say Mass, for he was a Jesuit and a chaplain of the 2nd Battalion. Afterward, the men stood quietly near their vehicles, eating sandwiches and coffee, and Father Suver, in his Jesuit way, mused on the difference between courage and fearlessness. "A courageous man," he decided, "goes on fulfilling his duty despite the fear gnawing away inside. Many men are fearless, for many different reasons, but fewer are courageous. I hope I have courage, for I will never again be fearless." They went in with the ninth wave – Suver, Captain Arthur H. Naylor, Second Lieutenant George W. Haynes, and a lot of others. The chaplain remembered now that, some days before, Wells had said he was going to get a flag from the transport. Haynes said, "You get the flag and I'll get it up to the top of Suribachi." Father Suver added: "You get it up and I'll say Mass under it."

On the next beach to the north, Major John W. Antonelli took Companies E and F of 2/27 in over Red Beach 1 in the first waves. Private First Class Harold L. Pedersen, a machine gunner from Williston, North Dakota, had no trouble remembering the date, it was his twenty-second birthday. Thirty-eight days later he walked off the island, carrying the only gun left of the dozen his company started out with. He also carried thirty-eight days of beard and was a good deal older than twenty-two years and thirty-eight days.

The 1st Battalion of the 27th went into action alongside the 2nd, landing on Red 2, led by Lieutenant Colonel John A. Butler. But the confusion was beginning. Company B went in on the left of Company C, instead of the right. There was no time to rectify this, so Company A was thrown in where Company B should have been, and the battalion quickly advanced across the southern end of Airfield No. 1. En route, the regimental exec, Colonel Louis C. Plain, was shot in the arm but finished an inspection and report before being evacuated. Crossing the beach, unreeling wire as he ran, Corporal Robert M. Blankenship 3rd, of Company A, smiled to himself. He remembered his sergeant's last words as they boated up on LST 756. Goldblatt, who had been in every invasion, it seemed, turned to his men and said: "I'll kill the first son of a bitch that says 'This is it.'" No one did.

Leading a machine-gun platoon of 1/27 past the southern end of the airfield, heading for the west coast, was a big-eared Italian boy, handsome and dark. It was Manila John or, more formally, Gunnery Sergeant John Basilone, and there were few things he liked better than soldiering. He never tried high school, but he did a hitch in the Army, and by 1940 was in the Marines. One night on Guadalcanal in October, 1942, he held off a Japanese assault with two machine guns and a pistol, hauling his own ammunition. His Medal of Honor was the first won by an enlisted Marine in World War II, and now he was back doing what he liked best. "I'm a plain soldier. I want to stay one," he had said, turning down a commission. Behind him was that afternoon in 1943, when 30,000 people turned out to honor him on Doris Duke's estate near his home in Raritan, New Jersey. He'd been kissed by a starlet, had his portrait unveiled in the town hall, and been given a $5,000 bond.

For Manila John there was now only one objective, the west coast, and he ran for it, his men behind him. It was barely 10:30 A.M. A mortar shell thudded and burst, and five men were dead, one of them Manila John. As he lay on his face, his arms sprawled in front of him, one could almost see the tattoo on his left arm – "Death Before Dishonor." The Navy Cross was awarded to him posthumously.

Navy Lieutenant Louis H. Valbracht, a Lutheran chaplain with the 27th

Regiment, was amazed at the humor in men about to face death. On the way in, a private hung over the side of the landing craft, watching the shells splash all around. "Boy, what a place to go fishing," he said. "Look at those babies jump." Another kid cried in mock hysteria: "Someone lied to me. The natives on this island ain't friendly."

Running for the terrace when his boat beached, Valbracht met a corporal from the previous boat, limping back. Shrapnel had torn off one of his shoes and several toes.

"Short war, no?" he said. He limped past the chaplain and into a boat for the ride to a hospital ship.

As the 27th turned north beyond the airfield, it came up against Major Tatsumi's 311th Independent Infantry Battalion. Of the 700 men, half survived D-Day; 23 lived through the battle.

In the ships at midmorning, it looked like a World Series broadcast; knots of men were gathered wherever they could find a radio.

"We're in 50 yards," said a Marine sitting in a jeep on the deck of a transport. "Tanks are up a hundred yards," he called out a minute later, and the sailors cheered again.

In radio rooms on the warships, men on watch got only fragments of the battle.

"Let's have some naval gunfire in Target Area 181."

"Air observer Fifth Division reports six friendly tanks on southern end of Airfield No. 1. Have stopped there."

"Air observer Fourth Division reports enemy gun position in TA 166 C-D (the Quarry)."

"Mission 11, enemy gun and mortar positions in TA 183 W-Q-D (behind Quarry) will be attacked by bombs, rockets, and machine-gun fire as soon as possible. 305 Lucky (16 planes) will expend all ammunition on this attack."

"Three torpedo planes with propaganda leaflets are now orbiting Point Sugar awaiting instructions."

Over the aerial observer frequency, a lot of men heard Ray Dollins singing. The major, spotting for the Fifth Division, sang:

Oh what a beautiful morning
Oh what a beautiful day,
I've got a terrible feeling,
Everything's coming my way.

After a moment of silence, the plane spiraled from the sky and crashed in the water among the assault boats coming in. One of the boats picked up Major Dollins' body and that of his pilot. The major's first child, a daughter, had been born eight days before.

Halfway across the island, Valbracht sank down at the foot of a shattered pillbox. As he lit a cigarette, his eye fell on a foot – a bare white foot, all by itself. The chaplain turned his head slowly to the right. In a shell hole 20 yards away, lay the tangled remains of four Marines, their uniforms still smoldering. One of them was missing a foot.

Chapter 3

The Fourth Division's beaches were the hottest. Before the first boat touched down, General Cates, watching the bluffs through glasses from the rail of his transport, shook his head gravely. "If I knew," he said, "the name of the man on the extreme right of the right-hand squad of the right-hand company of 3/25 I'd recommend him for a medal right now."

Guns and mortars on the heights had had the range for weeks, but there was no fire at first. The leading wave landed without trouble. "There's something screwy here," said Corporal Leonce (Frenchy) Olivier, remembering the first wave at Tarawa. 1/23 and 2/23 were across Yellow 1 and 2 without a shot. Then it began. Fire poured in from the front and the flanks, from pillboxes, ditches, and spidertraps. In front of the 23rd were two huge blockhouses and at least fifty pillboxes. The blockhouses were partly wrecked, but fire still came from them. Lieutenant Colonel Ralph Haas sent out the first call for artillery and tanks.

But Sergeant Darrell Cole of 1/23 wouldn't wait. He led his machine-gun squad against the pillboxes, firing into the slits as he passed. When his gun jammed, he ran behind the pillboxes, one after another, tossing grenades into them. Twice he ran back for more grenades, but on the third trip a Japanese grenade fell at his feet, Cole was killed instantly, but he had started his platoon off that murderous beach.

The day started off badly for Company A, 1/23. Captain John J. Kalen took them in on the third wave, landing over Yellow 1, and, almost immediately, his radioman was wounded. As the captain crawled toward him, he, too, was hit. His men, held in their holes by incessant fire, watched in agony for forty-five minutes as Kalen slowly bled to death.

Fifteen hundred yards offshore, Lieutenant Commander Robert L. Kalen, gunnery officer of the Chester, directed the cruiser's main-battery fire inland, trying to clear a path for the Marines. It was not until a month later that he learned his brother had died before the battle was an hour old.

First Lieutenant William E. Worsham took over Company A, and the 2nd platoon made it 250 yards inland, the 3rd platoon holding up a hundred yards back. Machine-gun fire from pillboxes ahead made it impossible to advance, and Worsham decided to make a run to the left around Company B. A moment later he was killed, and First Lieutenant Frank S. Deyoe, Jr., platoon leader of the 60-mm. mortars, took over. A bullet drilled him through the left shoulder, but the maneuver began. First Lieutenant Arthur W. Zimmerman led the men around Company B and up toward Airfield No. 1.

A blockhouse stood in the way, and Zimmerman went back to the beach for a tank. It was obvious that nothing else would do. He coaxed the Sherman into position, and its 75-mm. gun opened fire at close range. As the blockhouse fell silent, Zimmerman's men rushed it with demolition charges, and the platoon rolled over it. Through the afternoon they pushed on, and toward nightfall paused near the airfield to regroup. Zimmerman knew Kalen was dead, but he had not seen Worsham all day. Through the twilight came a gaunt figure, his left arm dangling. It was Deyoe, still in action. "I just wanted to tell you," Deyoe said, "that you've been in command for two hours." Zimmerman, a twenty-five-year-old Montanan, veteran of Roi-Namur and Saipan, smiled wryly. "I'm glad to know it's legal," he said. Deyoe turned and headed back for the beach. What was left of Company A, with its fourth commander in one day, began tying in for the night.

Also dead somewhere on that first wild day, was the 23rd's Lieutenant Howard W. Johnson, the Fourth Division's football star. At Camp Maui they named the baseball field "Smiley Johnson Field" in his honor.

On the beaches, trouble began almost immediately. As the enemy fire rose, so did the surf. Within twenty minutes the beaches began to clog up as the LVT's bogged down or were hit. Then came the LCVP's and real trouble. The light boats hit the beach hard and the surf broke over them, broaching some and swamping others. Other boats, some already disabled, piled in behind them and were hurled onto the beach by the waves. If this kept up, the beaches would soon be impassable.

On Blue 1, farthest north under the cliff, 1/25 came ashore and scrambled to get off the beach. Lieutenant Colonel Hollis Mustain rallied the men, and they struck out for the airfield to circle around and take the top of the Quarry. This was the key move of the whole day.

The heights must be captured to stop that terrible fire on the beaches. Early progress was surprisingly good.

Calls for tanks went out before the men had been ashore a half hour. The LSM's, far sooner than planned, were called in and three of them hit the Yellow Beaches soon after 10 A.M., landing sixteen Shermans for the Fourth Division. The Fifth Division sent its first tanks ashore in LCT's. Two of them made it, but the third fell into the water as a wave threw the landing craft off the beach. Lieutenant Henry Morgan radioed his superior: "Horrible Hank sank." The rest of the Fifth's tanks came in in LSM's.

The first three in were hit by gunfire, but the crews held them on the beach and the 15-ton Shermans began to crawl out. A bulldozer cut its way to the top of the terrace and began opening a road. A horned mine blew off a tread and, as the driver jumped, three big shells smashed the machine. The tanks ground up the terrace and into the minefield, bogged down, and began blasting with their 75-mm. guns. Engineer troops on hands and knees poked for mines with their bayonets and laid white tapes to mark the edges of the cleared lanes. Mine detectors were no good in the magnetic sand, and most of the beach mines were ceramic anyway. They had to be hand-picked or taken out the hard way, by exploding them.

Confusion mounted on the beaches. Coxswains were landing wherever they could find space. Beachmasters fought to follow the plan, but even the Marines thwarted them, ordering in this boat or that out of turn, because it had something they wanted. One LSM tried to land tanks on Red 1, but there was no exit yet. The skipper headed for Red 2, but the beachmaster hooted him off. He finally dumped them on Red 1 and they churned up the beach and found an exit.

LSM 216 took four hours to unload. The first tank down the ramp on Yellow 1 stalled in its track, blocking four more behind it. The ship moved a couple of hundred yards south and broached. The crew finally got it off, tried Yellow 1 again, and found the sand too soft. At 1 P.M., on the fourth try, the tanks finally landed. The infantry was already cursing them for drawing fire. "It's a ███████ toss-up," said a corporal, "whether to run away from them or crawl under them." But their 75's were most welcome.

The 133rd Seabees were unique – they made an invasion, landing right along with the Fourth Division. It was the first time this had ever been tried in the Pacific – and the last. The whole battalion, 1,032 men, was ashore by 4 P.M., and its casualties were heavy, the worst of any Seabee battalion in the war.

The "old men" had trained with the "Kids" on Maui for five months, and not a one was killed. It was different on Iwo. Chief Carpenter's Mate A. W. Barker, an ex-deputy sheriff in Arkansas, took a 40-man section ashore on Yellow 1 in the second wave. By nightfall, three of them were dead and fourteen wounded.

Chief Machinist's Mate Douglas Davis hit Yellow 1 at 9:30. A.M. with four 37-mm. guns in LCVP's. Mortar fire wiped out the first 7-man gun crew to land. Motor Machinist's Mate Second Class Neldon Day was crushed to death when he fell under a gun just as it bounced off the ramp. He was the battalion's best pitcher and had been saving money to get married. Carpenter's Mate First Class Robert Pirie, a small man who seldom spoke, was mashed to death under the same gun.

Cleveland Washington of Philadelphia was pretty sure he was the first Negro ashore, a place in history he had not sought. But he had made careful preparations. He had mailed $50 of his crap-shooting winnings to his church. He knelt to pray on the beach, but a Marine major ran by shouting, "You ███████ Seabees get the hell up that ███████ terrace!" From then on, Steward's Mate First Class Washington was just another "███████ Seabee," carrying ammunition up to the airfield.

Carpenter's Mate Third Class Delmer Rodabaugh was a "checker." He was supposed to sit on the beach and "check" things as they came across. He had five large notebooks filled with mimeographed forms – so many drums of gasoline, so many cases of ammunition, so many cans of water. It didn't work that way. The Marines up front were yelling for "ammo, ammo." He picked up a box and started up the terrace. At the top, a Japanese was staring at him. He sat very still in a hollow in the sand. He was in full uniform, every button buttoned, and he was dead. He looked very small, and very foreign. Rodabaugh trotted by and dropped his ammunition case near the airfield.

On the way back, he first noted the dead around him and the wounded stumbling or crawling back to the beach. He jumped into a hole to rest, and a Marine in another hole called out, "Better not lie there, they fire at that hole." Rodabaugh jumped in beside the

Marine and took a good look at him. He was not over seventeen, and Rodabaugh was a very old thirty-four. "What about you?" he asked, and the boy replied, "Oh, I'm all right. I'm up against this side, and the fire comes from this direction." It was Rodabaugh's first combat lesson, and a good one.

Seaman First Class Frank Riefle, thirty-six, a Yellow Cab driver from St. Louis, landed as a BAR man and dove for cover. Not fast enough. Shrapnel from a mortar blast sliced the wedding ring off his finger, barely breaking the skin. He did not stop to look for it. He would not forget he was married; he had six children at home. Riefle kept going forward, because it seemed that fire was always right behind him. Finally he stopped at the front, breathless and out of place. On consideration, he decided to work his way back to the beach and rejoin his outfit, a shore party.

Machinist's Mate First Class Alphenix J. Benard of Escanaba, Michigan sat in his bulldozer with the engine running. He was all ready, and behind him were another bulldozer, two tanks, and two retrievers. LSM 145 hit the beach and the ramp dropped. Directly in front of it was a pile of bodies, mostly Marine, some Seabee. Benard hesitated only an instant. He closed his eyes and the heavy treads ground over the bodies. The men at the front had to have tanks.

"I had no choice," he kept saying to himself as he used his dozer to open roads off the beach.

Chapter 4

Despite the shelling, the Navy beach-master parties went in directly after the first assault waves.

Lieutenant Commander John J. McDevitt, Jr. had eleven men for Green Beach – himself, a lieutenant (j.g.) for communications, a doctor, and eight signal men and radiomen. When the first wave had passed the Line of Departure, McDevitt said, "Let's go." It was the first landing he recalled (and he'd made Kwajalein and Saipan) where the enemy shrapnel came all the way out to the control boat.

"When the ramp hits," he told his coxswain, "put that thing in low and keep going." The LCVP made two lengths before it bogged. The men scrambled out with sandbags, radio, portable generators, bullhorns, and signal flags. For Marines the order was: Get off the beach before the mortars get you. For the Navy beachmaster parties it was: Stay on the beach and keep it open.

Well before noon, the beachmasters were in business. Their bullhorns – nine horns on a tripod – could be heard even above the gunfire and the roar of the surf. Colored banners, lashed between two poles, marked the beach limits, and the generators were sandbagged in holes. Radiomen talked to the ships, passing orders as the Marines called the turns – tanks, more men, ammo, artillery, water, gasoline.

Lieutenant Commander Gaston A. Hebert (he'd been in World War I, but nothing like this) had Yellow 1. "Wave off the LCM, wave off the LCM," he told his signalman. Then his bullhorn blared, "LVT, LVT, any room, any room?" A signalman wigwagged back "Affirmative," and the bullhorn roared, "Come in here, come in here, between the LST's, for casualties."

Behind Hebert stood his Marine aide,

First Lieutenant Carl C. Gabel, moving the stuff inland. It was mixed up, to be sure but, in general, the Navy landed it, and the Marines and Seabees moved it inland.

By noon the tempo of battle was furious. Destroyers were crowding closer in, and even the Tennessee was standing less than a mile off Suribachi, blasting at the mountain. The Japanese fire was intense, and unless it was stopped the beaches would be untenable. Smoke and dust rose from the island, and fire came from everywhere. Overhead in a Navy plane, William F. Tyree of United Press said the island looked like "a fat pork chop sizzling in the skillet."

The enemy was definitely suffering artillery loss. All heavy guns in Suribachi were silenced within three hours of the landing, as were many more in the hills to the north. Much small-arm and machine-gun fire had been wiped out in the neck of the island, but from the north the medium-calibre fire, both mortar and artillery, was extremely heavy. These guns, so artfully hidden, simply could not be found from a distance. And shortly after noon the rocket guns were given permission to fire. According to Kuribayashi's plan, the time had come. The enemy was solidly ashore, and now was the time to annihilate him.

The rocket guns were a freak. The 20-cm. ones (8-inch) fired from a barrel, and the 40-cm. (16-inch) from a wooden chute. Accurate fire was virtually impossible, but the huge shells lobbing through the air made a terrible rumble. When they did hit the beach, they cut a wide avenue of destruction. This was the first time the Japanese had used them, and Kuribayashi had been given seventy guns, with 50 rounds per gun.

The 28th had been calling for reinforcement, and around noon the remaining battalion was ordered in. Lieutenant Colonel Charles E. Shepard, Jr., a bald ex-sergeant, had given his men two objectives:

"1. To secure this lousy piece of real estate so we can get the hell off it.

"2. To help as many Japs as possible fulfill their oath to die for the Emperor."

His men, who concurred, began landing a little after one o'clock, in the hottest fire of the day. Suffering casualties all the way, they finally got across the beaches and inland, but not before late afternoon.

The tanks, now maneuvering inland, were helping, but there was a surprising amount of opposition left in the neck of the island. For days it had been saturated with naval and aerial bombs. Still the enemy lived on. Captain Masao Hayauchi's 12th Independent Anti-Tank Battalion knocked out several Shermans. When his guns were smashed, he led the last assault. Clutching to his chest a charge with the fuse lit, he splayed himself against a tank and blew himself up. Second Lieutenant Nakamura of the 8th Independent kept his gun firing all day and into the night.

But still the Marines landed. The last

battalion of the 27th, the 3rd, led by Lieutenant Colonel Donn J. Robertson, was ashore by noon, and by 3 P.M. the last battalion of the 26th, Lieutenant Colonel Daniel C. Pollock's 1st, was assembling inland.

Colonel Chester B. Graham's 26th Regiment, the last of the Fifth Division, had been boated since 8 A.M., bobbing around far offshore. At 11 A.M. it was ordered to the Line of Departure, but the beaches were impossible. Finally it was ordered in, and crossed the beach a battalion at a time, marching inland for the airfield.

The artillery had been boated for hours, but there was simply no place to land. The Fifth Division had sent only a few of its 31st Seabees ashore, according to plan. Chief Carpenter's Mate James L. Price of West Monroe, Louisiana took a 5-man demolition party in with the assault waves. Price was a seismograph man with Gulf Oil, and he knew explosives. So did his top man, Gunner's Mate First Class Pete A. Paris, a potash miner from Colorado Springs. By afternoon there was plenty of work for them, blasting boats off the beach. Unless the wreckage was cleared, nothing would move.

Seaman First Class Ben Massey of Plainview, Texas, brought the 31st's first bulldozer ashore at noon. He was promptly shot in the neck, and Machinist's Mate Hollis R. Cash, Jr., of Calera, Alabama, climbed into the seat. Soon there were more, all up and down the beach – caterpillars, bulldozers, cranes, shovels, LVT's – everyone straining to cut beach exits and level the terraces, towing jeeps, rocket trucks, and Dukws.

But artillery was vital, and by 2 P.M. it began to pile ashore, ready or not.

The reconnaissance parties and FO's (forward observers) had been ashore since morning. Now, Dukws carrying the 75's and 105's waddled ashore. The Fifth Division guns were first on the beach, but the Fourth Division's were not far behind.

General Cates had looked at the sun at 1:15 P.M. "I wish we had six more hours of daylight," he said, "or even four. Hell, I'd compromise for two. I'll have to shoot the artillery in soon." A short time later he gave the order, and the 14th Regiment started in.

The 13th's guns got over the south beaches somehow, and up the terraces. Within thirty minutes the crack of artillery, clearly recognizable to the foot soldiers, gave heart to the men on both fronts. Sergeant Joe L. Pipes' "Glamour Gal" was first to fire on Suribachi. At almost the same instant, Sergeant Henry S Kurpoat's 75 let go from behind Yellow 2, firing north.

They never settled the argument over which gun fired first, and it really didn't matter. Other guns were right behind them. The Marines shouted as the shells went over them. Dukws of the Army's 471st Amphibian Truck Company, their Negro drivers pressing ashore through the wreckage, landed the field pieces of the 13th Marines in a steady column.

Lieutenant Colonel Henry T. Waller's 3rd Battalion, with 105's, was first across the Suribachi beaches, followed at 2:30 by Major Carl W. Hjerpe's 2nd Battalion. At 4:45 Lieutenant Colonel John S. Oldfield's 1st Battalion landed, and the final battalion, the 4th, under Major James F. Coady, was ashore by 7:30. It was dark then, and two 105's were lost as Dukws swamped in the surf, but the guns ashore were firing. The Japanese no longer had it all their way.

On the Fourth Division front, only the 1st and 2nd Battalions of the 14th Marines got ashore on D-Day. Nothing could get the Dukws over Blue 1, so the 75-mm. pack howitzers of Major John B. Edgar, Jr.'s 1st Battalion were wrestled up the terraces by hand. The Dukws quickly filled and settled in the sand. Bulldozers strained, cables snapped, and towing cleats sheered; The Dukws were through. But the guns and the ammunition moved. By 5 P.M. most of the battery was firing. The fire-direction party set up in a captured blockhouse, throwing a Japanese body into a rear compartment and sealing it. Several times men said they saw eyes at the peephole, but it was eleven days before they knew for sure. A grenade exploded then, and when they opened the compartment there were two bodies, one very cold and one very warm.

When the 105's started to come in, more miracles had to be wrought. These one-ton guns had to move inland in the vehicles in which they came ashore. It took quick work and accurate timing to snake them off the beach before they bogged down or were smashed by enemy fire. Every one of Major Clifford Drake's twelve howitzers of the 2nd Battalion made it into position, but not until nearly nightfall. The 3rd and 4th Battalions were held off until the next day. Without even landing, the 4th Battalion had seven casualties from shells falling in the LST area off shore.

During the afternoon the 28th and the 27th began consolidating, preparing to throw the full weight of the 28th against

Suribachi. But the attack was not ready until 4:45 P.M., and by 5:30 it had made only 150 yards. It was time to draw in and hold for the night. If the Japanese ran true to form, there would be a banzai charge during the night.

In the northern end, the Fourth Division had advanced to within 200 yards of the airfield by noon; an hour later, the reserve battalion of the 23rd, led by Major James S. Scales, came in. The 1st Battalion fought to the end of the airfield by 2 P.M., and there was stopped. Scales' 3rd Battalion passed through it, fought on a little farther, and by 5 P.M. began digging in. The 2nd Battalion came in a half hour later on the right. Behind them was the 24th Regiment of Colonel Walter I. Jordan.

Dutch Hermle, the only general to land on D-Day, got ashore about 2:30 P.M. and set up the Fifth Division's command post near the south end of Airfield No 1. He told General Rockey there was no point in coming ashore that day; communications out to the ships were better than they were between units ashore. Around five o'clock, Hermle sent runners out to tell the men to button up for the night. Sunset would come at 6:45 P.M., and a Japanese attack could be expected.

The O-1 (First Objective) line had been drawn from the Quarry through the center of Airfield No. 2 to the west coast. By nightfall the troops were nowhere near it, except on the east coast. Lieutenant Colonel Chambers had been told to take the Quarry with 3/25, and he had, but not by much. Justice Marion Chambers was 6 feet 2, and he never walked – he bounded – so the men naturally called him Jumpin' Joe. He had been wounded at Tulagi, and when the Japanese raided the hospital, he drove them off nearly single-handed. At Saipan he had literally been blown off Hill 500 by a shell blast. Now he was back, leading 3/25 again, and when Colonel Pat Lanigan ordered the Quarry taken, it would be.

"Get the hell up there," Chambers

said, "before those Japs get wise and grab that ground themselves," and 3/25 started up, nearly 900 men.

Captain Elwyn W. Woods of Company I, farthest on the right, was wounded almost immediately. Company K's commander, Captain Tom Witherspoon, was wounded in the first half hour and by 3:30 P.M., all eight of its officers were casualties. By 4:30 P.M. Company L had lost five officers and Woods' company had lost six. But the remnants of two companies were across the ridge and it held. The battalion was down to 150 men. Company L was down from 140 to 18 effectives in the rifle platoons. But the Quarry was taken.

As night fell, Pat Lanigan borrowed men from 1/24 and began sending them up to the ridge to relieve Chambers. What was left of Company L came down from the line about 6:30, and by midnight the rest of the battalion had been relieved. They went into "reserve," with heavy mortar fire falling all around.

Chapter 5

The carnage of D-Day was terrible, and of a special kind. It was impossible to see the enemy, and his weapons could not be found. Throughout the day a live Japanese was rarely seen. No prisoners were taken, and only a few bodies were seen. Still the fire rained down on the mile and a half of beach from mortars and artillery sited in weeks before the landing, and wherever it fell there was a target.

Navy doctors and corpsmen, landing with the Marines, were engulfed in a welter of blood as the steady crump, crump of mortar bursts blasted among the beach parties. Inland, from the first airfield and the hills above it, from the rubble at the foot of Suribachi, automatic weapons fire rose steadily in volume, as if the Japanese had been untouched by the most intense bombardment in amphibious history.

Lieutenants Sidney Bond and William McHugh, landing with the sixth wave, set up a medical outpost in a Japanese revetment 75 yards inland. As the Marines advanced, so did they, moving several times during the day, losing eleven of their twenty-six corpsmen by nightfall. On one beach alone, two entire medical sections of a doctor and eight men each were wiped out.

Lieutenant Emil J. Kakascik, surgeon of 3/28, got ashore just at noon. After forty-two days in a transport, treating prickly heat and athlete's foot, he almost welcomed action. His first case was one of his own corpsmen, slashed in the foot by shrapnel on the beach. A short time later the doctor was inland, lying in a hole, and had his first chance to look around. Next to him lay a Marine on his back, his left hand up, his wristwatch keeping perfect time and the gold band shining in the sun. You could tell from the color of his skin that he had been dead some time. Nearby was another boy, lying on his right side, one hand under his chin as if in sleep. He was – forever.

A Marine motioned, and Kakascik went to him. Both legs were gone, but he talked quite rationally. Kakascik examined the stumps, brushing off the black sand, and took his blood pressure. It was zero. Pharmacist's Mate Second Class Tom Milne rigged a plasma bottle, and the Marine said "Thanks Doc." They left him – they had to – and he almost certainly died. Kakascik had been ordered to follow the 28th across the island, and it was time to go. With the corpsmen and his partner, Lieutenant Archibald W. Thomson, they emptied their three hand carts (useless in the sand) and carried their gear across the island. By late afternoon they dropped into the command post exhausted. Kakascik could not forget the Marine who had stopped him midway across the island, crying "My buddy needs an amputation, my buddy needs an amputation!"

"Go to the beach station," the doctor said. "I cannot stop now." It seemed heartless, but his orders were to advance at any cost and stay with his unit. As darkness fell, he and Thomson set up in a hole, arranging knives, dressings, and rifles for the night's work. Kakascik noticed for the first time that he was trembling, only partly from the cold.

It was impossible to imagine the condition of the beaches by afternoon; they had to be seen to be believed. The surf line was choked with smashed landing craft that surged with every wave, crashing onto trucks, crates, bodies at the water's edge. Just offshore the small craft swarmed, trying to make out what the beachmasters wanted, and looking for an opening. Everybody had "hot cargo," or thought he had, and every unit ashore wanted its own stuff.

The casualties piled up, not only those from the beach itself but from the front. Every man coming back for supplies brought someone with him, hobbling, dragged in a poncho, or carried in a litter. They were everywhere, sitting, lying, groaning, dying. Nobody knows how many died there, waiting, or how many shivered through the night, waiting for dawn and a chance to get off.

Most men stuck to their jobs, if they could. Machinist's Mate Third Class Marvin Nottingham, cigar in his mouth and carbine across his back, drove his heavy bulldozer ashore and began cutting a beach exit. When he had it open, he backed up to a Higgins boat and began hauling pallets of ammunition inland. He was praying, too.

Somebody told Shipfitter Third Class John C. Butts, Jr. to carry grenade cases off Yellow 1. He made five trips before a sniper killed him. Butts, twenty-four, left a wife and child in Salt Lake City. Somebody picked up the case he had dropped and carried it inland.

Second Lieutenant Benjamin F. Roselle led a naval gunfire spotting party inland. Two hundred yards from the water an artillery shell smashed his left foot. Somebody put a tourniquet on his leg, and the rest of the party went on. Roselle lay in the open an hour and a half, and shrapnel sliced both thighs and his left arm. Someone carried him to the beach and put him in a boat.

Russell G. Dalin, "the Deacon," best gambler in the 133rd Seabees, was ashore one hour when a mortar blast tore off his dice arm.

Seaman First Class Giovanni Jannacone saw an LCVP loaded with ammunition about to broach. He swam out through the wreckage with his buddy, Shipfitter Third Class Terry Terwelleger. They'd never been on an LCVP before, but they found the right levers and gunned the boat onto the beach. Then they unloaded it, and as they took the last cases off, a wave sucked it back into the sea.

Private First Class Leonidas M. Jones of Atmore, Alabama, found a 37-mm. gun on Green Beach. A bulldozer pulled it to the top of the terrace, and Jones and another private began firing toward

Suribachi. Then a bullet sniped the sciatic nerve in Jones' right thigh, and he lay in a hole until dark. Somebody dragged him to the beach and put him in a boat. It was Jones' twenty-second birthday and he was satisfied with the present of his life.

They started dragging out the Marston matting around noon. It was a good idea while it lasted. The first vehicle off the ramp pulled it out into a steel roadway 500 feet long and 10 feet wide. There wasn't enough of the matting, and it wasn't always in the right place, but it helped. Inside of three days, heavy vehicles chewed it into scrap metal, but by that time the beaches were opening anyway.

Gunnery Sergeant Raphael E. Kearns needed ammunition for the 23rd's mortar section. He couldn't find any on the beach but an amphtrac load of it was circling offshore. Jumbo Kearns swam out and guided it across the wreckage on the beach and up the hill. There it stalled. Kearns piled out and commandeered a work party to carry the shells forward. "There's more than one way to win this ~~war~~ war," he said.

From the sea the invasion looked unreal. As it unfolded, in bright sunshine, it looked like a set piece. Lieutenant Commander John McClain, forty, a Hollywood writer once with the New York Sun, thought of it as a movie, perhaps because that was his job. He was there with a staff of forty Navy and Marine photographers to record the operation in color film. He had done the same at the North African invasion under John Ford, and he had been at Normandy. But they were nothing like this.

This was a war in miniature, like a show being put on for the spectators. The entire island was visible, and all the forces, and it was barely possible to believe that men were being killed.

Robert Sherrod of Time-Life watched through glasses as the tanks climbed off the beach, like "so many black beetles struggling to move on tar paper."

Sherrod had made the landings at Tarawa and Saipan, and he had no wish to make a third, but he prepared to go ashore nevertheless.

John Marquand, chewing a dead cigar stump, watched from the open bridge of the Nevada. The Pulitzer Prize novelist, now in his fifties, had come aboard at Saipan at the end of a line slung under his shoulders over a rough, open sea. For D-Day, Commander Howard A. Yeager, executive officer of the battleship, had dressed him in flash gear. His pants were tied at the bottom and stuffed into long socks. Fireproof gloves covered his arms to the elbow, and he wore a lifejacket and a helmet. He carried a .45 pistol, a knapsack, and a gas mask. Wedged into a corner of the bridge, he watched for hours, still remembering the courage of the bloody LCI's coming back from the beach reconnaissance on D minus 2.

This was the biggest show of the war, at the moment, and nearly a hundred newsmen and photographers were present, representing the wire services, important American magazines, the radio networks, and British and Australian publications. The landing, an open secret for more than a week before D-Day, held the eyes of the nation and the world. As the first penetration of the Japanese homeland, it inspired particular dread.

Not all correspondents were going ashore, but those who were took special risks. They could not carry arms. The old hands accepted with amusement the advice that they were to be accorded treatment equal to a major. The enemy had little regard for rank.

Correspondents, the orders said, "may not land earlier than the fifth wave," or 9:17 A.M. None of them did, but James S. Lindsley of the Associated Press finally made it about 1:30 P.M. The beach, they said, had been stabilized.

"It doesn't look like it to me," said Captain John W. Thomason, 3rd, public relations officer of the Fourth Division, as a shell smashed a landing craft on the beach 100 yards away.

Lindsley and Thomason crouched in a hole on the beach. An officer ran by, shouting a question at one of his men in a nearby hole. "I'm sorry sir, I don't know," the Marine replied, then died, both his feet shot away. At dusk, Lindsley and the Captain scrambled up the terraces and dug in on the plateau as bullets spurted sand around them. Nearby, erstwhile sportswriter John Lardner ducked mortar shells. He had left Al Crocker of the St. Paul Dispatch on the control boat. Now Lardner muttered, "Smart man that Crocker, smart man." Thomason left Lindsley in a hole and began helping corpsmen carry wounded to the beach.

Sherrod left his ship about 5 P.M., wondering if the law of averages was about up for him. "I think the worst is about over now," said a Marine in the boat, and everyone felt better for the lie. At the control boat, Keith Wheeler of the Chicago Times, already on the way out, said, "I wouldn't go in there if I were you. There's more hell in there than I've seen in the rest of the war put together." Just then the colonel called "Ready?" and Sherrod heard his voice say "Sure." On the beach, in the cool of twilight, Sherrod smelled it again – death. He began to dig a foxhole for the night.

Casualties had begun to come out to the ships when the landing was less than an hour old, and by noon it was a bloody stream. Surgeons were waiting in the transports and hospital LST's and the cry rang out, "Man the casualty booms." Sailors lined the rails, staring in horror at the loads of "meat" bobbing in the little boats alongside. The dead and dying sprawled everywhere – in the boat wells, lashed to the bow deck, and lying on the motor hatches. As the wire baskets hoisted them aboard the ships, their eyes were closed or staring in silence, unseeing. There was, in all of them, a subtle change in personality. These were not the same men who had gone ashore a few minutes or a few hours ago. They had passed through a portal, with life on one side and death on another, and some of them had come back. These were the ones whose eyes were open, transfixed. Never again would anything on this side look the same.

All day and into the night the boats churned through the water, taking in the living, bringing out the dying. As the first day ended, nearly 600 men, ashore and afloat, were dead, and nearly 2,000 were maimed, but alive.

Chapter 6

Darkness came suddenly at 6:45 P.M. As the sun dropped into the sea, the Marines braced for the night. Nearly 30,000 men, and thousands of tons of equipment were ashore, jammed into a tiny beachhead more than 4,000 miles west of Pearl Harbor. It was a strong lodgment, but it was only 700 miles from Tokyo. In front of the lines, and even within the lines, were unknown thousands of Japanese. The Marine command, from Howlin' Mad Smith down, had warned repeatedly that the first night would be critical.

Along the front in the north, tired eyes strained to watch for movement, seeing movement that wasn't there. Nervous fire crackled. There were plenty of holes, and the digging was easy. Some units stretched string from hole to hole.

Inside the perimeter and on the beaches, the activity went on, and so did the shelling. Japanese mortars and artillery fell steadily. Supplies were stacked on the beach and terraces, the shore parties were dug in along the beach, and casualties were everywhere. More than a thousand men had been evacuated during the day, but hundreds still lay ashore, many dead or dying.

Offshore, the mortars boats put in a night-long fire above the Fourth Division positions, more than 10,000 rounds of 4.2-inch high-explosive shells in all. Star shells from the destroyers lighted the macabre scene through the night. Bulldozers droned, hauling cargo, cutting down the terraces, pulling equipment out of the sand, carving revetments for medical parties. Shore parties crawled in and out of the landing craft, bringing supplies ashore and carrying wounded back into the black holds.

By 11 P.M. Japanese fire was so heavy that the Yellow and Blue beaches were ordered closed. Farther south the men still worked, but only a few vessels tried to come in. During the night, the Third Division transports arrived in the reserve area, 80 miles southeast of Iwo Jima.

Inland, runners crawled in and out of command posts, bringing reports, carrying orders. And ceaselessly, throughout the night, the litter bearers trundled the wounded to the beach. Men everywhere were looking for their units and their equipment. So many men lost their units that no accurate count of the day's casualties could be made. But they were heavy – more than half as many in one day as the whole Guadalcanal campaign had cost.

During the night the battalions in front of Suribachi worked to unscramble the day's confusion. Colonel Harry B. Liversedge moved his command post 200 yards nearer the front, to be ready for the morning assault on the mountain. Harry the Horse, a tall, gaunt man of loping stride, had commanded a Raider battalion on

New Georgia. The man from Volcano, California, was going after another volcano.

Huddled under a tarpaulin, he studied a map and issued orders for the attack. Two feet away, his executive officer, Lieutenant Colonel Robert Williams, shaved himself carefully with a straight razor in the light of a lantern. His hand was perfectly steady.

Many Japanese were moving through the lines. Leading Seaman Jinzo Horii crept away from Suribachi about midnight. His gun had been smashed early on D-Day, and he had no more weapons to fight with. During the night he passed through the enemy zone without challenge. Horii went all the way to Kitano Point, where he crawled into a cave.

There were a few attempts at infiltration. A barge came in about 11:45 P.M. on the west coast. Riflemen of 1/28 picked the Japanese off one by one as they landed, thirty-eight of them. On the east coast a Seabee, Shipfitter Second Class Karl Friel of Smyrna

Mills, Maine, watched a log in the surf about 2 A.M. The current bore it south along the shore, but suddenly it made a sharp turn. Friel fired 13 rounds and at dawn found a riddled Japanese body at the water's edge.

Bunched in foxholes along the perimeter, the Marines took turns on watch, fighting to stay awake, waiting, waiting for the crazy banzai. Now and then, shouting and ragged fire broke out in hysterical patches as the rocks and bushes seemed to move in the eerie light of the star shells. Still the rush didn't come.

Attrition along the beaches was steady. Second Lieutenant Cyril P. (Pete) Zurlinden had come ashore in late afternoon to pick up copy from correspondents. He couldn't find the newsmen, and the press boat didn't show up anyway. He dug in for the night. About 10:30 P.M. a shell exploded so near that Zurlinden was stunned. Sergeant Roy Heinicke gave him brandy, and the lieutenant began to feel for his legs. He thought both were gone, but then he found the right one, doubled under him. The left one seemed severed, and he wondered if he should throw it away. He examined it critically, found that it was still attached, and laid it out straight, the way it should be. Then he fainted. About 8 A.M. someone put him in a boat, and there was Jim Lindsley, going out to file his story. Pete pushed himself up on his elbows and smiled. "You look shaky, Jim," he said. "Have some brandy."

Shortly after midnight, an artillery shell landed squarely in the command post of 1/23 on Yellow 1. Colonel Haas and his operations officer, Captain Fred C. Eberhardt, were killed instantly. The executive officer, Lieutenant Colonel Louis B. Blissard, moved over from the next hold and took command.

About the same time, a giant spigot mortar shell, wobbling down from the north, exploded on Green Beach near Suribachi. Corporal Arthur L. Natter of New York staggered away in a daze. Somebody put him in a hole and covered him with a tarpaulin. A Navy doctor looked in later with a flashlight, tied his torn right arm in a sling, ticketed him, and put him in a boat. By 7:30 A.M. he was bound for Hawaii.

The 25th Regiment's dump of 80-mm. mortar shells, gasoline, and fuel for the flame tanks – two full boatloads – was hit at 4 A.M. The blast caved in foxholes for yards around, and a Navy doctor, Lieutenant Commander W. W. Ayres, struggled for his life. With one free hand he scratched until he freed himself. Then he began digging for Major Leo A. McSweeney, who had been lying next to him. Finally his hands found a helmet, and beneath it was the major, his lungs bursting.

Ayres freed the major's mouth and kept digging. Around them the ammunition burned and burst. The doctor pulled McSweeney out, and they crawled to the terrace and lay there gasping.

Seaman First Class Abe Levine of Brooklyn came to hate wise guys that night. Standing security watch near the beach, he challenged a figure in the gloom. The password was any presidents' name; and the figure cried out "Fillmore." "All right you son of a bitch," said Levine, "one more like that and you're dead."

Levine's troubles were not over. Ship's Cook Third Class Claude L. Wallace was stopped, and in panic called out "Wallace." "Goddamit," said Levine, "it's presidents, not vice presidents."

At dawn, Bob Sherrod looked around him. "The first night on Iwo Jima can only be described as a nightmare in hell," he wrote.

"About the beach in the morning lay the dead. . . . They died with the greatest possible violence. Nowhere in the Pacific have I seen such badly mangled bodies. Many were cut squarely in half. Legs and arms lay 50 feet away from any body." In a shell hole not 10 yards away from him were eight dead Marines. On the other side were two unexploded Japanese mines. Within his short view he could count at least 50 men who were wounded but were still fighting.

"All through the bitter night," he said, "the Japs rained heavy mortars and rockets and artillery on the entire area between the beach and the airfield. Twice they hit casualty stations on the beach. Many men who had been only wounded were killed."

Nonetheless, he said, "My strictly unofficial estimate is that the conquest of Iwo Jima will take thirteen days, and that casualties will be slightly less than Saipan." He was wrong on both counts. It took nearly three times that long and cost nearly twice as much.

In a transport off the beach, the doctors finished their work about dawn. They had taken aboard seventy-four casualties the first day. Lieutenant Commander J. H. McCauley of Los Angeles was proud of his work on a shattered arm – he hated to amputate – and a colleague at the next table had performed brain surgery. "First time I've ever tried that in a ground swell," he said. The final count was: four dead, two critical, and sixty-eight fair to good. Lieutenant W. E. Wright, once pastor of the First Christian Church of Smithville, Texas, was with each of the four Marines as they died.

The first night was over, and there had been no banzai; it had been much worse. With little cost to himself, the enemy had steadily killed Marines through the night, hurling fire into the masses of men on the beachhead. Many a Marine cursed the planners for putting so many men ashore, penned as in a corral, waiting for death. But not Kuribayashi; it was his plan to keep them there and slaughter them.

Part Three

SURIBACHI ONLY THE BEGINNING

Chapter 1

The second day was cold and miserable, and a light rain was falling. The wind was rising from the south, and the surf pounded on the beach in waves 4 feet high. None of the men ashore had had much sleep; the heavy pattern of fire from the enemy never slackened.

The lines had been strengthened, however, and all regiments now faced firmly north, except the 28th. Liversedge's men stared down on Suribachi, which looked like an overturned cup. Between them and the base lay a wasteland of broken rock and stubble, still strongly held by an enemy who could not be seen.

At first light, the carrier planes came in, rocketing and bombing the sides, and dropping napalm bombs at the foot of the slope, where most of the fire was

237

coming from. The destroyer Mannert L. Abele **came in on the west coast to support Shepard's 3rd Battalion, and the minelayer** Thomas E. Fraser **on the east, to help Chandler Johnson's 2nd Battalion. Butterfield's 1st Battalion was in "reserve," rebuilding first-day losses from cutting the isthmus in half.**

The tanks had not arrived at 8:40 A.M., when the attack finally opened. Eight of them were ready, except for ammunition and gasoline that hadn't arrived from the beach. While the tankers scrounged among wrecks getting gas, the enemy mortars began falling on the tanks and they had to be moved at least three times. There was no place to hide them; the tankers were just trying to keep them whole until they could get into action.

The attack, backed by artillery, 75-mm. half-tracks, and the 37-mm. guns, gained less than 75 yards in the morning. The destroyers pumped in over 1,500 rounds of 5-inch, at ranges as close as 200 yards. Still the only way to advance

was with flamethrowers and demolitions, and it was slow, dangerous work. By late afternoon, Johnson's men had driven down the beach to the foot of the mountain, blasting nearly forty caves shut. Around them was the wreckage of the big coastal guns, smashed on D-Day and before by the naval bombardment. Machine-gun and sniper fire was still heavy. On the west side, Shepard's men counted seventy-three dead Japanese. They were the first bodies found, and a welcome sight. There were more, but the enemy was hiding them in the mountain.

Kuribayashi's plan specified that: "Even if the enemy does capture our positions, we will defend Suribachi Yama to the utmost, and even though all positions fall into enemy hands and organized resistance becomes difficult, we will continue fighting fiercely to the last man and inflict heavy casualties on the enemy."

Colonel Atsuchi felt this time was arriving, and he sent a message to the General Tuesday morning:

"Enemy bombardments from the air and sea and their assaults with explosions are very fierce, and if we ever try to stay and defend our present positions it will lead us to self-destruction. We should rather like to go out of our position and choose death by banzai charge."

This was exactly what the General did not want. Banzai charges were a luxury he could not afford. He expected every man in the mountain to die, but the enemy would have to come in after them at heavy cost. He did not reply to Atsuchi.

In the afternoon the tanks moved in, and the attack progressed. By nightfall, the 28th was 200 yards nearer the mountain. The 1st Battalion, in "reserve," had killed seventy-five Japanese in sudden and savage hand-to-hand clashes inside the line.

Blue and Yellow beaches were reopened at 6 A.M., but at 9:30 they had to be closed again. Fire was heavy and the shoreline was jammed with a churning mass of wreckage. The Navy underwater demolition teams reported to the beachmasters and began blasting the wreckage with TNT. From this time in, any vessel smaller than an LCT (120 feet) was barred from the beach. Only the larger vessels could hold the beach in the heavy surf or smash through the flotsam to reach land.

On the north, seven battalions were stretched across the island on a 4,000-yard front. They shivered all night in their holes, dropping off to sleep like the dead when they weren't on watch, and even when they were. Corporal Richard B. Wilson, twenty-two, a North Dakota farm boy, had never been so cold in his life, and he was mad clear through. This was his fourth landing, and he thought they must be nuts to put so many men on a hot beach. A couple of small engineer outfits should have opened the roads first, he thought, so the troops could get inland. But he got his men in, losing only one, and six of them lugged a machine gun near the airfield and set it up in some wrecked Japanese planes.

Just before dawn he sent four men back to the beach for ammunition, food, and "the dope." The man who had stayed with him crawled to the other side of the hole to relieve himself – and screamed. A Japanese arose from the plane wreckage and started for them. A BAR man in the next hole cut him down. Wilson went back to cleaning his carbine, fouled with sand. The Japanese lying there was the first one they'd seen, dead or alive.

Even before the attack began, the casualties started. A mortar shell fell in the command post of 2/25 at 7:15 A.M., up above Blue 1. The commanding officer, Lieutenant Colonel Lewis C. Hudson, Jr., and his executive officer, Major William P. Kaempfer, and operations officer Major Donald K. Ellis were badly wounded. An officer who had stopped in to ask the day's plans, the commander of Company B, 4th Tank Battalion, was killed. The executive officer of 3/25, Lieutenant

Colonel James Taul, arrived to take command. Because officers had become so scarce, he fought the rest of the battle with no executive officer.

The attack opened at 8:30 A.M., with the right end holding at the Quarry while the center and left came up to straighten the line. In the center, the 23rd, helped by tanks, moved forward, and by noon had overrun the airfield in spite of fierce machine-gun fire. A direct artillery hit on 1/25's command post at 11 A.M. killed six Navy corpsmen, and wounded seven more. Lieutenant Colonel Mustain was at the front and escaped the blast.

In the afternoon the new battleship Washington, arriving late on the scene, joined the bombardment. With air spotting, the battleship fired three full 16-inch salvos at a cliff line near the southern end of Airfield No. 2. The shelling brought down landslides, closing some caves, but in this small area there were more than three hundred Japanese strongpoints.

Somewhere in there, Second Lieutenant Nakamura, of the 8th Independent Anti-Tank Battalion, was killed. General Kuribayashi radioed to Chichi Jima that, between the landing and his disappearance on Tuesday, the Lieutenant had "destroyed one score of the amphibious tanks by handling, himself, the 47-mm. anti-tank gun and he died a heroic death."

This message was announced to the troops, along with the General's order of the day:

"First, one must defend Iwo Jima to the bitter end.

"Second, one must blast enemy weapons and men.

"Third, one must kill every single enemy soldier with rifle and sword attacks.

"Fourth, one must discharge each bullet to its mark.

"Fifth, one must, even if he be the last man, continue to harass the enemy by guerrilla tactics."

This was the last message transmitted to the men in Suribachi. Fifth Division engineers had found a buried cable, an inch and a half in diameter, and cut it. Colonel Atsuchi was on his own.

On the west coast, two battalions of the Fifth, 1/26 and 3/27, attacked to the north on fairly even ground. Aided by tanks, and probing through minefields, they advanced without encountering enemy strength. There was no cover from mortar and artillery fire from the north, but by the end of daylight the advance had carried 800 yards. The line was now nearly straight across the island, just north of the first airfield.

During the afternoon, Private Jacklyn H. Lucas, who had just turned seventeen, fought his way up a ravine. A grenade rolled down among the men. Lucas vaulted over them and fell on it, just as a second one went off. They left him for dead, but he lived.

Lucas, at the time, was at least a technical deserter. He had lied about his age and enlisted at fourteen (he stood 5 feet 8 and weighed 200 pounds). He had been brigged twice, for fighting and being AWOL. When the 26th was loading for Iwo, Lucas walked out of the Sixth Base Depot and onto the transport with them. He was tired of the depot, and he had a cousin in the 26th. The 26th was glad he came along.

Farther up the front, a Japanese crawled from a hole, put a mine in the road, and ran 20 yards away to wait for a tank. The blast tore off the tread and up popped the turret hatch. Second Lieutenant William O. Jarvis of Sparta, Tennessee came up fast, fired his .45, and killed the Japanese before he could fire.

Down south of the airfield the Fifth Division post office opened. Captain Leslie W. Babbin of Lynn, Massachusetts, was the postmaster. He was forty-three, the father of five children and a Purple Heart veteran of Chateau Thierry. Despite surf and beachmasters, he got his equipment ashore on D-Day. Six sailors with a stretcher helped him carry it inland.

Then they took the stretcher away for another use. Babbin got out a shovel and began "enlarging the post office."

The 2nd and 3rd Battalions of the 26th, on the west side of Airfield No. 1, began to suffer casualties from artillery during the morning.

Lieutenant Richard E. (Ed) Baker was watching a kid in a foxhole in front of him. A shell struck some concrete dragon's teeth nearby, and they shattered. As Baker watched, the boy's face turned to blood from his neck up and he fell without a sound. It was the beginning of Baker's combat initiation.

The 26th was "reserve," but still there were many bodies wrapped in shelter halves at the sick bay. Baker went forward with Colonel Trotti and Major Day to reconnoiter the route forward. Just after they passed the 27th's command post under the airstrip. Baker saw his first dead Japanese. He looked very small, perhaps because a huge Marine sergeant lay nearby on a stretcher. A tank was burning, and the smell of flesh inside was nauseating. Baker walked on. In the road, where a man had been run over by a tank, there was a square yard of entrails – yellow, purple, red, and gray. The fire was becoming intense and Trotti turned back. The 26th was standing by, ready to relieve the 27th if called. It wasn't called that day.

By the end of the second day, the Fifth Division had lost 1,500 men, killed or wounded, and the Fourth Division about 2,000. The first prisoners – three of them, all wounded – were taken the second day, but two of them died. Six hundred and thirty Japanese dead had been counted, but there must have been many more.

The hospital ship Samaritan arrived from Guam, and Secretary Forrestal went aboard to talk with the wounded. He was shocked at the grievous wounds he saw, and deeply moved.

The 21st Regiment was surprised when it got orders to boat for landing; the "reserve" being called in on the second day? Coming up from Guam on D-Day the men had listened in on the radios, and it sounded good. "Boating excellent, very light swells," and at 9 A.M. promptly, "First wave ashore."

"They won't need us," somebody said during the afternoon. "This thing will be over in five days." Some of the bandsmen struck up a little concert in the hold, playing snatches of classical music until a truck driver growled, "Can't you give us some boogie?"

The 21st began boating before noon, in rain and rough water. Dozens of men missed the drop into the bobbing boats, and when they were fished out, the boats went to the rendezvous line. There they circled for six hours, cold and wet, before they were ordered back to their transports. Some boats got lost and drifted all night.

But the rest of the artillery had to go in. The 105's of 3/14 had been afloat all Monday afternoon, unable to get ashore. They launched again Tuesday around 10 A.M. and finally were called ashore in the afternoon. By 5 P.M. they were sited behind Red 2 and Yellow 1, and opened fire at 5:28 P.M.

Lieutenant Colonel Carl Youngdale's twelve 105's also tried a landing Tuesday. The first Dukw out of LST 1032 wallowed a moment in the heavy sea. Waves surged over the side, the engine stopped, and the Dukw sank, gun and all. In horrifying procession seven more Dukws waddled out of the LST and sank, one after the other. Eight precious 105's were lost, and a dozen officers and men.

Four Dukws made it to shore, but two of them broached at the surf line and the guns were lost. At last, two 105's out of the twelve were safe ashore. Late at night they began firing northward into the blackness.

All day the front had been calling for artillery, more artillery, and at last the big ones – the 155's – began coming in. In late afternoon the huge snout of LST 779 smashed through the wreckage at Red Beach 1. The bow doors opened, and with tractors straining and cables whining the 2½-ton guns of Battery C, 2d 155mm Howitzer Battalion, were hauled up the terrace. By 6:40 P.M. all four guns were in position on the west coast.

Far up on Suribachi that night there were white and amber flares. Colonel Atsuchi was calling for artillery fire from the north to save the mountain. There was not much General Kuribayashi could do.

Chapter 2

By Wednesday morning the weather was declining. The wind had risen to 19 knots from the northeast, and surf 6 feet high was pounding the landing beaches. Admiral Turner was not getting the three days of good weather he had hoped for.

The 28th, supported by destroyer and cruiser fire, resumed the attack on Suribachi at 8:25 A.M. Just before that, forty carrier planes came in, strafing, rocketing, and bombing within 100 yards of Marine lines. It was the closest air support so far, and the last at Suribachi because the men were now too close to risk it. In the mountain, less than 600 Japanese were still alive.

It was grueling fighting all day. Where the terrain permitted, tanks and artillery gave some support, but chiefly it was the footsloggers, working with grenades and light arms, demolition charges, and flamethrowers. The 2nd Battalion worked down the east coast, some of the men along the beaches and others on a ledge 50 feet or so above. Don Ruhl, twenty-one, crawled out in the morning with his platoon guide, Sergeant Henry O. Hansen. They came to a bunker at the foot of the slope, and just as they peered over the log at the top, a grenade rolled into the shallow trench behind the bunker. Ruhl shouted to Hansen, vaulted into the trench, and fell on the grenade. He could easily have fallen down the slope outside the bunker, as his training had told him to do. The choice was clearly his own; he sacrificed his life so his sergeant might live. In just twenty-four hours in combat, Private First Class Ruhl from Columbus, Montana had also captured a blockhouse single-handed, rescued a wounded Marine 40 yards in front of the lines, and spent the night in an abandoned Japanese machine-gun pit, guarding the weapon so it could not be retaken.

During the day progress was not spectacular but was solid. These were the main defenses of Suribachi, and all day long LVT's trundled to the front with grenades, satchel charges, and flame oil. The 28th was blasting through some of the heaviest concrete and stone defenses ever met in the Pacific. More than thirty caves were found, many connected by tunnels, and the satchel charges roared as the caves were closed. The last Japanese command post at the south end of the island was blasted shut.

During the afternoon, as a cold rain set in, patrols went along the beach all the way to Tobiishi Point, on both coasts. They pulled back for the night, but the main line had advanced from 500 to 1,000 yards to the base of the mountain and partly around it. The Marines could hear the Japanese inside and sent flaming gasoline down the fissures. More than 200 Japanese burned to death or suffocated during the day, and Colonel Atsuchi was mortally wounded by a shell fragment. As he lay dying, his last order was that a squad of men try to break through to General Kuribayashi's headquarters and report.

Just before nightfall, "Tough" Tony Stein was wounded in the shoulder by shrapnel. They sent him to the beach for evacuation, but he was back in the line a few days later.

On the northern front, the battle began to fall into a pattern. The morning offensive opened with rocket and strafing runs by carrier aircraft, and artillery and naval gunfire barrages. On the west coast, where the terrain was still fairly even and tanks could help, the Fifth Division drove forward to large gains. But it was not easy. Japanese fire from the higher ground in front was relentless, and casualties mounted steadily. During the day the 26th and 27th Regiments advanced almost a thousand yards, but it cost them nearly 600 casualties.

Wednesday night, Captain Robert H. Dunlap of 1/26 finally came back into the lines. The twenty-four-year-old Illinois farmer had crawled far out in front on Tuesday to see where the heavy firing was coming from. He scrambled north to the base of cliffs where the broken ground started, to within 50 yards of the Japanese positions. He stayed there alone through Tuesday night, all day Wednesday, and into the night, calling down smashing naval and artillery fire against the enemy. He returned unhurt and fought on for five more days before he was shot through the left hip and evacuated.

In the center, above Airfield No. 1, and all the way to the east coast the Fourth Division found stubborn resistance. The 23rd met heavy fire and thick minefields and moved only 50 yards during the day. But the pressure, added to the devastating naval fire of preceding days, was enough to dislodge the Japanese 1st Battalion of the 145th Regiment. Major Mitsuaki Hara had had his command post north of the airfield since the convoys had sailed from

Saipan. His 3rd Company, behind Yellow Beach 2, had been annihilated on D-Day. Most of the men in his other two companies were now dead, killed in the fighting around the airfield. With what was left, Major Hara pulled out and moved north, to Nishi Buraku in the northwest.

On the east side of the airfield, 1/25 struck off to the northeast. But the advance did not go well, and Lieutenant Colonel Mustain started for the front to see why. Jumpin' Joe Chambers came bounding over from 3/25, and they talked a while, Musty pointing out the direction he intended to drive. Chambers started back toward his outfit, and saw two tanks come over a ridge near Mustain. He turned instinctively to call out, because he knew they would draw fire, but it was too late. The first burst killed Musty instantly. Chambers ran to his body. They had been together in the Fourth all the way. At Saipan, Musty had shinnied up a

Japanese telephone pole at Marpi Point to nail up the American flag. Chambers crouched by Musty's body until Major Fenton Mee came up to take over the battalion, then he went back to 3/25. Two days, two battalion commanders – Lew Hudson wounded, Musty dead. Only Chambers was left. A cold rain started in the afternoon, and Mee egged 1/25 on.

Company A was pinned in the ravines near Airfield No. 2 by fire from many points. "Preacher" Gray, a Bible-reading sergeant from Marvel Valley, Alabama, called his men back out of range. Ross Gray, twenty-four, had been a carpenter on Saipan, but when his buddy was killed he asked for combat. With three riflemen covering him, he ran forward with a huge satchel charge. He hurled it at an emplacement, ran back for another charge, and blasted another. Exhilarated, there was no stopping him. By late afternoon he had killed more than twenty-five Japanese, destroyed six positions, disarmed a minefield, and blown up enemy ammunition. His buddy's score was settled, and 1/25 made 50 to 300 yards along its front that day.

Not far away, a taciturn thirty-three-year-old Irishman from Chicago, Captain Joseph J. McCarthy, Silver Star winner from Saipan, lost his patience when steady Japanese fire held up Company G, 2/24. He charged 75 yards across open ground, blasted a pill-box with grenades, and killed two men running from it. With demolitions men and flamethrowers behind him, he charged another one and climbed into the ruins to kill the last Japanese with his own weapons. Then he called his men, and they swarmed over a ridge lying before the airfield. McCarthy was temporarily satisfied. His outfit made a hundred yards, but the Fourth Division was paying. It lost another 500 men and was down to less than 70 percent efficiency.

Fire on the beaches slacked off a little during the day, but signs of the terrible struggle were all around. Bodies and pieces of flesh lay everywhere. In the surf, the severed head and shoulders of a sailor bobbed in a lifejacket. With each wave the obscene remnant nearly beached, then the undertow sucked it out again.

The 21st Regiment – 3,000 fresh men – began landing late in the morning and by nightfall was assembled near Airfield No. 1. During the afternoon General Rockey set up Fifth Division headquarters south of the field, but General Cates remained afloat. His assistant, Brigadier General Franklin Hart, was ashore, but he advised Cates not to follow him for a day or so. Communications among units ashore were still bad, and Cates believed he had better control from shipboard.

Near Rockey's command post, in a hole beneath the runway, bulldozers droned through the day, laying out the Fifth Division Cemetery. The site had been selected before the invasion, from aerial photos, and the crosses were already coming ashore. Thousands of pieces of wood, cut to specifications and prepainted, had been bundled together for easy handling. Once ashore, they could easily be put together into neat white crosses. The bodies were waiting.

In order to relieve the beaches, Admiral Hill decided to release the pontoon causeways. They had worked well at Salerno and other landings, and the Admiral said, prematurely, "Thank God we brought them." Half of the 70th Seabees, a causeway specialist outfit, had come to Iwo with six sets of pontoons, slung sidesaddle on LST's and LSM's. Each section, 175 feet long, weighed 130 tons, and when Hill said "Go" they went.

In a rising sea, the result was chaos. Seaman First Class W. J. Brunner slipped between two bucking sections and his leg was smashed. Carpenter's Mate Second Class C. L. Branch fell between a pontoon and the side of his ship. He dived and swam out, unhurt.

Chief Carpenter's Mate T. J. Duffy

and his gang finally got one set of cause-ways chained together. Using Dukws for tugs they started for **Red Beach 1**, a mile away, some of the men riding flat on the whipping pontoons. The 260-ton rig smashed the beach head on, the Seabees dropping 3,000-pound anchors off the stern. Bulldozers hooked onto the shore end and began to pull.

For a few minutes they held, then the seaward end began to turn slowly. Duffy passed a cable to an LST. It strained and snapped. The whole causeway picked up speed and broached full on the beach, smashing everything in its way and adding 260 more tons of wreckage to the beach.

No other causeway got that far. They broke loose and churned around in the open sea, frightful hazards in the crowded roadstead. Some were captured. Others were never seen again.

"I pulled a boner," Admiral Hill admitted later. "I should have launched one to see how it went." He waited, but there was no word from Turner.

The smaller pontoon barges, 25-ton units with outboard engines, fared little better. They were scattered to sea, some with men aboard, or thrown upside down onto the beach. Four were salvaged to serve as landing stages alongside the hospital LST's, and one became a floating gas station. Chief Shipfitter E. B. Gandy and his men anchored it 400 yards off Yellow 1, and for seven days pumped fuel for small craft by hand, from drums. One detail had been overlooked – it had no lights. An LST rammed it on the third night and by the end of the week nearly every outside pontoon had been holed by amphtracs.

Just at dusk, the Japanese made one last try from the air. About 50 planes of the 2nd Mitake Special Attack Unit (kamikazes) left Hatori, outside of Tokyo, and stopped at Hachijo Jima in the Bonins to refuel.

The Saratoga, about 35 miles northwest of Iwo Jima, picked them up on radar 100 miles away and reported "friendlies." Six planes were sent out to make sure, and at 5 P.M. the word was passed: "Tallyho. Splashed two Zekes." Within minutes six Japanese planes broke through the clouds and the anti-aircraft guns opened fire. Two planes, both afire, struck the Saratoga near the starboard waterline, their bombs exploding inside the carrier. The old "Sara" had four or five hits in four minutes, but her power plant was unharmed and she built up 25 knots to fight fires. By 6:30 they were under control, but a few minutes later five more planes came in. Four were shot down, but the fifth grazed the flight deck and crashed overboard. Its bomb blew a hold in the flight deck. By 8:15 the Saratoga was ready to recover planes, and the first pilot aboard said, "Boy, I'm glad this isn't the Saratoga. You ought to see her."

The Bismarck Sea was not as fortunate. She was 20 miles east of Iwo Jima, in a circle of six escort carriers. In the failing light she took in a Saratoga plane and planes from the Wake Island and Natoma Bay. The deck was crowded and the planes were rushed below without degassing. At 6:45 a plane came in low on the water and a destroyer withheld fire, thinking it was another Saratoga plane. The kamikaze smashed the Bismarck Sea square abeam, blasting four torpedoes from a rack, severing the fire mains, and cutting the cables of the plane elevator. The elevator plunged to the bottom of the shaft and flames spewed up. The gassed planes caught fire and ammunition fell into the blaze. The executive officer took one look and recommended abandoning ship. Captain John L. Pratt agreed. The wind was 22 knots, and fires were roaring inside.

"Abandon ship!" was ordered at 7 P.M., and 800 men went over the side into rough seas laced with rain and snow. Within minutes a tremendous explosion blew out the carrier's stern, and she rolled over and sank.

Escort vessels closed in for the rescue, and the Japanese planes strafed the waters. Lieutenant Eugene R. Shannon of Freeport, Illinois, chaplain of the Bismarck Sea, died of his wounds just after he had been pulled aboard a rescue ship. His final prayer the night before over the carrier's public address system had been: "Almighty God, may we have ears to hear the call of battle, eyes to see the enemy wherever he lurks, and skill to save our ship, our planes, and ourselves from the hand of evil, that finally we may glorify Thee, the giver of all victory, through Jesus Christ Our Lord, Amen."

Three other ships were attacked. The carrier Lunga Point fought off four torpedo bombers without loss, and 50 miles southeast of Iwo Jima a convoy of LST's and net tenders was attacked. The net tender Keokuk, once a train ferry, was hit by a diving Jill and set afire. LST 477, carrying guns for the Third Division, was struck a glancing blow by a plunging kamikaze. The old Keokuk put out her fires, but lost 17 men killed and 44 wounded. The Saratoga had 123 men killed and 192 wounded, and was out of service for four months. Not a single plane returned to Japan.

During the attack, "Condition Red" for air attack was set ashore, and both sides took cover. Private First Class Joseph J. Leniart, twenty-three, of Union, New Jersey was sent out as a runner for 1/21 and told to eat his message if he were caught. There was no fear of that. Leniart had the feeling he was alone in a desert.

As the day ended, the hospital ship Samaritan sailed for Guam with a full load, 623 seriously wounded men. Casualties at the end of the third day stood at 2,517 men of the Fourth Division and 2,057 men of the Fifth Division.

No vessels came for the Japanese wounded, now or ever. Some crawled or were carried to aid stations behind the lines and then were placed in niches in the walls of the tunnels, to be tended by their comrades as best they could. Others bound up their own wounds and stayed with their units, to fight again if they could, or to work behind the lines.

Men whose units had been smashed began a curious life of roaming, without direction, from cave to cave as the war came near them. Still others were behind the Marine lines, some living under Airfield No. 1 even as the tanks rolled over them going to the front. At night they came out, looking for rations, or discarded clothing and weapons. A few were still full of fight. Many wanted to surrender but did not know how to do so without being killed. Others could not face the disgrace; they felt guilty at being alive.

Late that night something moved in front of the Marine lines up above the cliffs near Airfield No. 2. It was Petty Officer Second Class Chinichi Onodera and his buddy, Seaman First Class Seiichi Matsuno. They were trying to find Captain Inouye to tell him their coastal gun was smashed and the crew surrounded. Matsuno ran first and a machine-gun burst from the Marine lines cut him down. From behind a rock, Onodera watched his friend writhing on the ground. When he could stand it no longer, Onodera struck a grenade against his helmet and rolled it down on Matsuno. The blast killed him but drew more fire, and Matsuno's body danced along the ground. Onodera was horrified by what he had done, but he could not stay to face it, and ran on. If he lived – and he did – he would have plenty of time to worry about the morality of his mercy.

Chapter 3

Shozo Matsumura arose early and wrote to his parents. He said that he and his comrades had been fighting diligently, "but the time has now arrived for me to give the final measure of my loyalty to my country and love for my parents." He spoke of the terrible bombing of past days and the power of the enemy, "so rich in material things."

"Dear Mother and Family," he concluded, "I shall repay as well as I can all my obligations to you by suffering here, and I shall acquit myself well. Please, all of you, take good care of yourselves and do your utmost until victory comes. The battle is on.... I leave this, expecting to die." The letter was found, days later, but Matsumura never was.

It was a thoroughly bad day, with a

cold, hard rain beginning about dawn. The ground turned into gumbo, and the 28th went after Suribachi again, too close now for air support. It was handwork, picking through the rubble, blasting and burning. First Lieutenant Tom Mahoney's company alone smashed twenty-five pillboxes. Mortar fire still came from the mountain, and Corporal Clifton Taylor's platoon leader was cut down. Taylor lost his head, and jumped up shouting, "Come on, damn it, we gotta go." He ran forward suddenly, leading a charge. "I'll get 'em," he cried, and killed three Japanese in a bunker while his buddies got four more. Sergeant Everett Hedrick threw a grenade into a cave, forgetting to pull the pin. A Japanese threw it right back, also forgetting to arm it, and Hedrick drilled him with his carbine.

The 3rd Battalion cleared out the base of the north face of Suribachi during the day and sent a patrol around the west coast down to Tobiishi Point. There they met a patrol from the 2nd Battalion coming down the east coast; the mountain was surrounded. Above them, the slopes of Suribachi were so scarred by shelling that no path up could be found.

In the afternoon, Sergeant Robert L. Whitehead of Company 1 scrambled partway up the north face of Suribachi, above the wreckage of a large gun. He returned to report no Japanese in sight and asked if he should continue up the mountain. But it was late, and Liversedge decided to put off the final assault until morning.

Perhaps 300 Japanese were still alive inside the mountain. That night they talked about whether they should stay or attempt to fight their way north. About half of them decided to stay. The others crawled out in the dark and began to go north. Incredibly, about twenty of them made it through both fighting lines and reached General Kuribayashi's headquarters near Motoyama. They were assigned to new units.

Up on the west coast there was no lull even through the night. About 4 A.M. a small band of Japanese arose from the rubble on the west coast and started south. The 27th, preparing to leave the line that day, turned them back with a steady mortar barrage. An LCI close to shore fired 40-mm. shells flat across the Marine lines into the cliffs rising before them.

After daylight, the 26th began moving in to give the 27th a rest. Mortar fire was intense, coming from the higher ground ahead and in the center of the island, and the passage of lines became confused. Colonel Trotti, commanding 3/26, tried to get his unit headed in the right direction. Ed Baker ran forward toward the tip of Airfield No. 2 looking for Trotti to tell him the men were moving. He was too late. As he ran, the shelling from the bluff increased with every yard. First Lieutenant Arthur I. Chappell came to meet him.

Chappel, the communications officer, was very pale and there was blood on his face. He said Trotti and the operations officer, Major William R. Day, were dead, and he pointed to a shell hole, still smoking.

"Dick Fagan is on the way up to take over," Chappell said. In the meantime, Captain Richard M. Cook of Company G took command. The battalion's executive officer, Major George F. Waters, Jr., had been wounded and evacuated two days before. Major Richard Fagan, Fifth Division inspector, arrived about noon and relieved Cook. The battle went on, with the 2nd Battalion moving into the center of the Fifth Division line. This was its first real action, but the battalion already had many casualties from fire falling on the "rear" since D-Day afternoon. The 26th, with its 1st Battalion along the west coast, made about 300 yards during the day, but it was still short of the heights to the north, and the cost was bitter.

On Thursday ten Fifth Division officers were killed, the same number as the day before. In four days the division had lost 35 officers. Among the day's killed were the 28th Regiment's surgeon, Lieutenant Commander Daniel J. McCarthy, Colonel Trotti, two majors, two first lieutenants (Angelo M. Cona was shot squarely between the eyes), two second lieutenants, and a Navy lieutenant (j.g.), Steven W. Holmes, who was with the 5th Tank Battalion for naval gunfire spotting.

In the center of the line, the fresh troops of the 21st Regiment began moving up about 4 A.M. to relieve the 23rd, which had been fighting since D-Day. In the darkness, pierced now and then by the light of parachute flares, the 1st and 2nd Battalions of the 21st darted from hole to hole, past the airfield, where the smashed Japanese planes stood out starkly, past the bodies of men of the 23rd, still not carried from the field. Men of the 23rd gathered in little groups and waited. They had been three full days in the center of the line with no hot food, no sleep, no relief from steady fire. "I could kiss you," said a dirty, bearded gunner when a man tapped him on the shoulder and motioned to the rear. Back they went, into "reserve," where the shelling was almost as bad, but you might get coffee and two hours' sleep.

The 21st's initiation was rough. In the rain and heavy fire, full relief of the 23rd took nearly six hours, but an attack of sorts got off at 8 A.M. Company F moved out on the left, against strong fortifications between the airfields. Within fifteen minutes Captain Gerald G. Kirby, the company commander, was killed, bracketed by mortar bursts. First Lieutenant Richard H. Strauss took over, but by noon less than half the company was left, and the other two companies of the 2nd Battalion had to relieve them. In his knapsack, Strauss carried a small picture of the company officers. It showed him sitting next to Kirby; both men were smiling. Throughout the day the battalion made about 50 yards.

The 1st Battalion gained up to 250 yards in places, paying a price for each yard. The commander, Lieutenant Colonel Marlowe C. Williams, was slashed in the arm by mortar fragments but refused to leave the front until nightfall, when his executive officer, Major Clay Murray, took over.

In the rocky ground above the east cliffs the 25th Regiment could do little more than hold all day, waiting for the 21st on its left to try to come abreast. 1/25 made some advances, but 3/25, still shattered from its battle at the Quarry on D-Day, badly needed rest and reforming. It clung to its positions during the day and at about 4 P.M. began digging in for the night.

A corporal ran up and told Jumpin' Joe Chambers his rocket truck was loaded and ready to go. He wanted to unload it against Charlie-Dog Ridge. Chambers said okay and began striding toward the rear. There was a burst of fire, and Chambers just had time to classify it mentally as light machine gun when a bullet struck him in the left collarbone and he fell.

In a daze he heard the corpsman say, "It's a sucking wound," and realized someone was stuffing gauze into it. Then the regimental surgeon, Dr. Michael Francis Xavier Kelleher was there, working over him. The bullet had traveled through his lung and out his back.

Jim Headley came up, kicked Chambers gently on the foot and said, "Get up, you lazy bastard. You were hurt worse on Tulagi." But Chambers could not get up. His men put him on a stretcher and carefully snaked down to the beach. Now it was D-Day plus three, and the 25th had lost all three battalion commanders.

Captain Headley took over. He and Chambers had fought up Hill 500 at Saipan, and after Chambers was blown off the hill Headley took command, though twice wounded. He began to pull 3/25 together.

All day long Major Treitel's 1/24 worked along the east coast above the landing beaches, blasting caves and pillboxes, trying to cut down the mortar and sniper fire. One shell from the cliffs caught an Army Dukw of the 473rd Amphibian Truck Company coming in with one of the Marine 105's. It cut the rudder cable, and the boat slewed in the heavy seas, swamped, and sank. First Lieutenant George B. Weill and his Negro driver, T/5 Henderson Crockett, were lost.

On the beaches, surf was so heavy in the afternoon that it was no longer safe to try to get the wounded out to ships. LST's dumping ammunition on the beach took in Marine work parties and fed them steak, spaghetti, and coffee. It was warm and dry in the big holds, and some men had their first shower and shave in five days. They washed their clothes and hung them over the engines to dry, and a few even had the luxury of naps in bunks. Wounded lay wrapped in blankets all around them, and in the background a radio played "I'll Be Seeing You."

In one LST, Chief Commissary

Steward Elihu Schlosburg thought he had fed at least 3,000 Marines "and they're still coming." Fifty yards away on top of the terrace, artillery fired steadily to the north, and on the decks of the LST's sentries cracked away at the cliffs and suspicious movements in the water. Sniper fire was still coming from somewhere, and a man on the beach was hit just at dusk.

When night fell, the LST's withdrew, with the exception of LST 807, which volunteered to stay on the beach all night as an emergency hospital. Her doctors, working through the night treated 200 casualties, losing only two.

The Fourth Division Cemetery opened during the day, and burials began, including a foot a corporal had found up near the airfield, where a Fourth Division tank had been smashed by a direct hit. The foot was still in a Marine field boot with a serial number on the tongue. The foot belonged to a tank crewman who was missing, and it was buried in a regulation grave. Six days later word came that its owner was in the hospital at Saipan. The foot was exhumed.

The Seabee boss, Captain Robert C. Johnson, came ashore during the day, to set up headquarters of the 9th Naval Construction Brigade. Johnson, a lanky, gray-haired man of fifty, would soon have 7,000 Seabees working under him, transforming the island into a giant airdrome. That was, after all, the whole reason for this fighting and dying.

Task Force 58 sailed at sundown for the second raid on Tokyo, and that night naval gunfire was rationed. Since the first night it had been heavy and wild, pouring out all night whenever the Marines asked for it, keeping the skies aflame and the Japanese in their holes. But now Marine artillery was ashore, and Navy ammunition was running low. From this night on, all requests for Navy fire or parachute flares were centralized and granted on a priority basis. Iwo was settling down to grim, ferocious land fighting.

In a bomb crater up on the west coast, just at midnight, Private First Class Fred Harvey watched a grenade roll down the side of the hole. He reached for it, juggled it, and batted it away. The blast stunned his legs and he could not move. A second grenade rolled down behind him and impulsively he sat on it, pressing it into the sand. The explosion tore away his buttocks, and he remembered no more. Nine months later he left a hospital in Hawaii.

It was indeed a ferocious fight.

Chapter 4

Friday was the day to take Suribachi. The bald, gray dome, so formidable only a few days ago, was now still, the caves and chambers nearly empty, the blockhouses torn from their roots by the naval guns, the pillboxes blasted and agape, the tunnels closed and smoking.

Sergeant Sherman B. Watson of 2/28 set out at eight o'clock, scrambling up the north face with three privates from Company F: Louis Charlo, a Montana Indian, Theodore White of Kansas, and George Mercer from Iowa. Once out of the rubble at the base of the mountain, footing was good and they climbed up warily. It was very quiet, and in forty minutes they were at the cone, peering into the defunct crater. Nearby was a battery of heavy machine guns, ammunition stacked alongside it, but no

Japanese. The patrol slid down the mountain to report.

Now was the time for Lieutenant Wells' flag. Colonel Johnson sent a runner for Lieutenant Harold G. Schrier, a slim, tall ex-Raider. When Schrier got to the battalion command post the colonel told him to seize the crest and hold it.

"And put this up on the hill," Johnson said, handing him the flag.

Schrier, executive officer of Company E, started out with 40 men, putting out flankers to cover the advance. The patrol was plainly visible as it moved up the face of the mountain, and all over the southern end of the island dirty, tired Marines watched.

"Those guys ought to be getting flight pay," said a bearded corporal.

Still there was no opposition, and at 10:15 Schrier and a small party of men tumbled over the rim into the crater. There were no Japanese in sight.

There, nearly 600 feet above the sea, a moment in history was taking shape.

The patrol scouted through the crater, rifles ready; a couple of the men found a piece of pipe, about 20 feet long. They lashed the flag to one end and thrust the other into soft ground near the north rim of the crater. The flag rose above the mountain, clearly visible from land and sea, and snapped out in a brisk wind. Sergeant Louis R. Lowery, a photographer for Leatherneck magazine, stood in the crater taking pictures, while Private First Class James Robeson jeered, "Hollywood Marines." He refused to get in the picture.

As the shutter clicked, two Japanese darted from a cave. One threw a grenade and ran toward the flag, his sword drawn. Robeson shot him, and his body rolled down the inside of the crater, snapping off his sword under him. The other Japanese hurled a grenade toward Lowery, and the sergeant vaulted over the rim, sliding 50 feet down the mountain before he could stop. The camera was smashed, but the pictures were safe inside, and the flag was up. Six men raised it: Schrier, Platoon Sergeant Ernest I. Thomas, Jr.; Sergeant Henry O. Hansen, Corporal Charles W. Lindberg, Private First Class James R. Michels, and the Crow Indian, Private Charlo.

This was the flag raising on Iwo Jima that thrilled the troops. The one that thrilled the world was still to come, nearly two hours later.

On the sandy terrace below, tired men wept in their foxholes, unshaven men on the beaches thumped each other on the back and shouted. Across the ships, whistles, horns, and bells rang out. Private Charles S. Ranger, nineteen, tried to raise himself from his deck cot on the hospital ship Solace. He could not be with Company D, 2/28, on Suribachi, because his left thigh and knee had been smashed by a mortar. He could not cheer very loud either, but he cried a little.

And near the base of Suribachi, a few feet in from the surf, a man said, "This means a Marine Corps for the next 500 years." He looked like any other Marine, but he was Secretary of the Navy Forrestal. Chance placed him on the beach just as the flag went up, and with him stood Howlin' Mad Smith, a Navy party that included two admirals, and Forrestal's Army aides, Major Mathias F. Correa and Colonel Cornelius V. Whitney. Forrestal wore khakis and a sweatshirt against the cold wind.

The party had just stepped ashore from a Higgins boat, not for the flag raising but because Forrestal had insisted on visiting the beachhead. Smith, afraid of repercussions if anything happened to Forrestal, had tried to talk him out of it, but the man who had gone ashore at Normandy would not be dissuaded. Later, in Washington, Forrestal remarked that "it was as safe there as it is right here in this room." To which a Navy captain countered: "Yes, it was safe there. Twenty-three men were killed on that section of the beach that morning."

To Colonel Johnson, one implication

of the flag raising was instantly apparent. "Some son of a bitch is going to want that flag," he said to Wells, "but he's not going to get it. That's our flag. Better find another one and get it up there, and bring back ours." Wells sent his runner, a lisping corporal nicknamed Wabbit, racing for the nearest LST.

Joe Rosenthal was thirty-three, stout, and so myopic no branch of the service would have him. He was also a photographer – not a special one, just a photographer like hundreds of others. He had been in the Pacific since March, covering the war for the Associated Press and making the landings with the Marines or Army at Guam, Peleliu, and Angaur. At Iwo Jima he landed about noon on D-Day with Fourth Division troops, riding in on a Higgins boat with a load of mortar ammunition. In the next few days he took dozens of pictures and made several trips out to the ships for rest, caption writing, and dispatching of his pictures.

Friday morning he decided to work the southern beaches, and on the way in aboard an LCT the boatswain said he'd heard on the radio that a patrol was going up Suribachi that morning. When Rosenthal got to the 28th Regiment command post they told him he was too late, but he decided to go up anyway. He started up with Sergeant William Genaust, who had a color movie camera, and Private Robert Campbell, a combat photographer.

About that time Wabbit returned from LST 779, the first LST to beach at Iwo, and still beached on Green Beach. The communications officer, Ensign Alan S. Wood, had given him the ship's flag. It was 56 by 96 inches, twice the size of the one then flying on Suribachi and nearly new. Wood had found it in a salvage depot at Pearl Harbor, and it had been flown from the LST's gaff on a few Sundays. Wood's only thought at the time was that the Marine runner looked filthy and exhausted, and that the Marines were really having it rough ashore.

When Rosenthal got to the top, the first flag was coming down.

"We're going to put up a bigger flag and keep this one for a souvenir," a Marine told him. Rosenthal decided to try for a shot of the first flag coming down and the new one going up, but he couldn't get into position in time so he backed off about 25 feet, to try for a shot of the second raising. He frantically piled stones to get some height, climbed on the pile, sighted his camera and clicked, one shot at 1/400th of a second, lens setting between f/8 and f/11. He had in his black box one of the most famous photographs of all time, but at the moment it was just one of seventeen other photographs he took that day and sent off to Guam by plane that night. It bore the caption: "Atop 550-foot Suribachi Yama, the volcano at the southwest tip of Iwo Jima, Marines of the Second Battalion, 28th Regiment, Fifth Division, hoist the Stars and

Stripes, signaling the capture of this key position." In the confusion, Rosenthal had not even been able to get the names "from left to right," though he had tried.

As a matter of fact, it was not a good news photograph. Of the six figures in the picture, only one face could be seen, and that could not be identified. One figure stood almost alone, at the base of the pole, and the other five were huddled together so that two of them were scarcely distinguishable. It was a bad news photograph, but a masterpiece of composition. It had movement and drama, and it told a story that needed no caption. The moment it began to come up in the developing tank at Guam it was recognized for what it is, a military work of art.

When it became important to know who the men in the photograph were, it took weeks to find out. The official "left to right" was finally determined to be: Private First Class Ira H. Hayes of Arizona; Private First Class Franklin R. Sousley of Kentucky; Sergeant Michael

Strank of Jamestown, Pennsylvania; Pharmacist's Mate Second Class John H. Bradley of Antigo, Wisconsin; Private First Class Rene A. Gagnon of Manchester, New Hampshire; and Corporal Harlon H. Block of Weslaco, Texas. Chance determined that they should represent nearly all sections and origins of the American people. Hayes was a Pima Indian; Sousley, a Kentucky mountain boy; Strank, the son of Czechoslovak immigrants; Bradley, a Mid-westerner and a Navy man; Gagnon, a new Englander of French-Canadian stock; and Block, a Texan.

But the Marines on Suribachi were not concerned with picture taking. They were busy holding a mountain. For the rest of the day they scouted out the crater and down the sides of the mountain, but there was little opposition left. Navy shelling and five days of fighting had finished the 1,200 Japanese inside. Kuribayashi had hoped they could hold out two weeks.

The 14th Marines rushed echo and flash-ranging equipment to the top, hoping to spot the Japanese artillery and fortifications in the north. But it didn't work very well. Too often the island was covered with fog patches, dust raised by the shelling, or sulphur vapor. And the Japanese were well hidden behind the ridges.

And the war didn't stop because Suribachi had fallen. General Cates, the perpetual cigarette holder gripped in his teeth, came ashore during the morning and staked out a command post just under the long runway of Airfield No. 1. It was a shattered Japanese gun pit, the stone sides giving good protection. Buried deep nearby was a wrecked plane fuselage; his communications and planning sections went in there.

General Schmidt also landed, at last able to take command of the largest Marine force ever fielded. In the afternoon he and Cates met at Rockey's command post, and the three generals assayed the position. After five days the landing force was firmly ashore, Suribachi had fallen, and resistance in the south had ceased. All forces, nearly three full divisions, could now concentrate on the drive north. Since the high ground lay up the middle of the island, it was agreed that the Third Division would press straight up the center, opening the flanks for defilade through the ravines leading to both coasts. The Fifth on the west and the Fourth on the east would also try to move forward with the Third. The full weight of naval guns, aircraft, and Marine artillery would be laid onto an ever shrinking area. Tanks of all three divisions would be placed under the command of Lieutenant Colonel William R. Collins of the Fifth Division, for support of the main thrust in the center.

It seemed that with such power of explosive against him, Kuribayashi must soon be wiped out, but they knew from experience there was no hope of his capitulation.

Bob Sherrod caught up with Harry

Schmidt after the meeting and asked him how long he expected the campaign to last. "Five days more after today," the General replied. "I said last week it would take ten days, and I haven't changed my mind."

Friday was a good day on the beaches. More exits were opened, the clearing of derelict equipment was beginning to pay off, and supplies were flowing steadily inland. A good number of LSM's came in, 2,500 rounds of 81-mm. mortar ammunition were landed (it had been in short supply for five days), and LST 646 put ashore twenty-five tanks of the Third Division. Despite the surf and the enemy shelling, 267 of the 400 LVT's were still in service and 190 of the 250 Dukws. One of the LVT's was definitely missing. It was "Mama's Bathtub," with Corporal Bruno C. Laurenti in command. After five straight days running supplies, his luck gave out. At nightfall, no LST would open its doors to him, and suddenly "Mama's Bathtub" was alone on a cold, dark sea, out of gas and drifting steadily away in a strong off-shore current. Two days later, a destroyer found it with Laurenti and a couple of privates, William Seward, Jr. and Alex Hebert, Jr., freezing and exhausted. As the sailors lifted them aboard, "Mama's Bathtub" slowly filled and sank.

Through the day, naval gunfire was the closest yet. The Idaho laid 162 rounds of 14-inch fire within 400 yards of Marine lines just before the morning attack opened, and the Pensacola added 390 rounds of 8-inch. The Navy-Marine SFCP's (shore fire-control parties) were in the front lines, working well at calling fire.

But the wind was shifting to east, meaning high surf on the east beaches. Admiral Hill therefore requested General Schmidt to prepare to receive cargo over the western beaches for several days, in the Fifth Division's zone.

And despite the flag on Suribachi, fighting remained bitter in the north. The Fifth Division fought hard all day on the west side, with virtually no advance and with the same searing losses. At noon a shell fell in the command post of 2/26, and the commanding officer, Lieutenant Colonel Joseph P. Sayers, was hit with shrapnel in the arm and side. He'd been limping since D-Day anyway, with a sprained knee, and now he was sent out. His executive officer, Major Amedeo Rea, once Eastern Intercollegiate middleweight boxing champion, took over the battalion. It was destined to bear the heaviest casualties of any battalion on Iwo Jima.

In the center, the Third and Fourth Divisions concentrated on the approaches to Airfield No. 2, one of the most important objectives of the campaign. General Kuribayashi was aware of its importance, and he had assigned Colonel Ikeda's 145th to defend the field. They were the best Japanese outfit on Iwo Jima, and their 47-mm. anti-tank guns were sited to fire straight down the runways.

The 21st Regiment bore the brunt of it in a four-hour battle. Major Clay Murray, taking over 1/21 for his first day, figured that if he could find the weakest point and destroy it he could then knock off the supporting positions one by one. He lifted the telephone to give an order and a machine-gun burst smashed the phone in his hand. Two bullets tore through his left cheek and out his open mouth, taking five teeth with them, and the rest of the burst sheared the knuckles off his left hand and ripped open his left ear. Major Robert H. Houser became 1/21's third commander in two days.

Company C was absolutely unable to move, with enemy pillboxes everywhere. Finally the commander asked Corporal Hershel W. Williams, "Can you do anything?" Williams, twenty-one, the last of nine flamethrower operators in the company, said, "I can try." Covered by four riflemen, Williams moved forward, his flamer hissing. On the right, a Japanese popped up repeatedly from a buried oil drum to fire. The corporal finally caught him on the upbeat. Four more men rushed him, and Williams dropped to one knee and incinerated them. Running on, he thrust the flamer nozzle into one pillbox after another, and burned them all out. The company moved on, but not far; there was always another line of pillboxes ahead.

Private First Class George Smyth, eighteen, of Brooklyn, had never seen such Japanese. They were 6-footers, and they never retreated. Smyth's buddy fell beside him, a pistol bullet through his head, dead center. It came from a captured Marine .45. On the other side, a Japanese came down with his sword, both hands grasping the hilt. The Marine put up his right hand to ward off the blow, and his arm was sliced down the middle, fingers to elbow. As Smyth ran forward, a Japanese disappeared before him into a hole. Smyth dropped at the hole to finish him off, but the Japanese was already rising from a tunnel behind him. Smyth turned just in time to kill him. The ground was giving Ikeda's men every advantage, and they were using them all. By nightfall, nearly every gain in the center had been nullified.

Behind the lines – a phrase still evoking bitter humor – men in "reserve" spent the day mopping up, cleaning weapons, resupplying. Some even got hot coffee, the first since Monday morning. The Fifth Division moved its tank park back 500 yards; the northwest corner of Airfield No. 1 was still too hot for it.

By the end of the day, the spectacular phase of the Iwo Jima campaign was over. Secretary Forrestal left for Guam at 4 P.M. Task Force 58 had pulled out the day before, for the second raid on Tokyo. Now, aerial support was limited to that provided by the small carriers in the daytime and by the Enterprise's night fighter group. The Marines were solidly ashore and forty-four men were guarding the top of Suribachi – all that

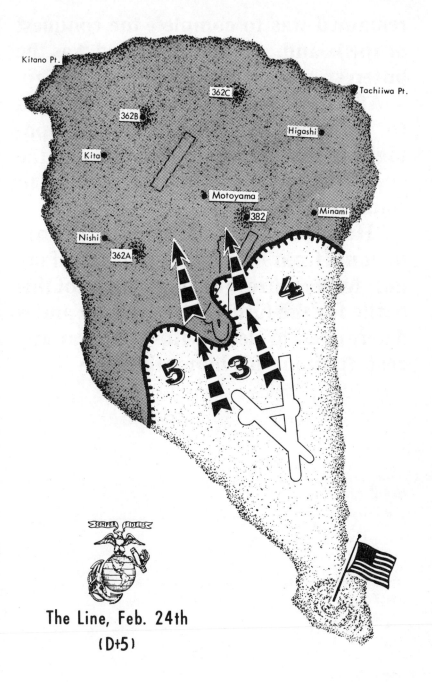

Kitano Pt.

Tachiiwa Pt.

362C

362B

Higashi

Kita

Motoyama

Minami

382

Nishi

362A

4

5

3

SEMPER FIDELIS

The Line, Feb. 24th
(D+5)

remained was to complete the conquest of the island. All that remained was the bitterest, bloodiest part of the campaign.

Admiral Ichimaru knew it. He cabled to Admiral Toyoda that night, apologizing that he had not annihilated the enemy at the waterfront, according to tradition.

"However," he said, "real battles are to come from now on. Every man of my unit fully realizes the importance of this battle for the future of the nation and is determined to defend this island at any cost, fulfilling his honorable duty."

Chapter 5

Tactically, the first phase of the battle ended on Saturday, a day of intense activity.

In the rear, men and machines were pouring ashore in an unending stream. Mortar fire still fell on the beaches occasionally, but nobody paid any attention to it. General Schmidt's staff came ashore, and General Erskine and Colonel Howard N. "Red" Kenyon, the waved ends of his luxuriant mustache curling skyward, brought in the last of the fighting forces, the 9th Regiment. More of the artillery and the last of the Third Division's tanks climbed the beaches and snaked inland.

The replacements were coming in steadily, too. Private Johnny Lane, eighteen, from Brooklyn, moved up to the front as a replacement in the 25th

Regiment. His instructions for battle were a brief statement of military wisdom. The sergeant said: "This here is G Company. We're going to move out this morning. This won't be no straight line, so when you see a Jap, shoot him. You know what a Jap looks like. Don't shoot any Marines." The sergeant was gone. What more could a guy need to know?

Lane crouched in a hole, waiting, clutching the rifle he had never fired in combat. He waited all day and nothing happened. At nightfall he was ordered back, and he ran across the open ground, still clutching the rifle. Someone nabbed him to serve as a runner, and he never saw the front again. He never fired his rifle, and he never saw a live Japanese.

Nor did he ever see again many of those friends who had gone ashore with him that morning. Holcomb, who had been a singer on a small radio station in North Carolina, was killed before sundown. His guitar, which he took to bed with him, was still back on the transport.

Koski, a big Finn from Quincy, Massachusetts, was killed by machine-gun fire, and Lane helped carry his body to the cemetery. Kolbmayer pulled the pin on a grenade one night, then dropped it. He jumped from his foxhole and was instantly killed by the Marine in the next hole. "With the goddam Japs jumpin' around all night what the hell could I do?" Windbegler, who was always thirsty, stepped on a mine while prowling for water. Lane saw no Japanese, but he knew they were there. Every morning he had to crawl from hole to hole, taking the names of those from G Company who were still alive. The list got shorter and shorter.

By Saturday morning, 2,000 Seabees were ashore, and the 31st Battalion started to work on Airfield No. 1. With riflemen covering them, they crawled up the runway on hands and knees, probing for mines and picking out shrapnel. This was supposed to have been the 133rd's job, but it was so badly shot up on D-Day that it still had not reorganized. All day the Seabees and some of the Corps' 2nd Separate Engineers sifted the dirt on the runways, with hidden Japanese still sniping, and every once in a while the enemy artillery dropped a few salvos on the runway.

All command was now ashore, and more than 50,000 troops, Seabees, Army units, and work parties. The narrow part of the island was jammed. The 28th Regiment, still mopping up on Suribachi, had counted more than 600 Japanese dead and estimated that another thousand were sealed in caves, probably forever. Some were still alive, and you could hear them talking at night inside the mountain. The Marines were content to wait for them to come out, if they ever did. The Navy seaplane base off Suribachi was functioning, and nets and buoys were being set out to protect the harbor. The south was a giant construction site.

But in the north the battle for Airfield No. 2 began. All artillery massed fire on the center of the island, and the Idaho and Pensacola put in shells from the sea. The carrier planes made bombing runs, but only twenty-six of the bombs were 500-pounders. The rest were 100-pounders, and General Cates put in a complaint. He wanted Army bombers to come in from the Marianas with heavy stuff. All tanks were again under Colonel Collins, and the 2nd and 3rd Battalions of the 21st moved out in the center.

It was hard going. More than eight hundred pillboxes ringed the field, mostly on the high ground to the north, and the artillery fired straight down the runways. The attack was off at 9:30, with the 3rd Battalion in the center and the 2nd on the left. At the 3rd's command post, Lieutenant Colonel Wendell H. Duplantis told his men simply: "We have to get that airfield today."

Captain Rodney L. Heinze, commanding Company K, lasted forty-five minutes. As he reached the edge of the runway, two grenades went off. Heinze slid into a hole, the inside of his thighs ripped open by shrapnel. The grenades came from a hole with a metal cover, and the next time the lid lifted it was the last. A BAR man blasted the Japanese inside. Captain Daniel Marshall took over the company.

To the right, Captain Clayton S. Rockmore led Company I straight at the pillboxes. He was a tall, rugged, impatient man of twenty-two. He had quit Cornell to enlist, been wounded at Guam, and now he stormed out against the pillboxes. A bullet struck him in the throat, killing him instantly. Within minutes three lieutenants were wounded and sergeants took over the companies.

Then up came First Lieutenant Raoul Archambault, rallied the men of both companies, and started them rushing across the runway. A lot of them knew him from Guam (Bronze Star) and Bougainville (Silver Star), and when he led they followed. Running across with the air full of steel, Archambault thought, "This is fighting on a pool table," but he made it, and so did the men with him, and behind them the mortarmen, throwing up a storm of 60- and 81-mm. shells. As the men ran, the machine guns stitched up the ground all around them, and they scrambled into the ridge on the other side.

First across the center was Lieutenant Dominick Grossi. Only twelve men of his platoon were left, but those twelve kept going. Once they were knocked off the ridge, but Grossi led them right back up with a bayonet and grenade charge, and they stayed. The hill on the far side was honeycombed with tunnels and trenches connecting the strongpoints, and the men plunged in, attacking with anything at hand.

In the wild fighting they fell on Ikeda's men with rocks, rifle butts, bayonets, knives, pistols, and shovels. In ninety minutes it was over. Archambault and his men were on top of the ridge, the advance had covered 800 yards, and the line was breached. Through the gap poured tanks, bazooka men, mortar- men, and machine gunners, cleaning up as they advanced.

After nightfall, amazingly, a tractor came plowing up the ridge, pulling a trailer loaded with hot food, water, and ammunition. Warrant Officer George Green, out front as an artillery spotter, couldn't see the driver but concluded he was either crazy or lost. If the men had not stopped him, he would have gone straight on to Kitano Point. But Green was so happy to have the food he only called the driver a son of a bitch for tearing up his wire. After eating, Green crawled back, found the break, and spliced his wire.

Archambault, his long, thin figure draped around a hole, concluded ruefully that this was worse than Guam or Bougainville. In the jungle, men died quietly, out of sight.

Here they were torn to shreds in full view, and there was not even time to bury them. Just steady firing, he thought, as if they were all trying to use up their ammunition before the war ended.

In late afternoon, Corporal William J. Middlebrooks started back to his ship. He was a combat correspondent, and he was going to write how Archambault and his men had stormed the airfield. Middlebrooks was twenty-three, and he had been at Guam and Bougainville. Just before he landed on Iwo Jima, he had written that this would be old stuff to the veterans, but for the new men "it will be a terrible and horrifying experience." While he waited for a boat out to his ship, he offered to carry some ammunition up to the 2nd Battalion. On the way back he was shot, and by nightfall he was dead.

Near the coast, the Fourth Division held its lines all day Saturday, but the 24th attacked over Charlie-Dog Ridge, trying to reach Airfield No. 2. It was fairly easy going in the early hours, and by 11 o'clock the 2nd Battalion was only 150 yards from the runway. But Ikeda's men were waiting, and at about 11:25 they opened fire with anti-tank guns, automatic fire, and rifles. The Marines called for artillery fire, rolled a 37-mm. gun to the front, and brought down mortar fire. The 3rd Battalion, just to the east, caught the full force of the Japanese counterattack.

Kuribayashi was fighting for the core of his central-island defense now. Just beyond the airfield lay Hill 382, highest point in the north, and the Amphitheater, Turkey Knob, and Minami. Here lay a complex of hills and crags, ravines and valleys, all rock and concrete and brush, tunneled and fortified with great skill. The 24th was beginning to hit an important enemy nerve, and the Japanese replied with heavy mortar fire. By 3 P.M. 3/24's casualties were so heavy that it was necessary to lay down white phosphorous smoke in order to carry out the wounded.

Just after four o'clock, mortar fire fell in the command post. Three men were killed and the commander, Lieutenant Colonel Alexander A. Vandegrift, Jr., was wounded in both legs. His father was also a Marine; was, in fact, the

Commandant of the Corps. Major Doyle Stout took command and the fight went on. By nightfall the 24th was firmly atop Charlie-Dog Ridge and never gave it up.

One of the day's casualties was Second Lieutenant William K. Webb of Prairieville, Louisiana. He was killed, but he didn't have to be. He had been wounded in the thigh on D-Day. As soon as he could walk he left the hospital ship without permission, hitched a ride to the beach, and rejoined his unit. Many men were like him – they would rather be with their unit at any cost. It cost Webb his life.

Across the line, deep in a ravine near Higashi, a Japanese Navy lieutenant and several men arrived at Inouye's command post. The lieutenant, his uniform torn and stained with blood, reported that they had escaped from Suribachi.

"You traitor," the captain roared, "why did you come here? Don't you know what shame is? You are a coward and a deserter."

"Under military regulations a deserter is executed summarily," Inouye shouted. "I shall condescend to behead you myself."

He drew his sword and raised it in samurai-fashion, both hands on the hilt. The lieutenant, who had said nothing, knelt and bowed his head. Aides rushed up and wrested Captain Inouye's sword from him. The Captain turned away, weeping. "Suribachi's fallen," he muttered, "Suribachi's fallen." His orderly, Petty Officer Riichi Koyatsu, led the lieutenant to the sick bay for treatment of his wounds. Captain Inouye, when he recovered his composure, was absolutely determined on one thing: No Navy man would leave Iwo Jima alive.

At the end of the day, after six full days of battle, the cost to the Marines was 1,605 men killed, 5,496 wounded, and 657 cases of combat fatigue – a total of 7,758 casualties.

For this the Marines had bought one-third of a very small island.

Part Four

KURIBAYASHI'S
LAST STAND

Chapter 1

The terrible two weeks began on Sunday morning, quite unspectacularly.

It was clear that the only way to take the remaining two-thirds of the island was to go up the high ground in the middle. From the relatively flat plateau, the ground broke to east and west and ran down to the shore in gullies, canyons, and arroyos. The shelling had churned them into masses of broken stone, their sides riddled with caves, holes, tunnels, the ridges broken and strewn with boulders.

On the west coast, the Fifth Division was faced with one ridge after another, each one meaning a fight up the slope and over the top, only to meet another ravine with another ridge beyond it. Japanese fire down the canyons would be murderous. The enemy would have to be driven from the high ground in the center, and even then the advance along the coast would be expensive.

The Fourth Division on the east faced a battlefield stripped of all cover. Where once the oaks had grown, there were only shattered rock, tangled brush, and defiles running to the sea like spokes from the hub of a wheel. Rising from this frozen sea of stone were Hill 382, the highest point on the island excepting Suribachi, a bald little hill someone had named Turkey Knob, and a natural bowl that quite easily took the name of the Amphitheater.

Far beyond, toward the sea, was the headquarters of Major General Sadasue Senda, and all through the rock lay his 2nd Mixed Brigade, unseen and waiting. There was a smashed radar station on top of Hill 382, and on the far bluff of the Amphitheater could be seen cave mouths and tunnel entrances. Not a gun barrel could be seen, but at every turn and fold in the rock were cross-lanes of fire for machine guns and mortars, automatic weapons and rifles, light artillery, and rapid-fire cannon. Behind them were the men, some with sabres or pistols, bamboo lances, and sacks of grenades, waiting.

In the center, General Erskine took back the 21st Regiment from the Fourth Division and for the first time had all his troops then ashore under his own command. The 21st went to the rear to re-equip and rest, and the 9th went into the line. All artillery of the Corps, the Fourth and the Fifth Divisions were in place, and the remainder of the Third Division artillery was landing. The drive up the center began.

A battleship and two cruisers opened the assault, firing for twenty minutes in slow, deliberate salvos from their main batteries. The artillery followed with 1,200 rounds across the front, and carrier planes with 500-pound bombs came in just ahead of the line.

At 9.30 A.M. the men moved out, and it was as though the guns had never fired. Japanese fire sweeping across Airfield

No. 2 was strong and accurate.

Twenty-six tanks were available, and there had been talk of riding the infantry across the strip on them. This idea was discarded, and the tanks lumbered out, with Ateball, Agony, and Angel at the point.

Angel and Agony were hit and flamed immediately. Ateball was stopped by a shell hit. Corporal William R. Adamson of San Jose, California squeezed out of Agony's hatch and dropped to the ground alongside his tank. A bullet nicked his leg, and he sat in a pall of smoke from the burning machine, tearing up his pants leg to bandage the wound. From the corner of his eye he caught sight of a muzzle flash. Crawling toward Ateball, he crouched in the open, 30 yards from the muzzle of its 75, and waved wildly toward the flash. Ateball fired, again and again, and the Japanese gun was silent.

In succession, Adamson then pointed out four machine guns, a Japanese running up with a satchel charge, and 30 infantry sneaking up along a ravine. Atebal 1 broke them all up, and a tank retriever came for Ateball. On the way it rolled over Adamson and picked him up through the escape hatch. Other tanks rolled on. By day's end, nine tanks had been knocked out.

The 1st Battalion of the 9th fought five hours and advanced 100 yards, to the foot of Hill Peter. The 2nd and 3rd made better advances, and by the end of the day the line was north of Airfield No. 2 at all points except the extreme right tip.

Erskine was not satisfied (he rarely was) and he called in Colonel Kenyon, the 9th's commander. Were the men prepared for a night attack, the General asked. The Colonel ran his arm over his sweaty red face. "They're mighty tired," he said.

The General reared back and began to talk of World War I. He told how, at Soissons, he came back from a patrol, one of four men left out of thirty-eight, and the company commander told him to go out again and throw a rock at a

German machine gun so that they could spot it.

"I did what he told me," the General said. Then he turned to Captain Oscar Salgo of the reconnaissance company.

"I want you to go through the Jap lines in a night attack and blow up and burn out some of these pillboxes that are holding us up."

The Captain said he was willing to try, but which pillboxes did the General have in mind? The map showed only a few, but everybody knew there were many. The General, his eyes flinty, canceled the night attack, but he put the idea away for another time.

The Fourth Division, using the 23rd and 24th Regiments, moved off into the Meat Grinder. No one knew where the name came from, but everybody knew what it meant. It meant the area from Hill 382 down through Turkey Knob and the Amphitheater, the area where the men were ground up into meat – fresh, red meat.

They laid on the artillery, the navy

gunfire, with mortar boats and LCI's firing up the draws, carrier planes plunging down in, and the LVT (A)'s firing from offshore. They sent the tanks around through the Third Division's area, because they couldn't get over the rubble in front, and armored bulldozers chewed away at the shattered rocks, trying to clear roads. And the men fought all day, and by nightfall they had made about a hundred yards.

The Fifth Division took it easy. That is, they didn't press the battle, waiting for the Third to move in the center. They took it easy, and they still had 163 casualties, with mortar and artillery fire dropping off the ridges up north. In the afternoon, the Fifth's artillery had one bright moment. Against all orders, some Japanese artillery began moving north in daylight, high up on the west coast. A plane spotted them about 3 P.M., and the Fifth's artillery enthusiastically poured on nearly 600 rounds. Three Japanese artillery pieces were smashed, and an ammunition dump was set afire.

Colonel Kaido had warned against such folly. For the rest of the campaign, no more artillery moved by day.

Behind the lines, it was as though there was no dying up front. An east wind piled high surf on the east beaches, but LSM's and LST's held the beach, and trucks and cranes unloaded them. Bulldozers and Dukws waddled inland on the roads taking shape; poles went up to get the wire off the ground. Artillery cracked incessantly, and work went on under the belching muzzles. The Navy began surveying the western beaches, and Fifth Division engineers opened the first water distillation plant on the west coast, on a ledge 45 feet above the sea. Intake pipes were driven into the natural springs, and the water came out so hot it had to be cooled with sea water. But there were showers for some, and the dirt ran off the men in mud waddies.

The 31st Seabees, using some heavy equipment borrowed from the 62nd, finished blading and rolling the north-south runway on Airfield No. 1. By nightfall a strip 1,500 feet long and 150 feet wide was ready for light planes. A plane came in from the Marianas and dropped some mail. Corporal Joseph P. Whittam, twenty, of Chicago, opened his. It was a civics lesson from the Marine Corps Institute.

All day the casualties streamed to the beaches, and nine ships left for Guam. This time the cargo was men – 1,469 casualties. The Third Division opened its cemetery just off the runway of Airfield No. 1.

While the 21st Regiment rested, Corporal Leniart of the 1st Battalion made his first trip to the beach to get replacements. After the corporal's four days at the front, these men looked to him as if they'd just come off liberty in San Diego. He led them forward, 50 or 100 at a time, and turned them over to the noncoms. Once in a while he got to watch as the new men were given a BAR, or a bazooka, or a machine gun. Someone showed them how to fire a few rounds, and from then on they were "ready." They had missed the hell of D-Day, but a special kind of ordeal awaited them.

Far off to the north, Task Force 58 went in again after the Japanese mainland. The weather was very bad, and the planes, flying in from 190 miles off Tokyo, could find only secondary targets. The strike was canceled at 12:15 P.M.

Late that night, in a cave with a single bulb hanging from the roof, Baron Nishi poured a drink for himself and his aide, Okubo. During the afternoon, at Airfield No. 2, the Colonel had watched a Marine run forward with a flamethrower. The Baron had ordered firing stopped, but Okubo winged the Marine, and they brought him in and turned him over to the surgeons. In his pocket was a letter from his mother, in which she said she was praying for his return.

The Baron thought of his own children, and Okubo thought of the stories he had heard that the Baron was pro-American. Nishi said he had wanted to question the Marine for intelligence.

"If I tried to save that American, that has nothing to do with my background," the Colonel said. They talked some more, about the chances Nishi had had to stay in America and of his opportunity to avoid the Iwo Jima assignment. After Okubo went to bed, Nishi finished the bottle. The next morning he was advised that the American had died.

The second week of the Iwo Jima campaign began on Monday morning, unnoticed. In seven days of fighting the Marines had captured two-fifths of the island and paid for it with more than 8,000 casualties. (Tokyo Radio said the part of the island held by the Americans was "not more than the size of the forehead of a cat.") There was no cause, and no time, to mark this anniversary. The men who had crossed the beaches on D-Day – every hour there were fewer left at the front – could not think in terms of time as long as a week. They measured it in spans of hours: of hours still alive; of nightfall and sunrises, still alive; of short, sharp stabs of pain when the word went around, "Charley got it." "That leaves only six of us," a man would think to himself, and the skin would tighten a little more over his cheekbones, and he would look a little grayer, a little older.

And mostly they would hunch over a little more, and move forward. But when it was Harold's turn, they stopped. He was leading a rifle squad on the west coast, and they saw him fall, cut down by a swathe of machine-gun fire. His own brother, Luther Crabtree, saw it, from where he was blowing up caves as a demolitions man. Private First Class William C. Erler saw it. He and Harold and Luther had been together every day since they enlisted together in Columbus, Ohio nearly two and a half years before.

"We can't leave him out there," Erler said, and the company commander agreed to hold up a minute while they tried for the body. He shouldn't have; this had nothing to do with the battle, but he threw up a smoke barrage, and Erler and two other privates ran forward with a stretcher.

They had no trouble finding the spot; it was where the lines of fire crossed from two Japanese pillboxes, and they rolled the body onto the stretcher and raced back into the lines. Luther got there just as they arrived, and for an instant in time the war stopped for Luther. They had landed in the same assault wave, eight days ago, and now Harold, his older brother, twenty-two, was dead. And Luther and Harold and Erler had never been apart before. They took the body to the rear, the smoke barrage dissipated in the light airs above the hills, and the war went on.

If you didn't know about Harold Crabtree or the more than 200 other men around him who were killed or wounded that day – or maybe if you looked at it from a different angle – it was a good day on the Fifth Division front. They made about 300 yards by nightfall, and the 26th overran Japanese Wells No. 4 and

5, the last water wells the Japanese had.

Twenty LVT(A)'s of the 2nd Armored Amphibian Battalion were out most of the day, bobbing off the west coast and firing their 75-mm. guns up the draws. They knocked out at least three enemy strong points, but in the late afternoon choppy seas forced them to stop firing. The rocking guns were sending shells into Marine territory.

Up ahead, nearly 800 yards away, you could see Hill 362A, the next big objective, and during the day they had flushed some Japanese and killed them as they ran. It was the first time they had seen the enemy in the open, and it gave the men a tremendous boost in morale.

Down on airfield No. 1 the first planes came in, two little OY-1's of the Fourth Division (VMO-4), their wheels kicking up spurts of dust as they touched down. Dirty engineers and Seabees lined the runway and cheered as the little spotter planes rolled to a stop. The Grasshoppers (Stinson Sentinels), or "Maytag Messerschmitts," stayed only a few minutes and then they took off again, to fly over Turkey Knob and the Amphitheater to spot targets for the Fourth Division. As they left, the first of the 133rd Seabees' rollers and scrapers climbed up onto the runway. After a week of fighting, and heavy casualties, and reorganization, the 133rd was ready to start on the job it had come for.

In the center of the island Colonel Kenyon's 9th Regiment opened the second day of its assault on Hill Peter. Eight bombers and fighters were out in front of the lines, their bombs falling far up ahead. The Marines cursed them, and the formal language of the Third Division report said this type of support "was entirely inadequate to meet the requirements of the situation. A much larger number of aircraft employed in mass against targets holding up the advance of infantry was clearly indicated."

The 1st Battalion, Ninth Regiment did succeed in getting a flamethrowing tank around behind the hill, and a few

Japanese running from a tunnel were incinerated. Petty Officer Third Class Isamu Okazaki, twenty-two, a Navy rocket gunner, came out of a bunker and was surprised to see Marines about 50 yards away. A bullet hit him in the chest and he fell. Okazaki threw a grenade and killed the Marine who had wounded him, and then he threw three more grenades, scattering the Marines. He crawled a half mile to the field hospital under Motoyama. A surgeon sprinkled disinfectant on his wound and told him: "I can't do anything more now. Go into the cave and rest until I can come back to you." Okazaki crawled far back into the cave and fell into a stupor. (When he came out, the battle had passed him by, and maggots and time had healed his wound. He lived by his wits among the Americans until April, when a soldier tapped him on the shoulder and took him in.)

The 9th fought all day long around Hill Peter, again using massed tanks as assault guns, but at the end of five hours there was no gain, and eleven tanks had been knocked out. Private First Class James Golden of Boston, a rifleman, did not finish the day. He was sent back to the beach in the morning, covered from head to foot with heat rash. But he didn't know anybody at the beach, and he missed his outfit. He walked back and found his squad working around the face of the hill. Shortly before noon a bullet drilled him squarely between the eyes, just under the helmet line.

The Fourth Division struck out again for Hill 382 and Turkey Knob. Colonel Lanigan's 25th, strengthened by replacements after the severe losses of the first four days, went back into the line, replacing the 24th, and ran into very strong fire from Turkey Knob and the Amphitheater. The ground was so bad tanks could not be used, and even the 75's and 37's could not get into position. But around the East Boat Basin the final nests of snipers were wiped out, and at last the beaches were clear of all close fire. General unloading began on the

Fourth Division beaches, and the Columbia Victory arrived with artillery ammunition. Parties worked all night moving ammunition up for the guns. Corps artillery had a record day, firing 5,652 rounds.

The 23rd worked through minefields on the taxiways at the east end of Airfield No. 2 and on the slopes around the shattered radio station lying before Hill 382.

Starting up the slope toward Hill 382, Private First Class Douglas T. Jacobson of 3/23 was seized with a frenzy. For the moment he ceased to be a rifleman and became a bazooka man. He grabbed the weapon from a man who had gone down, ran to a Japanese 20-mm. gun position and knocked it out. Running on, he destroyed a pillbox and a blockhouse with fire and demolition charges. Still he ran on, into the enemy lines, and before the fires within him subsided he had killed at least seventy-five Japanese and captured sixteen Japanese positions. Company I was a good way up the southwest slope by late afternoon, but the enemy still held the top. The 23rd had to withdraw for the night.

It was plain that the Japanese were no longer retreating. The Marines were now in the main line of defense, and the Japanese had to stand. Captain Awatsu's 309th Independent Infantry Battalion, or what was left of it, stood fast. By nightfall it had ceased to exist. The 309th had been falling back slowly since D-Day, from in front of Airfield No. 1. The 23rd now drove it to the southeast, over against Lanigan's 25th, which finished it off. Net gain for the day on the 23rd's front was 200 yards.

Off Japan, the weather was so bad before dawn that Admiral Mitscher saw he could not get into position to raid Nagoya, the day's target. For the time being, at least, Task Force 58 was through with the great showpiece raids on Japan. The force broke up, part of the carriers leaving for Ulithi. The others fueled west of Iwo Jima and set out to raid Okinawa.

For the first time that night there was no mortar fire from the sea. All thirty of the LCI(M)'s had left that day for Saipan. In a week of supporting the Marines with close-range fire, only one had been damaged, by a near-miss at the beach. Their night firing, in particular, had given the Marines a good feeling.

The Army's 506th Anti-Aircraft Battalion finished landing during the day and began lobbing 90-mm. shells at Kama and Kangoku Rocks off the west coast. Occasional mortar and rocket fire had been coming from there, harassing the Fifth Division troops.

In the evening the weather cleared (it had rained a little in the afternoon), and a bright moon came out. A large group of Japanese, a company or more, started down the west coast, apparently hoping to recapture the wells lost that day. Lined with concrete rings, the wells were only 25 feet deep, and the water in No. 5 was heavy with hydrogen sulphide, but they were the last ones Kuribayashi had. The Marines welcomed the sight of the enemy, and those in the front line watched with great satisfaction as their artillery and destroyer fire from the sea smashed the raiding party. From now on the Japanese would have to rely on rain or stored water.

On Tuesday, the island was roaring with activity, at the front and in the rear.

Bobbie Erskine goaded the Third Division forward in the Hills Oboe and Peter again, and Doug Watson finished the job he had started the day before. Private Wilson D. Watson, twenty-four, a tall, hollow-cheeked farm boy from Alabama, had led his squad forward on Monday, brandishing a BAR and subduing pillboxes with fire and grenades. On Tuesday morning he ran to the top of a hill, firing the BAR from the hip and holding the crest alone for fifteen minutes. He was not scratched, and killed at least 60 Japanese before his platoon joined him.

At 12:40 P.M. the artillery laid down a ten-minute barrage, and suddenly the

9th Regiment was moving. Lieutenant Colonel Randall's 1st Battalion swarmed over Hill Peter, down the back slope and up Hill Oboe. The 2nd Battalion, under Lieutenant Colonel Cushman, kept pace on the left, pushing ahead 1,500 yards. After three days of heavy fighting, the Third was coming out on the plateau, with relatively flat terrain ahead, and Airfield No. 2 was cleared.

Not so on the right. The Fourth Division, with five battalions abreast in the line, went off after a heavy barrage, including 300 rounds from the Corps' 155-mm. cannon. It was hand-to-hand fighting for the 23rd, hitting Hill 382 again and again. The top of the hill had been hollowed out and rebuilt with artillery and anti-tank gun pits. Grenades and even satchel charges were hurled up and down the slopes, into the night as well as during the day. The 23rd clawed around toward the northwest slope of the hill and made some progress. But the artillery at the top commanded the ground and forced the tanks back.

The 24th, pushing around the south of Turkey Knob and the Amphitheater, made nearly 200 yards along the east coast but accomplished little penetration of the two bastions. The 23rd, despite the fierce combat, was back at its line of departure by nightfall. The day had cost the Fourth Division 792 casualties – the worst single day it had had, or would have, in the whole campaign, excluding the first two days of slaughter across the beaches. But General Senda's 2nd Mixed Brigade was suffering too. These were mostly Kanto soldiers from around Tokyo, considered a cut below the Kyushu troops, but they were giving their best performance of the Pacific war. They still stood atop Hill 382, and late that night they sent up flares, calling for medical supplies and ammunition. Just before 1 A.M., the Marines saw parachutes falling behind the hill; planes had come down from the Bonins for the last time.

The 25th had one surprise during the day. Three Marines came on Superior Private Kunimatsu Kato, asleep near a cave, or pretending to be. In his hand was a stick with a white Marine sock on it. Kato, thirty, a medical corpsman with the 309th, sprang up when a Marine poked him with a bayonet and readily started toward the rear. He told intelligence officers he had been on Iwo Jima fourteen months and seen at least twenty men die of malnutrition. The caves and the water gave the men colds and paratyphoid. Diarrhea, he said, had a pitiful effect on the men wasting away from poor food and water. He was glad that he had been "overpowered," and he readily agreed to try to convince other Japanese to surrender. At last he could think, too, of returning to his wife in Tamuragen, Fukushima-ken.

Not all Japanese were surrendering. The 5th Reconnaissance Company, closing out a week of hunting stragglers in the "rear" areas, had killed 515 Japanese. There were still many left, and

Intelligence was revising its estimates. It now concluded that there must have been more than 20,000 Japanese on the island on D-Day, instead of the forecasts of 14,000. Enemy dead were already estimated at 5,483, though few bodies had been found. It was also said that it was still not known if General Kuribayashi himself was on the island, though he was thought to be.

On the west coast, the 27th relieved the 26th and assaulted the approaches to Hill 362A behind heavy artillery preparation. Marine guns, both division and corps, fired for thirty minutes, followed by destroyer fire, salvos from the rocket trucks, and carrier plane attacks with bombs and rockets. The advance, hard-scrabbling all day long against caves and pillboxes, carried 400 yards on the right and 500 yards along the shore. The hill was almost within reach.

During the assault, the 3rd Battalion lost a "gunny." Gunnery Sergeant William G. Walsh, twenty-two, led a platoon charge up a ridge, and they were thrown back. He led a second charge, and this time a few men made it into a trench on top. They lay there panting, and a grenade rolled in. Without an instant's pause Walsh rolled over on it. The rest of the men held the ridge and that night got his body out.

Nearly one-third of the island was now freed, and it was jammed with men and machines. Some order was beginning to emerge. The 31st Seabees moved to the west side of the island, into a foxhole camp that resembled the city dump. But the pipefitters tapped a hot spring and set up gang showers. The galley opened, and men no longer had to feed themselves; they were free to work.

Roadways and beach exits for the western beaches were ready to handle small craft, but Japanese fire from the north was still too strong.

Near the east coast, the Fourth Division post office opened in an abandoned cistern. Captain Emmet E. Hardin, forty-two, in private life a New

York postal inspector, announced the first mail plane would leave for Saipan that night, and he was equipped to handle 100,000 V-mail letters daily for all three divisions. The troops never liked V-mail, but they wrote, and reducing the letters to microfilm was the only way the volume could have been handled.

For the first time, whole blood was moved up to company medical stations. Freshly drawn in Los Angeles, San Francisco, San Diego, and Portland, it had come all the way by plane, packed in ice, and it was welcome. A truck load rolled up to a Third Division station, and Lieutenant Commander Leo Theilen shouted, "Break it out, boys, on the double." In a few minutes the fresh scarlet blood flowed in the tents behind the sandbags. "Bless it," said Captain C. P. Archambeault of Brooklyn, a Third Division surgeon.

A Navy evacuation hospital, the first of its kind in the Pacific, set up on Purple Beach and by nightfall had two hundred beds ready. The Fourth Division Hospital, at the north edge of Airfield No. 1, had seventeen doctors working in four operating teams around the clock. The Army's 38th Field Hospital, 22 officers and 182 enlisted men, began landing. In the coming days, its six surgeons would perform 592 operations, 360 of them major surgery.

Major General James E. Chaney, head of the Army garrison force, came ashore with his staff and parts of the 147th Infantry Regiment and the 7th Fighter Command. The Fifth Division's first spotter plane landed in the afternoon, First Lieutenant Roy G. Miller piloting. He had been fired off LST 776 by Brodie gear, a giant slingshot that hurled the little Grasshoppers into the air. Ten more planes followed in the next three days (one fell into the sea before it could be fastened into the catapult), and the front-line soldiers were glad to see them. The ground crews rigged the little planes with bazookas, rockets, bombs, and the pilots flew low over the enemy lines, looking for targets – both for themselves and the artillery. Japanese fire dropped sharply when they were overhead. The enemy could not risk revealing the position of his artillery and mortars. The number of Japanese guns was shrinking fast enough. But the pilots paid for their "sport." Three of the Fifth Division's five spotters were killed. Second Lieutenant Mont Adamson, flying for the Fourth Division artillery, did twenty missions out of Airfield No. 1 and was not scratched. He died of multiple sclerosis before he was discharged.

Navy search planes, the big PBM flying boats, came in from the Marianas and began operating from three tenders off Suribachi. Planes from the Anzio sank a submarine a few miles west of Iwo Jima. It was the I-368, carrying kaitens, the one-man suicide submarines. These little subs, fastened to the deck of the regular submarine, were fired off like guided torpedoes, never to return. Japanese vied for the honor of this kind of death for the homeland. The day before, Anzio planes had sunk a regular submarine, the RO-43, west of Chichi Jima, and the destroyer escort Finnegan had bagged another kaiten-carrying sub, the I-370, between Iwo Jima and Saipan. The Japanese submarine force was making its last forays.

General Smith told correspondents "We expect to take this island in a few more days." He conceded that there would be heavy fighting, but he said that the Japanese were short of water and having trouble caring for their wounded. They were becoming jittery, he said.

On Wednesday, the tenth day ashore and the last day of February, the Marines held less than half the island. This was the day General Harry Schmidt had predicted the battle would end.

The Third Division did make good gains in the center of the island.

The 21st began moving into the line before dawn, relieving the 9th. Even then, snipers and enemy patrols were busy, and soon after dawn a Marine of 2/9 crumpled in a ravine, blood welling from a neat hole in his neck. Pharmacist's Mate Second Class Floyd L. Garrett, twenty-three, who had spent a good deal of time as a surgical assistant, recognized immediately that the jugular vein had been pierced. He knelt, slit the wound with a knife, laid the vein bare and clamped it. Then he stuffed the hole with gauze and motioned for the bearers. At the battalion aid station the Navy doctor, Lieutenant (j.g.) Cloyd L. Arford, whistled in admiration at the surgery.

By 9 A.M., the 9th was out and the 21st was in. Backed by its own artillery and Corps' 155's in a rolling barrage, the 21st Regiment moved forward. Almost immediately, Company I was confronted with tanks rising from the earth. These were Colonel Nishi's tanks, flushed at last from what had appeared to be hillocks. They churned forward, throwing off mounds of dirt, shrubbery, and rocks, and firing rapidly. The

Marines faltered in shock before the heavy fire, and for moments the battle teetered. Captain Edward V. Stephenson, who had fought at Guam with great valor, rushed forward and rallied his company. Massing flame-throwers and bazookamen, he led a counterattack that smashed the tanks. Three were destroyed on the ground, and planes caught two more of them with 20-mm. fire. Nishi now had only three tanks left.

During the morning, gains of 400 yards were made, but by noon the momentum stopped. The 21st was off again at 1 P.M., with artillery support, and the 3rd Battalion smashed through what had been the village of Motoyama. Where once General Kuribayashi had been greeted by schoolchildren, strewing flowers and waving tiny flags, there was nothing. The village had been swept clean except for the ruins of a concrete building. Beyond the village, the 21st settled in for the night. It was now firmly on high ground, having breached the center of the enemy lines, and off to the northeast could be seen the unfinished strips of Airfield No. 3.

The Fourth Division continued its assault on Hill 382, virtually surrounding it. Company A of 1/23, reaching the back slope around 2:15 P.M., began attacking from the east. The rocket trucks got in a good day, rushing up six at a time, firing double ripples of 4.5-inch rockets and retiring in less than five minutes. The heavy artillery lent support, and bazookamen blasted the fortifications. Still the hill held out, fire coming now from the east to help the enemy still inside. The fighting was extremely bitter, and Company A lost a brave man and a celebrity. Sergeant Fritz G. Truan, twenty-seven, of Cody, Wyoming, leading the assault platoon of Company A, as he had since D-Day, was killed during the afternoon in a burst of fire. He was billed as World Champion Cowboy, and rodeo people all over the country knew him. In 1940, he was best all-around rider at

Madison Square Garden, and the next year he won $5,000 and the Sam Jackson trophy at the Pendleton Roundup. His last prize had been taken at Honolulu Stadium less than a year before, when he won the bronco-riding championship and $1,000. For the 1945 rodeo, 6,000 people stood in the darkened arena in Honolulu while Truan's riderless horse was led around the ring. Private First Class Robert L. Mather of Clinton, New York played taps. He had been with Truan on Hill 382.

The 25th continued battering against Turkey Knob and the Amphitheater, trying to fight around north of the Knob. In desperation, the Marines hauled up a 75-mm. howitzer on a Dukw, took it apart, and reassembled it at the front, to fire point-blank into the stone and concrete emplacements. Eighty-five rounds failed to destroy the fortifications but did wonders for morale. First Battalion troops, with tank support, nearly accomplished an encirclement of the Knob, but on the southeast side,

Japanese high up in the ravines showered down grenades and mines and laced the cut with machine-gun fire. On the other side, to the northwest, tanks blasted at a concrete structure on top of the Knob. The Shermans' 75-mm. shells did no harm, and it was obvious a juncture could not be made around the Knob. Both prongs fell back. Gain for the day – zero. Nearer the coast, 3/25 advanced easily and held up only to avert gaps in the line. In seven days the Fourth Division had had more than 4,000 casualties, but the Japanese still held Hill 382, Turkey Knob, and the Amphitheater.

That night, General Erskine made his first request for the 3rd Regiment, nearly 3,000 fresh men, still in transports off the beach. General Harry Schmidt endorsed the request; casualties were already well over 8,000. The request was rejected by Howlin' Mad Smith, backed, for once, by Admiral Turner. It was the start of a disagreement still not resolved.

The Fifth Division, with the 27th

Regiment in the line, pressed forward all day toward Hill 362A, which rose bare and sharp ahead. The 3rd Battalion reached the foot of the hill by noon, and Company I fought all the way to the crest by 4:30 P.M., but the position could not be held. During the assault up the hill, Pharmacist's Mate First Class John Harlan Willis, twenty-three, was wounded by shrapnel and ordered to the rear. He was back in a short time, and into the melee again. Running out front, he jumped into a hole and rigged a rifle to give plasma to a wounded Marine. A grenade fell in the hole. Willis threw it back. He threw back seven more of them, and then his luck, far over-extended, gave out. The grenade went off in his hand, killing him.

Late in the afternoon, Company H on the right, up against the Third Division line, beat off a party of about 100 Japanese in hand-to-hand combat. But the 27th was forced to dig in for the night about 100 yards short of the top of Hill 362A. In the rear, the 26th spent the day re-equipping and resting, and the 28th, conquerors of Suribachi, began moving north.

During the day, all three Marine field hospitals, of Corps, Fourth and Fifth Divisions came into full operation. Along with the Navy and Army hospitals there were now enough beds ashore, and transfer of casualties to ships was discontinued. The four hospital LST's were released and sailed for Saipan fully loaded with casualties. In ten days they had treated 6,100 men. Toward evening, two torpedo bombers from one of the carriers sprayed the lower half of the island with DDT to prevent spread of disease by flies. Three twin-engine Navy planes and transports of the 9th Troop Carrier Squadron, USAAF, made the first air drops of medical supplies and vital parts. Thousands of Marines watched and cheered as the red and green parachutes billowed down along the western beaches. Only four fell into the water, and small boats rescued three of them. In all, nearly 5 tons of supplies were dropped, saving many days over ship supply from the Marianas.

At home, President Roosevelt flew in from the meetings with Stalin and Churchill at Yalta. His aide, Jonathan Daniels, told newsmen he had never seen the President looking better. "He is in grand spirits, in great shape," Daniels said. Rumors persisted that, in fact, he was exhausted and quite unwell.

That night, the Japanese made their last attempt to recapture Wells 4 and 5. They sent down a special force, equipped with rocket guns and mortars. Not a single Japanese returned from this mission.

Admiral Ichimaru had one of his last messages from Toyoda. It was dispiriting. The Commander in Chief said the Navy would be ready for the next expected American thrust by the end of April, but that all plans depended on the outcome at Iwo.

"I regret that except for full submarine support and some air support, we cannot send reinforcements to Iwo. However, in view of over-all requirements, I earnestly hope you will maintain calm and fight staunchly by any means," Toyoda said.

Ichimaru had understood perfectly, right from the start. He had never expected reinforcements, and he had been pulling his forces back slowly, exacting the highest possible toll. The retreat had hurt morale, but it was inevitable. One man had written in his diary: "We don't fight, we just retreat. The enemy is right before our eyes and we retreat."

On the last night of the month he recorded that he had just learned that First Lieutenant Nakahara and Second Lieutenant Hanazawa had been killed on patrol. "As the saying goes, 'When one braves the dangers, death goes along hand in hand,' " he wrote. He finished in disgust: "Ordered to withdraw again."

Chapter 2

There was no rest in the rear in the early hours of March 1. Shortly after midnight Japanese artillery, firing from new positions in the north, began shelling the west coast alongside Airfield No. 1, an area crowded with unit headquarters, supply dumps, vehicles and artillery, and the foxholes of men of many outfits.

At 2:15 A.M. a shell struck the Fifth Division's main ammunition dump, and it caught fire. Within minutes the blaze was roaring, burning flares arced into the sky, lighting it up like a Fourth of July show. Small-arms ammunition crackled, mortar shells detonated, and artillery projectiles were flying through the air. The entire southern end of the island was aroused by the wild spectacle, and at 2:38 A.M. the air-raid alarm went off. At 3 A.M. somebody tripped the gas

356

alarm, mistaking exploding white phosphorous projectiles for gas shells. The gas alert was canceled within ten minutes, but the air alert remained until 4:30 A.M.

After the first shock, men of all units raced for the burning dump. Fifth Division service troops, disregarding the rain of explosives in the air, ran into the edges of the fire and carried out shells. Men of the Headquarters & Service Battery of the division's artillery regiment, the 13th Marines, pitched in to save the dump, and Army units helped. Major Harry Edwards and Warrant Officer Harvey Richey of the 473rd Amphibian Truck Company ran into the fire again and again and were burned many times by hot shrapnel or knocked down by explosions.

At the height of the blaze, around 5 A.M., a burning 105-mm. shell was hurled into the Corps' fire-direction center a hundred yards away. The shell detonated with a low-grade explosion, enough the set the wire lines afire, knocking out communications to the artillery. The dump of Corps telephone wire also caught fire, and nearly all of it was destroyed.

Fifth Engineers brought in bulldozers, and the drivers fearlessly pushed sand over the main dump. Gradually, with dozens of men helping, the fire was brought under control. By 7 A.M. it was out. The Fifth Division had lost 25 percent of its ammunition, but not one man was killed. In a tent near the fire, Lieutenant E. Graham Evans, a Fifth Division surgeon, had made his decision. Exhausted by endless days of operating, he had decided to stay in his cot instead of searching for a foxhole. At dawn he rolled over; the tent above him was shredded. As far as he could see the ground was littered with shell fragments, but not one man had been hit. "Foxholes are a wonderful invention," he concluded.

But the day was only beginning. The air-raid alarm had not been false. A low-flying plane, probably from the Bonins, dropped a torpedo near the destroyer Terry at 2:45 A.M., a few miles off Kitano Point in the north. The destroyer rang up full speed and the torpedo passed 50 feet astern. But the Gerry pressed her luck too far. Passing the point at 7:20 A.M., about 2½ miles off shore, the destroyer came under fire from a 6-inch coastal gun. Before it could get out of range, hits on the main deck and in the forward engine room killed eleven men and wounded nineteen. The battleship Nevada and the cruiser Pensacola closed in to give her protection, and the Terry escaped. The same day, Lieutenant Commander William B. Moore buried his dead at sea and transferred the wounded to a hospital ship; the Terry started for Pearl Harbor, limping on one engine.

On the Fifth Division front, the 28th went back into action for the first time since Suribachi, and it was a bloody return. The 1st and 2nd Battalions swept to the top of Hill 362A in an early morning rush, but now they were on an

80-foot cliff dropping into a ravine behind the hill. Both sides of the ravine were pocked with caves hiding Japanese riflemen, and an anti-tank ditch ran across the bottom in the middle. The only way in was around the shoulders. Company A started around the right, B around the left.

Captain Wilkins of Company A, a hero of the D-Day charge across the island, asked for volunteers. Corporal Tony Stein, cited for the Medal of Honor on D-Day, nodded and crawled out with a 20-man patrol to clear the ridge of snipers. Seven men came back. Stein was not one of them. Within the hour, mortar and gunfire killed Wilkins. He was the last original company commander in the battalion. Captain Russel J. Parsons came forward and the attack continued.

Around the other shoulder, Company B found the fire just as intense. The company commander, Captain Robert A. Wilson, was wounded and taken to the rear. For the second time, First

Lieutenant Charles A. Weaver took over the company. The first time had been on D-Day, after Bobo Mears was mortally wounded assaulting a pillbox. The attack continued all day, the 3rd Battalion making good progress nearer the shore, where the ground flattened out. But somewhere down behind Hill 362A, where fire poured from the reverse cliff, and from Nishi Ridge up ahead, three other men of the 28th lay dead. One of them was Henry O. Hansen, the slim sergeant from Somerville, Massachusetts. Private Ruhl had given his life before Suribachi so that Hansen might help raise the first flag on the mountaintop.

Somewhere else in that jumble of rock and ravine, Corporal Harlon H. Block was killed. His hands had thrust the pole into the soft volcanic tuff at the top of Suribachi as the second flag went up and Joe Rosenthal snapped the famous picture.

Sergeant Michael Strank, third man from the left in that photograph, was pinned in the ravine for four hours by heavy fire. "We better send a runner to tell them where we are," he said, and knelt to draw a map in the sand. Corporal Joe Rodriguez, nineteen, faced him, leaning over as the sergeant's finger traced in the sand. Four other men hunched around, and a Japanese mortar found the range. Rodriguez remembered only the blast, and when he came to, Strank lay sprawled on his back, his arms above his head. It had been a long road for Strank, nearly six years in the corps, from the Russells to Bougainville to the top of Suribachi. The last journey for the rough son of Czech immigrants was to Grave 7179 in Arlington National Cemetery, within sight of an heroic-sized bronze statue of six men raising a flag, one of them Michael Strank. Block, the twenty-year-old Texas oilfield worker, lay for a time in Plot 4, Row 6, Grave 912 of the Fifth Division Cemetery, near Airfield No. 1. Eventually he went home, to private burial in Weslaco, Texas.

The day had cost the Fifth Division

six more officers killed, a first lieutenant and four second lieutenants, besides Captain Wilkins. The map for the day showed only the crest of Hill 362A in Marine hands.

In the center, the Third Division pounded forward from Motoyama Village, gradually turning east as the island widened. The fighting was unspectacular, but death was everywhere. Mortar shells rained down on front and "rear"; aid stations were full, and doctors moved from one table to the next, cramming a lifetime of surgery into one day. And there were not only wounded. In the afternoon a very young Marine, hardly out of boyhood, wandered into an aid station 200 yards behind the line. He said he had chills and fever, but he was not ill. Or more precisely, he had not been hurt. He was frightened, and when Dr. Arford suggested that he go back to his outfit the boy began to cry. He walked about 40 feet away, toward the rear, and sat down, sobbing softly. About thirty minutes later a mortar shell exploded at his feet, blowing off his drooping head. In the aid station, corpsmen lifted another bloody Marine onto the table and the doctor bent down again, scalpel in hand. The gain for the day was 500 yards, it said in the report.

The Fourth Division held back along the coast, concentrating again against Hill 382 and Turkey Knob. The hill was assaulted from the front and the sides and was nearly surrounded. At one time, Company G of 2/24 was astride the top, but still there was no quarter. The attackers fought with rifles and grenades, with flamethrowers and satchel charges. Still the defenders would not give up, even though their own fire fell on them from the ridges further east. These were the men from Kumamoto in Kyushu, an historic battlefield of the 1877 Civil War, and they would not give up. Not even when Major Kenro Anso died, burned from head to foot by a flamethrower. He led the 3rd Battalion, 145th Regiment, in defense of the hill. So great was his inspiration that at his death he was promoted two full ranks to colonel. By nightfall, the 24th and 25th had made some progress toward both objectives, but both the Hill and the Knob were still in Japanese hands. The day's toll was 374 casualties, and the Fourth Division's combat efficiency was rated at 55 percent. In eleven days of fighting it had paid 5,595 casualties for a small share of one-half of an island.

Some changes were appearing in the enemy's tactics. Japanese artillery seemed to be growing more sporadic and disorganized. Mortar fire was decreasing, and rifle fire was more discriminate. Back around Airfield No. 2, Robert Sherrod noticed that a company of Marines could walk along the runways without drawing fire, but small groups drew sniper fire. The Japanese were not wasting fire. Ammunition must be running low. The most significant change of the day was not known to the Marines. General Kuribayashi left the center of the island and moved to his underground headquarters in the north.

A few Korean laborers were captured during the day, and they said food and water were also low. But their word could not be trusted; they hated their conquerors, the Japanese. There was another bag of prisoners on Thursday. First Lieutenant Goro Wakatsuki, a gun-battery commander of the 8th Independent Anti-Tank Battalion, stumbled into the open below Airfield No. 2, leading 8 enlisted men. As far as he knew, they were all that was left of 180 men in the battalion. They had been hiding inside the American lines for a week, but they were exhausted and could not hold out. Wakatsuki explained that he had not escaped because he was wounded in the foot. He knew nothing of intelligence value, since the battle had long since passed by. The prisoners were put in a barbed-wire compound until they could be shipped to Guam.

During the day, Marine planes parachuted in sixty-nine sacks of mail. All of it was for the Third Division, infuriating the Fourth and Fifth Divisions. At sea, a second destroyer, the Colhoun, was hit by shore fire a little after 10 A.M. One man was killed and seven were wounded. The most tense moment came when the Japanese opened fire on the Columbia Victory, as it was moving in on the west beaches to unload ammunition. Mortar fire from Kama and Kangoku Rocks straddled the vessel, one shell falling close enough to wound a man on the fantail. The merchant ship immediately turned and headed for the open sea. "You could almost see the sweat pouring from her brow," said a Fifth Division officer. Howlin' Mad Smith was also watching. He stood with General Schmidt at Corps headquarters on the west beach. If the ammunition ship went up, the whole west coast of the island might be devastated. Thousands of Marines were working there. As they watched, the second salvo fell ahead of the ship. "The next one's going to hit her square," said Smith, but neither he nor

Schmidt moved. It fell astern, and by now the Columbia Victory was rapidly drawing out of range. Everybody went back to work.

Off to the southwest, Mitscher's carriers raided Okinawa. There was no reaction from the ground, and damage was light, but the fliers got excellent photographs for the invasion, just one month away. That night Task Force 58 headed for Ulithi; the two-week foray, in which the Navy had placed such hopes, was over. It claimed to have destroyed over 600 Japanese planes; the cost was 134 planes and the lives of 95 pilots and crewmen. The enemy still had hundreds of kamikazes poised for Okinawa, and some Marines still say, with bitterness, that Task Force 58 might better have tended to the knitting at Iwo Jima.

The final battle for the Meat Grinder began on Friday morning, March 2, though no one was aware of it at the time.

The main assault, for the sixth day, was straight ahead against Hill 382, with

Lieutenant Colonel Rothwell's 2/24, captors of Charlie-Dog Ridge, leading the way. Around to the south, units of the 23rd and 25th Regiments again attacked the Amphitheater and Turkey Knob from both north and south, trying to reduce these strongholds. The objective was to cut Japanese fire from there onto Hill 382 and open the way to the village of Minami. In this area lay the whole of the enemy's strength in the east.

All artillery was now ashore and sited, and under central Corps' direction. After a heavy barrage, and supported by tanks and rocket trucks, two companies of 2/24 moved on the hill. Major Roland Carey's Company E was on the left, Captain Walter Ridlon's Company F on the right. By 9 A.M. one of Carey's platoons, led by Second Lieutenant Dick Reich, was under the smashed radar antenna on top of the hill. Two of Ridlon's platoons, led by Platoon Sergeant James Bedingfield and Sergeant Tom Cottick, were held back by heavy fire. Carey crawled over to where Reich was, and Ridlon came up. They decided Carey would send a platoon around to the right, with two tanks, to cut off the Japanese fire. As he bounded down the hill, Carey was hit by machine-gun fire. So heavy was the fire, it took one hour to get him off the hill. Captain Pat Donlan took over the company, and by noon he thought things were looking up. None of the men had been able to move, but more of the enemy were coming out, driven from the hill by something, perhaps sulphur fumes.

About two o'clock, Donlan was hit by mortar shrapnel. As First Lieutenant Stanley Osborne came in to relieve him, there was another mortar burst. Osborne was killed instantly, Donlan's right leg was blown off below the knee, and two other officers were wounded, one mortally. Reich, still holding under the radar screen, was in command. He was the only officer left in Company E.

At 2:50 P.M. Ridlon's platoons finally got going. "Almost on high ground,"

Ridlon messaged to Rothwell. Working around to the rear of the radar, Bedingfield's platoon came under heavy fire. The sergeant, trapped behind a rock one foot high, called in mortar fire on what he thought was the machine gun pinning him down. Then he asked for four quick rounds covering him and sprinted for the rear. His men closed in, and Jack Frazer, the cigar-smoking corporal, led the final rush around the crest. At 3:27 P.M. Ridlon messaged: "Company F is on top of radar hill." The hill was overrun, but it was not subdued. At the end of the day, Rothwell's exec, Major Frank Garretson, noted, "Day's progress, a little over two touchdowns." He was an ex-backfield star at the University of Washington, and he liked to record gains in terms he understood – 10 yards was a first down, 100 yards a touchdown. The division report for the day did not claim the capture of Hill 382. It was not yet sure.

The 23rd and the 25th, burning and blasting all day at the Amphitheater and

Turkey Knob, could make no claims either, but they were reducing the fortresses. The 75's blasted at point-blank range against the concrete communications blockhouse on top of Turkey Knob, and more than a thousand gallons of flame oil were hurled against it. At one point, patrols from the north and south were less than 65 yards apart, but devastating fire forced them to draw back. It would not fall.

Saturday morning it started all over again. First Lieutenant William Crecink, who had taken over Company E on the previous afternoon (its fifth commander in one day), was wounded at 9 A.M. on Hill 382. Reich was again in command until Captain Charles Ireland arrived, but 2/24 moved steadily ahead, making 350 yards against intense resistance. Ireland was shot in the leg Sunday morning and once more Reich took over. The last officer was Captain Robert M. O'Mealia, the regimental band officer. He was killed instantly by a mortar blast. Reich did not take over.

Company E had ceased to exist. What was left was merged into Captain Ridlon's Company F. After nine days, Hill 382 had been taken, once and for all. All that was left were shattered banyan trees and high ground.

The Amphitheater and Turkey Knob refused to fall. All day Saturday, tanks and engineers blasted away, partially reducing the blockhouse on Turkey Knob and closing dozens of caves and pillboxes in the Amphitheater. On Sunday it was the same thing, again with heavy support from the artillery, battleships and destroyers, and carrier planes rocketing and dropping flaming napalm. Up in the front, sappers of the 23rd used 2,200 pounds of demolition charges in one day.

By Sunday night, both sides were exhausted. In eight days of fighting, the Fourth Division had sustained 2,880 casualties and its efficiency was rated at 45 percent. It had, without the satisfaction of sure knowledge, cracked the backbone of General Kuribayashi's defense. Hill 382 had been taken, the Amphitheater and Turkey Knob had been stunned into silence and bypassed. The Meat Grinder was closed.

During the same three days, the Third Division rammed eastward, seeking the sea, but the Japanese resisted at every hill and rise and rock. Every fold in the earth was cut with trenches and tank traps and covered by mortar and machine-gun fire. Artillery was sited across the unfinished runways of Airfield No. 3, and the roads and edges of the field were strewn with mines. From Hill 362B, north of the airfield, fire came straight down into the flanks of units moving east. The enemy was making a last organized stand, and doing it well. This was Kuribayashi's order. He had estimated that losses on both sides had been about equal until the end of February. He felt these early days of March to be the crucial ones and believed that if he could apply enough force, possibly even a counterattack, the

Americans might fall back, or at least halt. If not victory, he would buy time, which is all he really hoped for. His belly was, indeed, "packed full of strong fighting spirit." But he had a match, and a master, in the Marines across the line.

On Friday, General Erskine received permission to attack north, across the line into Fifth Division territory, to get at Hill 362B and stop the fire into his flanks. After artillery fire, including some of Corps' 155's and destroyer fire from the sea, Lieutenant Colonel Boehm's 3/9 moved out toward the hill. But the way lay across flat ground, covered by level artillery fire from the hill and hidden smaller arms. Tanks were called in, and the 37-mm. guns, and with the help of the mortars, 81's and 60's, 3/9 bulled its way across the open ground to the foot of the hill. On its right, 2/21 fought into the shoulders of the plateau leading off from Hill 362B. At day's end the battalion commander, Lieutenant Colonel English, was wounded for the second time and his executive officer, Major George A. Percy, assumed the command. Percy, a New York stockbroker, had joined the Marines at forty-five as a paymaster, but combat command was his aim. He now had it.

As his battalion lay alongside a runway at the north edge of the airfield, a mortar shell fell on the edge of a foxhole, burying Corporal Russell M. Hanson under dirt and asphalt. His buddy, Corporal Jack Wiecks, dug him out and called for the corpsmen. Hanson's leg was broken, and as they carried him away he said, "How much money you got, Jack?" Wiecks dug out a $5 bill. "Let me have it," Hanson said. "I got a million-dollar wound and no cash for liberty." Back in the States, Hanson was married, his leg still in a cast. Wiecks went back to his foxhole. The $5 caught up with him months later, after the war was over.

The rest of the front made no progress eastward during the day. Saturday morning both regiments turned to drive eastward, the Fifth Division sending 2/26 in to take Hill 362B, relieving 3/9. Major Rea still commanded 2/26, but not one of his four companies was under the commander that had brought it ashore D-Day, and the ranks were filled with reserves. The battalion, relatively fresh on its second day back in the line after four days of rest and reorganization, attacked with vigor. Companies D and E were sent against the hill, where Captain Inouye defended with about 3,000 sailors. The Captain forced him slowly back. By early afternoon the two companies had relieved 3/9, and at four o'clock they started up the hill, burning and blasting in the rocks and gullies. An hour later they held the top. Both company commanders had been wounded, and the battalion had nearly 300 casualties in one day. Inouye fell back, but not far.

Major Percy sent 2/21 off to the east early Saturday morning and by 9 A.M. it had gained 400 yards toward Hill 357. By 11 A.M. the hill was captured, and in the afternoon the 21st Regiment turned southeast to help the 9th Regiment against Hill 362C, the last impediment between Motoyama and the sea. Progress was slow, and when the men dug in for the night the division line was not yet abreast of Hill 357. The day had been warm, with the temperature rising to 75 in the afternoon, but after sundown it turned cold, and the sulphur smoke mixed with the night mist. Off to the left of 2/9, Lieutenant Colonel Cushman's outfit, the enemy seemed quieter than usual. The Japanese had fought hard all day off the eastern end of the airfield; perhaps they were tired too. As the night wore on, however, the enemy was reported moving in front of 1/21, Major Robert Houser's outfit. About 1:30 A.M., both battalions were aroused; some 200 Japanese were pressing in between Houser and Cushman. The mortars threw up flare shells, and in the eerie mist both sides fought bitterly, with knife and gun and grenade.

In ninety minutes it was over, and in the morning the Marines counted 161 Japanese bodies in front of their lines. It was a grand sight.

For the rest of the day, little was accomplished. Units were slow getting into position, and instead of attacking at 7:30 A.M. As ordered, they were not ready until nearly noon. Both artillery and destroyers fired heavy opening barrages, followed by a rolling barrage. The 9th and the 21st moved out and were stopped immediately by steady Japanese fire. Rain fell at times, and visibility was bad. The men tried, but they were very tired. In nine murderous days they had moved 3,000 yards. They welcomed the order that fighting would stop at 5 p.m., and that Monday, March 5, would be a day of rest.

On Friday morning, after four days of re-equipping and spotting reserves through the ranks, the 26th Regiment attacked up the middle of the island, west of the Third Division. The rest of the line, all the way to the west coast, fell to the 28th, including Hill 362A and Nishi Ridge, 200 yards to the north of it.

Chandler Johnson, whose men had taken Suribachi, advanced around the left shoulder of the hill, and Jackson Butterfield's 1/28 headed around the right end. Again they drew heavy fire from Nishi Ridge and from the sharp north face of Hill 362A. The back of the hill was worse than the front. At least four separate tunnel systems honeycombed the hill, the largest having 1,000 feet of tunnel and seven entrances, at the sides and rear. Two others had outlets in the cliff face and shafts running to the top of the hill for ventilation and servicing of guns. Fire came from every opening, some of them high up in the cliff face, but both battalions pressed on.

Sherman tanks maneuvered for position in the ravine before Nishi Ridge, hampered by the wide anti-tank ditch running north from the cliff to Nishi. Armored bulldozers of the 5th Engineers crunched down into the ravine, the tanks firing alongside them and demolition men blasting out the cliff face. The three heavy machine guns and tanks with heavy planks strapped on their sides were worked into the ravine. Time after time the Japanese ran to the tanks and plastered demolition charges on them, but the planks absorbed the blast and the tanks kept firing. Finally, the bulldozers filled in the anti-tank ditch and the Marines were in the ravine to stay, firing forward at Nishi and backward at the cliff face of Hill 362A. By afternoon, they were at the foot of Nishi Ridge, and there they clung. Johnson, whose drive and courage had lifted his battalion off the beach on D-Day, ran forward from his command post to check his lines. Just at 2 P.M. he was struck squarely by a high explosive shell and killed instantly. His battalion was staggered; they had loved this gruff Annapolis man, so brave, so contemptuous of danger. The shell that killed him may have been from his own artillery. His executive officer, Major Thomas B. Pearce, a decorated veteran of New Georgia and Bougainville, came forward to take command. The battalion held its ground.

There was another change of command nearby. The 2nd Platoon of B Company 1/28 lost its third commander since D-Day. Private First Class Carl B. Wozniak took over. The next day things improved a little bit – a corporal relieved him, and after that it took two days to find a lieutenant to take back the platoon. Sixty officers of the Fifth Division had already been killed.

On the coast, 3/28 moved forward, blasting caves with 37-mm. guns, heavy mortars, and demolition charges. There was a brief gas scare in the morning, when the Japanese fired shells that gave off green smoke. The two attacks, at 9 A.M. and again about 11:30 A.M., caused some vomiting and headache. The gas was heavy, drifting into depressions, but did not spread far and affected only a few men. The battalion moved on, blasting nearly seventy caves during the day, and no more was seen of the gas. Officers concluded it was picric acid.

The 26th moved ahead to the north and east, trying to keep in touch with the Third Division on the right. By General Rockey's order that day, any unit "creating a gap by advancing will be responsible for filling that gap." The order sounded unusual but the meaning was clear – there was no longer any reserve to fill gaps. On its front, the 26th was finding fewer concrete fortifications, and more rock barriers and tank ditches. It was also finding more abandoned equipment, including a generator truck behind one ridge and a 150-cm. searchlight behind another. While extending its lines to the sides, the 26th made as much as 500 yards that day.

On Saturday the Fifth Division smashed forward all along the front, moving on sheer courage and will, in the bitterest fighting since D-Day. On the right, the 26th captured Hill 362B to relieve the Third Division on the east, and drove north as much as 600 yards, into the broken ground toward the north coast. The enemy resisted fiercely, fighting for every gully and cave, and the 26th suffered. One company (H) lasted ninety minutes in the line before it had to withdraw, and the regiment sustained casualties of eight officers and 273 men.

In the center, the 28th swept up and over Nishi Ridge, through what was left of the tiny village, and 200 yards beyond. During the day the division lost eight officers and 127 men killed, and total casualties of 518, the worst since D plus 2, and the worst that any division would have until the end of the campaign.

On this day alone, five men of the division won the Medal of Honor, a record probably unmatched. Corporal Charles J. Berry, twenty-one, of 1/26 and Private First Class William R. Caddy, nineteen, of 3/26 leaped onto sputtering grenades and gave their lives to save their comrades. Pharmacist's Mate Second Class George Wahlen went the whole 600 yards forward with 2/26, treating casualties all the way. Wounded for the third time in six days, this time very seriously, he refused to quit and was still crawling forward when he collapsed.

In the shadows of Nishi Ridge, Sergeant William G. Harrell was on watch before dawn when a grenade broke his thigh and tore off his left hand. With his right hand, he drew his pistol and killed a Japanese poised above him for a sabre blow. Then he fell, exhausted, and another Japanese ran in to place a grenade under his head. Harrell killed him as he ran away and pushed the sputtering grenade as far out as he could. The blast tore off Harrell's right hand and killed another Japanese. At dawn, bodies of a dozen Japanese were found around him. Harrell had killed at least five of them and his post had not been taken. He was carried to the rear, still alive.

Jack Williams, twenty, won the fifth medal. He was a corpsman, Pharmacist's Mate Third Class, and he ran out during a grenade battle to treat a Marine. As he knelt in a shell hole, a sniper shot him three times, in the abdomen and groin. Williams finished treating the Marine, bound his own belly wounds, gave first aid to another man, and started back for the lines. Again the sniper fired, and Williams fell dead, short of the lines.

The 28th lost another man that day. Platoon Sergeant Ernest I. Thomas, Jr., who had helped raise the first flag on Suribachi, was shot through the head as he telephoned to the rear. It was his twentieth birthday.

Charlo, the Indian, was also killed in battle. Three of the six lived through the campaign: Lieutenant Schrier, Corporal Charles, W. Lindberg, and Private First Class James R. Michels. The two enlisted men were wounded. A queer trick of fate has left them in obscurity, but these were the six whose flag on Suribachi rallied the corps and, in truth, is remembered by a nation.

On Sunday the Fifth Division was slowing down, as were the other two. From here on, the ground was so rough that artillery and tanks were nearly useless. From here to the northern coast it would be hand-to-hand combat, with flamethrowers, demolitions, grenades, and rifles. The battle was bitter, the gains meager. The front fell quiet at 5 P.M., preparing for a day of rest. On the other side, even the enemy seemed to welcome a respite.

The fact was that the island defenders were in a bad way. Most of their artillery and tanks had been destroyed, and 65 percent of the officers had been killed. On Saturday, March 3, General Kuribayashi estimated that he had 3,500 effectives left. Communications had broken down to the point that General Senda was virtually isolated in the east. Captain Inouye still commanded a small remnant of sailors near Airfield No. 3. Admiral Ichimaru was in the north, in touch with Kuribayashi but no longer having effective control over Inouye. In the northern corner of the island, no organized force remained – only small groups of survivors of individual units, acting locally and almost independently. Spirit was still strong, however, and in no unit was there the thought of surrender.

The Army and Navy chiefs in Tokyo messaged Kuribayashi and Ichimaru jointly on Saturday, expressing great thanks to the Iwo Jima garrison and urging continued resistance. Ichimaru replied to Toyoda that the enemy was "pressing us hard, but we will hit back." On the same day, Sherrod's "unofficial estimate" of a thirteen-day campaign had run out. He had been nearly right on his estimate of casualties – over 3,000 Marines had been killed and nearly 13,000 wounded – but the end of the campaign was not in sight.

Chapter 3

During the past three days of desperate fighting, great changes had occurred behind the lines.

The Navy opened the western beaches on Friday, March 2, and general unloading proceeded on both sides of the island. The Army garrison forces and the rest of the staff and equipment of the 9th Naval Construction Brigade arrived. The assault shipping completed unloading on Saturday, and empty ships sailed for the Marianas, riding high in the water.

Thousands of men were still living in the ground, like prairiedogs, but underneath the confusion there was order and purpose. By Saturday both the Naval evacuation hospital and the Army field hospital were in full operation near the north end of Airfield No. 1, just in time for the flood of casualties from the center-island fighting.

Lieutenant Evans at the Fifth Division hospital wrote his wife: "We had 375 patients through here yesterday, to give you an idea. I've seen all the war surgery I want for a while." He was amazed at the Marines. "They come in with wounds that make you sick to look at, and all they want to do is 'Get back at those sons of bitches.' You tell them they must be evacuated and they cry."

Roads became highways, with traffic regulations and sprinkler trucks to hold down the dust. Signs went up for "Maui Boulevard" and the inevitable "Broadway"; jeeps and trucks moved night and day. Tank parks, repair shops, post offices, water points, showers, ammunition dumps, supply depots, and communication wire (hundreds of miles of it, underfoot and overhead) were everywhere. The day's most familiar cry became, "Get your truck off my goddam wire." Somewhere in the jumble, the Fifth Division bakery opened, and the first hot doughnuts started for the front.

Shortly after dawn on Saturday, Iwo Jima began to realize its purpose – the first plane arrived from the Marianas. It was not a fighter – not yet – but a Navy C47 hospital plane, "Peg O' My Heart." The pilot, Commander Clarence A. Keller, looked down in consternation. The dirt runway, now 3,000 feet long, was barely visible in a dust storm churned up by tanks, bulldozers, and trucks. The "control tower" was a radio-equipped jeep, and a windsock flapped from a long pole at one end. Keller, carrying medical supplies, a ton of mail, and a Navy doctor and corpsmen, circled the field and set down. The landing was bumpy but successful, and the plane followed a jeep over behind a hill, stopping near the Navy hospital.

The door of the plane opened and out stepped a woman, Barbara Finch of Reuters, the first woman to set foot on Iwo Jima. She was just thinking how like a classic Japanese print it looked, with Suribachi in the background, when a mortar shell whistled by. Corporal Joe Purcell of Boston shouted, "How the hell did you get here?" and led her to a tent. Inside lay two Marines, their heads wrapped in bloody bandages, plasma running into their arms from hanging bottles. Another shell exploded nearby, and a huge colonel thrust her outside and under a jeep, roaring "Down on your face and stay down." In a half hour she was gone, "Peg O' My Heart" winging back to Saipan.

The next plane in to Iwo, a short time later, was an R5C (Curtiss Commando) of Marine Transport Squadron 952, carrying 2½ tons of mortar ammunition. Lieutenant Colonel Malcolm S. Mackay called the field from 5 miles out and was told to come in downwind.

"What's wrong with the upwind approach?" he asked.

"Better not try it. Get the hell shot out of you," was the reply.

Mackay landed downwind, from the south, touching down between two abandoned Japanese steamrollers. The plane ran down along a line of parked grasshoppers, past a disabled carrier plane and stopped just before a sand bunker at the northern end of the field. Close under the bunker, pocked with foxholes, Marines lounged in the sun, drinking from canteens. In a barbed-wire enclosure, half a dozen stolid Japanese prisoners squatted in the dirt while curious Marines sauntered by. A live Jap was a rare sight on this island.

Mackay taxied back to the south end of the field, and pretty soon a truck arrived. A Marine with a bandaged hand said, "Japs dropped three shells on this field when that first transport landed. They do that all day long. Got artillery up there," and he waved to the north.

"Plenty of it," he went on. "Got the field zeroed in, too. It ain't safe anywhere on this damn island yet."

Considering his cargo of 81-mm. shells, Mackay did not attempt to prolong the conversation. In twenty minutes the unloading was finished, and as he took off, Mackay said to his co-

pilot, "Worst-looking island I ever saw."
He spoke as an expert; he had taken the
first plane in to Peleliu, while the
Japanese were still firing from Bloody
Nose Ridge.

So great was the shortage of 81-mm.
shells that other C-47's flew up from
Saipan that day, dropping the ammunition near the front lines. Far below, the
crews could watch Marines run out for
the bundles and hustle them away while
Japanese fire kicked up dust around
them. At the beach, every remaining sea-
worthy Dukw (about 100 of them) was
pooled under Corps command to bring
ammunition in from the ships. Trucks
waited at the shore to take it to the front.

Sunday afternoon, Radioman J.
William Welsh, guarding the air-sea
rescue frequency on the Auburn,
finished the ship's daily crossword
puzzle. The ship was anchored a mile
and a half off Iwo Jima, and no carrier
planes were up because of rain and mist.
Welsh looked around for something to
read, and suddenly the speaker above his

head croaked out:

"Hello Gatepost, this is Nine Bakecable. We are lost, give us a bearing."

"Hello Nine Bakecable, this is Gatepost. Who are you?" Welsh asked.

Back came the reply: "We are a monster, short on fuel. Give us instructions, please." The last word had more than a hint of pleading in it.

Marine Major J. B. Bertelling grabbed a call index, ran his finger down it, and whistled: "B-29. They raided Japan this morning. Guess he's trying to get back to Guam." The first crippled B-29, the Dinah Might, was about to try an emergency landing on Iwo Jima. Within minutes Admiral Hill was notified, transport planes coming in from the Marianas were warned off, all other planes were ordered off the frequency, a Navy Catalina anchored near Suribachi was sent out, and the field was cleared for "a big one."

The Auburn fixed the B-29 by radar and direction finger, and men crowded into the radio room from all over the ship. Admiral Hill called once, then he called again. This was a big moment for Iwo. This was what Iwo was all about.

In Nine Bakecable the radioman, Sergeant James C. Cox, pressed the receiver pads hard on his ears and heard the Auburn say:

"Turn on your IFF [radio gear for 'identification, friend or foe']."

He did.

"Look for Kita Iwo, 30 miles north of Iwo Jima."

"We see it. We see it."

"Roger. Course 167 for 28 miles. Do you prefer to ditch offshore or try to land on the strip?"

"We prefer to land."

"Roger. We will have the field cleared for you."

Cox had not waited to ask the pilot, First Lieutenant Fred Malo, which choice he would make. He knew Malo and he knew the the decision had already been made – try for a landing.

Malo's trouble was bomb-bay doors and a bad gas valve. After dropping his bombs over Tokyo in a precision run through ice and sleet, the bomb-bay doors would not close. The extra wind drag cut his gasoline supply, and when he called for the spare tanks the valve would not open. It was Iwo or nothing.

"Have you sighted Iwo yet?" the Auburn asked.

"We have sighted Iwo," Cox replied.

On the first pass, Malo caught a glimpse of the dusty runway, far down under Suribachi, then it disappeared under his wing.

On the second pass he could see a little more, including Marines and Seabees running for the field from all directions. Malo, twenty-four, and only five weeks out of the States, was not reassured by what he saw. He thought of the ten other men with him and of the falling gauges before him; he took a firmer grip on the wheel. The third time would have to be it.

The 65-ton plane, looming bigger every second, came in slowly on the west side of Suribachi and hit the south end of the runway with a "warhumpf." Co-pilot Lieutenant Edwin Mockler set the brakes hard, everything held together, and the plane skidded down the runway – the left wing felling a telephone pole and the engines setting up a giant dust cloud. A thousand men along the runway danced and cheered as Nine Bakecable came to a halt at the bitter end of the runway. In the sand hills a few yards beyond, mortar and artillery shells spurted. The Japanese sure wanted that first monster.

Malo turned the B-29, taxied down under Suribachi, and cut the engines. The crew rolled out. Marines rushed out to embrace them, and Seabees wanted to know "How's the runway? Did we leave any bumps?" "Stay overnight and we'll give you a thousand more feet tomorrow."

But Malo and Mockler said no thanks. In thirty minutes the valve was fixed and the spare gas flowed (there was no gas on Iwo yet for the big planes). The crew climbed back in, Nine Bakecable taxied onto the runway, Malo gave her full throttle, and the plane began to move. It gathered speed slowly at first, then faster, and 50 feet from the end of the runway she was airborne. Barely off the ground, Nine Bakecable banked out to sea through a curtain of Japanese anti-aircraft fire and disappeared to the southeast, climbing slowly.

The Marines had just bought eleven lives for the Air Force. Six weeks later, ten of the eleven, including Malo, were dead, shot down over Kawasaki or killed in a take-off crash at Tinian. Only the right gunner, Sergeant Robert W. Brackett, survived. He was, oddly enough, still on Iwo Jima. Malo had left him there to guard the Nine Bakecable when he made a second emergency landing April 12.

The same day the Dinah Might landed, the 62nd Seabees began work on Airfield No. 2, using equipment operators from all Seabee battalions. They were far behind schedule; in the original planning the field was to be ready March

2. Even now, Japanese shelling interrupted the work several times a day. Bulldozer operators crawled under their machines after each salvo, then resumed work. One day the 62nd's commanding officer, Lieutenant Commander Frank B. Campbell, was pinned behind a jeep for an hour by a sniper. A bulldozer finally uncovered the enemy rifle pit, and Marines shot the sniper as he scurried out.

At almost the same time Malo was taking off, hot sulphurous steam began issuing from hundreds of fisures on the north slope of Suribachi. While shooting at Japanese forced out of the mountain by the fumes, Marines stuffed cans of rations into the cracks. In fifteen minutes they had piping hot food. There were not many Japanese still alive in the mountain, but the day's rain had just given them three days' water supply. The subterranean fires were their undoing. They were buried in a special prisoners' cemetery, opened that day at the foot of Suribachi. Nearby, a permanent stockade for live prisoners was under construction. There were only 81 of them – 36 Japanese and 45 Koreans – but 12,864 Japanese bodies had been counted.

If Secretary Forrestal wanted better press coverage for the Navy, he got it at Iwo Jima. Newspapermen, photographers, magazine writers, novelists, columnists, radio broadcasters, feature writers, and sportswriters came from all over the globe to be in on D-Day. Most of them represented American interests – the news services, radio networks, picture agencies, and a dozen newspapers from the big cities – but British and Australian correspondents were also there. The newsmen were on ships, in planes overhead, in the landing boats, on the beaches, and even crouching in the foxholes with the Marines – at least for the first few days.

In addition, each service, Navy, Marine, and Coast Guard, had dozens of correspondents in uniform. The Navy had a special forty-man movie unit to shoot the whole operation in color, complete with scenario. (Two of the three men selected to be followed, from liberty in Honolulu right through the campaign, were killed at Iwo Jima.) Fifty still and motion picture photographers from the Fleet Motion Picture Office were sent along, with six officers.

Three LCI's and 2 LCVP's were assigned to the press for D-Day, and more later. On the first day, more than 8,000 words of press copy were transmitted by radio from the beachhead by radioteletype, the first time this had been done. Before nightfall, the first press plane, a Navy amphibian, took off for Guam with stories, photos, newsreels and, in the words of the official Navy record, "some remarkable photographs taken by the civilian pool photographer, Mr. Joe Rosenthal of the Associated Press." "Mr." Joe's most remarkable photograph was still four days away.

In the next few days, seaplanes

delivered to the Navy at Guam 301 bundles of press stories, photographs, thousands of feet of film, many recordings, both civilian and service, and a vast quantity of material handled by Marine public relations itself. On the eighth day of the campaign, Admiral Turner and Howlin' Mad Smith were interviewed from the beachhead by Don Pryor of CBS, for a nationwide pool broadcast by CBS, Mutual, and the Blue Network. It was the first time a commander in chief had made a live broadcast from the scene while the battle was still in progress. A newsreel sequence of Turner and Smith was shot by the only sound-film crew in the Pacific, and Sergeant Thomas, one of the flag raisers, was taken out to the flagship Estes for a radio broadcast and interview. Six days later he was dead on Hill 362A. In the first week, two Marine correspondents were killed and thirteen more wounded, including two officers. In the first twelve days, Navy radio at the beachhead cleared 1,168,875 words of press copy.

The first pictures from the beachhead reached the United States in seventeen and one half hours, compared to eight to fourteen days at Saipan and Guam.

If anything, the coverage was too good. Much of it was excellent writing, composed in the heat of battle and set down within sight of blood and smell of death. There were many references to Tarawa, and Saipan, and Peleliu, and even back to the carnage at Soissons and the Marne. Forrestal himself added to the picture in a nationwide broadcast from Guam, directly after he had returned from the beachhead. He spoke of the terrible Japanese guns set on "that grim and barren island so that there were streams of converging fire at the beachhead over which the Marines had to come scrambling in from the sea."

From all that barrage of words and pictures emerged an image for the people at home – certainly no worse than it really was – yet building into a picture so grim and terrifying as to shock the nation.

Thus the stage was set for Rosenthal's picture of the flag raising on Suribachi. Here at last was the meaning of it all, of all the courage, and the blood and the dying. The picture reached the United States in time for many Sunday morning papers – February 25. The New York Times and many others used it on page one. Businessmen pasted it in the windows of their stores, people framed it for their homes. Willard Ross, 14, wrote to the Kansas City Star suggesting it be the model for a bronze memorial to Kansas City's war dead. Representative Hendricks of Florida introduced a bill in Congress that such a monument be built in Washington as a tribute to "the heroic action of the Marine Corps as typified in this photograph."

There was rising concern, however, over American casualties. The early communiques had said "No estimate of casualties is yet available." Finally, the communique of February 22 said: "At 1800 (6 P.M.) as of February 21, our casualties on Iwo Island were estimated at 644 killed, 4,108 wounded, and 560 missing." The newspapers pointed out that this was worse than Tarawa. After that, the Navy communiques made no mention of American casualties at all. Nearly every communique, however, gave the latest estimate of Japanese losses. But the news coverage from the island left no doubt that the Marines were in one of their costliest battles.

On February 27 the subject sprang into national prominence. The San Francisco Examiner, in a front-page editorial, said that while the Marines would no doubt capture Iwo Jima, "there is awesome evidence in the situation that the attacking American forces are paying heavily for the island, perhaps too heavily."

"It is the same thing that happened at Tarawa and Saipan..." the editorial said, and if it continues "the American forces are in danger of being worn out before they ever reach the really critical Japanese areas."

Then the real intent of the editorial

emerged: No such thing happened in General MacArthur's campaigns.

"GENERAL MacARTHUR is our best strategist.

"He is our most SUCCESSFUL strategist.

"He wins all his objectives.

"He outwits and outmaneuvers and out-guesses and outthinks the Japanese.

"HE SAVES THE LIVES OF HIS OWN MEN, not only for the future and vital operations that must be fought before Japan is defeated, but for their own safe return to their families and loved ones in the American homeland after the peace is won.

"It is our good fortune to have such a strategist as General MacArthur in the Pacific war.

"Why do we not USE him more, and indeed, why do we not give him supreme command in the Pacific war, and utilize to the utmost his rare military genius of winning important battles without the excessive loss of precious American lives?"

That night nearly a hundred Marines rushed the Examiner office. Someone shouted "Let's go!" and they tramped up the stairs, brushed aside copy boys and editors, and crowded into the office of William C. Wren, the managing editor. Some frightened staffer turned in a riot call, and police and the Shore Patrol started for the scene.

The Marines demanded an apology or a chance to reply. Wren, chewing on his cigar, stood his ground. "Look," he said, "I only take orders from my commanding officer, just like you do." He said the editorial had come direct from William Randolph Hearst. "Call him," the Marines said. Wren put in a call to San Simeon but was told "Mr. Hearst is too busy to be disturbed."

The Shore Patrol and the police arrived, and gradually the Marines calmed down and withdrew after Wren assured them they would get a chance to reply. A Marine officer said he did not think there would be any action against the Marines; they were off duty and acting as individuals. "Apparently they read the editorial and didn't like it," he said, in a remarkable understatement.

The San Francisco Chronicle didn't like it, either, and said the next day:

"The recapture of the Philippines remains competent, energetic, and immensely heartening to the American people. We are proud of that job.

"To slur the United States Marines in one type of operation, however, to draw odious comparisons between theirs and the type of operations conducted by General MacArthur, is to raise a sinister fantasy. To hint that the Marines die fast and move slowly on Iwo Jima because Marine and Naval leadership in that assault is incompetent is an attempt at a damnable swindle of the American people.

"The Chronicle does not propose to engage in controversy over the relative merits of our fighting forces in the various theaters of war. But neither does the Chronicle propose to remain mute when the United States Marines, or any force on the world battle line, is butchered at home to make a Roman holiday."

Three days earlier, First Lieutenant Nion R. Tucker, Jr., of the Fifth Marine Division, had died of wounds he sustained in the D-Day assault on Iwo Jima. He was the only son of Phyllis de Young Tucker, who, with her three sisters, owned the San Francisco Chronicle.

There was no doubt that the struggle and bloodshed at Iwo Jima was affecting the nation in a strange way. Not even Normandy – the largest, and one of the most crucial, amphibious assaults in history – had aroused the emotion engendered by tiny Iwo Jima. Other great events filled the newspapers – the American flag was raised again over Corregidor, the B-29's were burning

Japanese cities to the ground. Allied forces were sweeping into Germany, and the Russians were driving from the east – still the holocaust of Iwo Jima wrenched the heart of the nation.

Time magazine said the name of Iwo Jima would rank in history "with Valley Forge, Gettysburg, and Tarawa." All the way across the Pacific, Secretary Forrestal stopped at hospitals to talk with the wounded, and when he arrived in Washington March 5 he disclosed at a news conference that 2,050 Marines had been killed on the island thus far. It was the first casualty figure that the country had received in nearly two weeks – and fully confirmed the worst fears.

Three days later, Bob Sherrod of Time magazine brought up the question at a news conference on Admiral Turner's flagship. Apparently a little behind on the news from home, Sherrod said: "It will not be long before John's boss, Mr. Hearst, [John R. Henry of Hearst's International News Service was in the room] will start writing editorials about the casualties at Iwo Jima. There are some people trying to sell the idea that the Marines waste lives. I think you ought to make the point stronger about Iwo's defenses being heavier than we expected."

Admiral Turner replied that he was "not going to get into any controversy" over American casualties. "Naturally the press is concerned with losses, but so are we all."

In the same week in Washington a newspaper had declared: "Give our boys a break – gas the Japs."

As a matter of fact, the question of using gas had come up extensively, but most secretly, in the highest military and political circles. The records are still shrouded, but this was apparently the sequence:

It was clear that some targets were ideally suited to gas warfare, among them some of the Pacific islands strongly held by Japanese troops but with few or no civilians present. Early in 1944 the Joint Chiefs of Staff asked the British for an opinion, because of their experience with gas warfare and their relative objectivity as to Pacific targets. The report, by Major General John Sydney Lethbridge (thereafter known as the Lethbridge Report), recommended the use of gas against certain objectives. To preserve secrecy, further development of the idea was turned over to the Office of Strategic Services. Its director of research and development, Stanley P. Lovell, flew to Pearl Harbor late in June, 1944 and discussed the subject with Admiral Nimitz.

Lovell told Nimitz that the Lethbridge Report recommended that the Iwo Jima radio transmitter be jammed and then the island be soaked with gas shells. Part of the plan, he said, was to change the yellow color banding on the shells so that the gunners would not know they were firing gas shells. Lovell said that Nimitz "was for it, I thought," but that when he got back to Washington he learned that the plan had been approved at all levels except the White House. It had come back marked: "All prior endorsements denied – Franklin D. Roosevelt, Commander-in-Chief."

There were powerful arguments for gas. Experience in World War I showed that gas caused over one-quarter of the casualties in the AEF, but only 2 percent of them were fatal, in contrast to 25 percent fatalities from other types of wounds. Two nations had not signed the Geneva Convention outlawing gas warfare – the United States and Japan. But the United States was the victim of its own propaganda. When the Germans introduced gas in 1915, against the French and Canadians, the moral storm raised by the Allies (because they had no defense at hand) so outraged the world that gas was banished from the arsenal of weapons. Gas was stockpiled for Iwo Jima, as it was for every other campaign, but only to be used in retaliation. It was never used, at Iwo Jima or elsewhere. History will not miss the irony: A nation that ruled out gas warfare against an exclusively military target, at the same time used fire bombs and atomic bombs that wiped out whole cities of civilians.

No one in authority publicly discussed gas warfare at the time of Iwo Jima, or for years afterward, but the question of casualties could not be ignored. On March 16, the Navy disclosed that it had received "a number" of letters, and released one as typical.

A woman wrote:

"Please, for God's sake, stop sending our finest youth to be murdered on places like Iwo Jima. It is too much for boys to stand, too much for mothers and homes to take. It is driving some mothers crazy. Why can't objectives be accomplished in some other way? It is almost inhuman and awful – stop, stop!"

The Navy said that Secretary Forrestal had replied:

"On December 7, 1941, the Axis confronted us with a simple choice: Fight or be overrun. There was then, and is now, no other possibility. Having chosen to fight, we had then, and we have now, no final means of winning battles except through the valor of the Marine or Army soldier who, with rifle and grenade, storms enemy positions, takes them, and holds them. There is no shortcut or easy way. I wish there were."

The Navy would not divulge the woman's identity, and said it did not know if she had a son or close relative at Iwo Jima.

On the same day, Admiral Turner and General Smith held a news conference on Turner's flagship at Iwo Jima. The nearest they came to disclosing losses was to say, that they were less than one-fifth of the Japanese. To newsmen, this meant that about 4,000 Marines had been killed.

The next day Admiral Nimitz' communique finally gave the figures through March 16, when the battle was declared officially over: 4,189 killed, 441 missing, 15,308 wounded.

It was worse than that: Full losses were not yet known, and the battle was not over.

Chapter 4

On Monday, March 5, two weeks after D-Day, the Marines rested. That is, by Corps order, no attacks were launched. In other respects, the day was much like those before.

Artillery and mortars were active on both sides of the line, and there were small actions in straightening of the lines, regrouping of units, and hunting down of Japanese pockets behind the Marine lines. The 133rd Seabees completed setting up six portable water distillation units at the foot of Suribachi and began sending water to the front, three canteens per day per man. Tank crews worked on their machines to get ready for the new assault, and some men got new uniforms and replacement weapons. In the rear, barbers set up shop

417

on boxes and some Marines went swimming off the east beaches.

Admiral Spruance left for Guam in his flagship, the Indianapolis, and there was a more significant departure. The 3rd Regiment sailed away, after two weeks at the beachhead, never having left its ships. Harry Schmidt, laconic and phlegmatic by nature, was aroused. The night before, he had formally requested, for the second time, that the regiment be sent into the battle. Iwo Jima was Schmidt's responsibility; as commander of the largest Marine force ever committed to battle, it was his job to take the island. Supported by the three divisional generals under him – Rockey, Erskine, and Cates – he asked for the regiment because fresh men were urgently needed in the line. Schmidt felt the regiment could substantially shorten the campaign, with a significant saving of lives.

On Monday, Howlin' Mad Smith came ashore, and there was a showdown meeting at Schmidt's command post. Smith was his superior – not in the battle, but in the Corps. Smith took out a notebook and read from it words to the effect that Admiral Turner would not release the regiment unless Smith would certify that the island could not be captured without it. Smith put this to Harry Schmidt and, of course, he had to decline. There was no question but that the island would be taken – two-thirds of it, including all three airfields, were already in Marine hands. The question was, at what cost would it be taken? Turner's main reason for refusing the new troops appeared to be that the island was already too crowded. One place it wasn't too crowded was at the front. Nearly 10,000 fighting casualties had already been taken from the island – more than three times the number of fresh troops Schmidt was pleading for. Colonel James A. Stuart and the 3rd Regiment sailed away to garrison duty on Guam.

Lieutenant Colonel Butler was a tall, dark, intense man. He was from New

Orleans and, like many Marine officers, a graduate of the Naval Academy. On the day of "rest," he went out in the afternoon to look at his lines. The 1st Battalion, 27th, was then beyond Motoyama, in the vicinity of a ruined sugar mill, where Japanese high-velocity artillery had been active for some days. His jeep driver came to a road junction and stopped. At that moment, a shell decapitated Butler and wounded two other men in the jeep. Later that day, Colonel Wornham called his operations officer, Lieutenant Colonel Justin G. Duryea.

"You want your battalion back?"

"Hell, yes," said Duryea, who had trained 1/27 at Camp Pendleton. He went up and took over.

The 1st Platoon of Company B, 1/28, finally got a new commanding officer, its fourth. Second Lieutenant Frank Wright, who had led it ashore, was wounded and evacuated March 1. Sergeant William W. Woods took over and was killed before nightfall. Another sergeant took over and held it until Second Lieutenant John S. Hyndman came up from a replacement draft. He would last four days, be knocked unconscious by a shell, and spend a year in the hospital.

The day of rest ended. There had been more than 400 casualties on the line where there was no fighting. The men got ready for the next big push.

The rest period ended Tuesday morning, March 6, with the heaviest artillery barrage the Marines had ever fired in a comparable area. Eleven battalions of artillery – 132 guns – rocked the island with thunder, firing first on the western half of the front for thirty-one minutes, then on the eastern front for thirty-six minutes. In sixty-seven minutes the guns fired 22,500 shells, from 75 mm. up to 155 mm., as close as 100 yards to the Marines lines. Then they began a creeping barrage, moving slowly forward. A battleship and cruisers added 50 rounds of 14-inch fire and 400 rounds of 8-inch. Three destroyers and two landing craft added their fire, and carrier planes bombed, strafed, and dropped napalm. It seemed no defense could withstand such a pounding.

The Marines attacked at 8 A.M. on the western end of the line and, an hour later, on the eastern end. The Japanese fire was instant, accurate, and intense. It was incredible, but the barrage, seemed not to have affected the enemy at all. As soon as the barrage lifted, he was alert and eager for battle and both sides fell into close and bitter fighting. The Japanese had little artillery left, but they had plenty of hand weapons and the skill and the cover to exploit them. They would have to be burned and blasted out every inch of the way. General Schmidt asked that from now on planes be armed with "maximum amount napalm for duration operation," for which he said there was "urgent need in ravines along northeast coast." Flame and demolition were the best weapons left.

In the Third Division zone Lieutenant William H. Mulvey and two platoons of G Company, 3/21, fought their way to the top of a ridge and there, 400 yards away, was the sea. It was an inspiring moment, but the enemy would not allow enjoyment of it. Fire was so heavy the platoons could not move forward or backward. Mulvey called Corporal Jerome J. Radke and asked him to take another man and go for help. On the way to the rear the other man was wounded, but Radke made it. He rounded up flamethrowers and demolition men – six of them were quickly killed and the other two wounded. Radke went back alone, found Mulvey, and led the platoons to safety. The corporal had often said he would "go through hell" for Mulvey, and today he had.

Gains on all fronts in the day of the big push were negligible. Not that there wasn't action – vicious action. Down behind Turkey Knob on the Fourth Division front, Second Lieutenant Herman "Chuck" Drizin and thirteen men of 2/23 found themselves out front and unable to get back. They kept going forward. Drizin sent Sergeant Edward A. Aldridge for help, but even company headquarters was pinned down by mortars. Drizin began circling, came upon a tank. Private First Class Eugene J. Fredericks, Jr. put a bazooka shell on the turret, and the riflemen picked off the crew as they jumped out. Corporal Harry T. Price ran in with a short-fused bundle of TNT and was blown down by his own blast as it destroyed the tank. Fredericks picked off a second tank with a bazooka bull's-eye from 200 yards, and the Marines raced back into their own lines. Fredericks and Price picked up more bazooka shells, gathered a few riflemen, and went out again. There was a dug-in tank out there, with a 47-mm. gun. It made little show back in headquarters, where they move the colored pins on the maps, but it cost 500 casualties for the day.

Robert Trumbull of The New York Times wrote that day that General Kuribayashi "is conducting his now hopeless defense like a German field marshal, making the Marines pay as heavily as he can for every yard gained." The General would have been pleased if he had read that.

Five bodies found in front of the Fourth Division lines during the day were those of Japanese, fully dressed in Marine uniforms. The enemy had captured much American equipment, and that night a Japanese wrote in his diary "I tasted Roosevelt's rations for the first time, and they were very good."

Planes from the Marianas were using Airfield No. 1 regularly now, for supply and evacuation of casualties. Ensign Jane Kendleigh, a 108-pound farm girl from Oberlin, Ohio, flew in with the first group of Navy nurses. After their C-47 waited eighty minutes in the air over the island, until the morning's big barrage ended, it was loaded up with serious cases and took off for Guam. The sight of the girls was, perhaps, better than whole blood.

A short time later, Brigadier General Ernest C. Moore brought in the first echelon of the Army's 7th Fighter Command – 28 P-51 Mustangs and 12 P-61 Black Widow night fighters. As they roared into the field, skidding down the runway, General Cates and the rest of the Marines dived for their foxholes. The next day, Moore took over as Commander Air, Iwo Jima, from Colonel Megee and the Marines.

By the end of the day, the Navy Evacuation Hospital had two operating rooms and an X-ray section functioning, and three hundred beds in service. After sundown, four 1,00-pound Japanese rockets fell in the center of the compound of the Army's 38th Field Hospital nearby, one of them 20 feet from the surgery. There were no detonators on the giant shells, and the bomb disposal squad was called.

In the Fifth Division hospital, Lieutenant Evans was noticing a change in the type of wounds coming in. They were bad ones, from close-range sniper or machine-gun fire. The earlier wounds, mostly from mortar bursts, had been numerous and ragged, but not so penetrating. The whole blood was being used as little as twelve days after it was given on the West Coast, but often it could not help. "Some of these kids get as much as five units (500 cc) of blood and five of plasma without a response," the surgeon wrote to his wife. After fourteen hours of surgery every day, he was still living in a foxhole, writing by flashlight, and his back was lame. He was amused, however, by the captured Japanese comic books. The characters did not have slant eyes.

About noon on Tuesday, the 31st Seabees began the road up the north face of Suribachi. The Army wanted to put trucks on top of the mountain, with radar, weather, and navigational equipment for the assault on Japan by the B-29's and the fighters. Lieutenant Horace H. DeWitt decided to try to get his bulldozers to the top first and work down. The ground at the top was soft loess, easily worked by the dozers, but it was all rock at the bottom. Some of the Seabees went to work there with compressors, jackhammers, and dynamite, while others and Marine parties dug out land mines and unexploded shells. The Army didn't want just a trail; it wanted a two-lane roadway, 35 feet wide and nearly a mile long, with no grade over 10 percent. Japanese were still inside Suribachi, but there was no fight left in them. They came out only at night, searching for food and water. Every day there were fewer left.

The Seabees worked all night by the light of flares and star shells, and early Wednesday morning Machinist's Mate Third Class James D. Ballard drove the first bulldozer over the lip and into the crater at the top of Suribachi. Two more followed, driven by Albert L. Patterson and E. C. Cagle, and the Seabees set up a cheer. The Marines guarding the top of the hill were unhappy. Their foxholes in the sides of the crater rim were bulldozed over the side of the mountain and their privacy was gone. From now on, those too lazy to climb up could ride.

General Erskine's chance finally came on Tuesday night. When he was ordered to attack as usual at 7:30 the next morning, with artillery support, he proposed instead a surprise attack at 5 A.M., without artillery. He had wanted to try a night attack for a long time, and the failure of Tuesday's heavy artillery barrage carried the argument for him. Permission was granted.

There wasn't much time, but Erskine began at once. Lieutenant Colonel Boehm's 3/9 was ordered into the line, to attack southeast and capture Hill 362C, 250 yards away. Silence in the lines was ordered, and mention of the attack by radio was forbidden. In the black night, with rain falling, the commanders of the two assault companies, K and L, went forward and talked with the company officers of Major Houser's 1/21. They pointed off to the front and said that was Hill 362C. In the light of Navy star shells, the K and L commanders shot azimuths to the hill. The assault companies began assembling at 3:20 A.M., moving as quietly as possible in the darkness. All illumination over the front was ordered to cease at 4:50 A.M. Five minutes later, the artillery, which had been firing random high-explosive shells through the night, would cover Hill 362C with smoke shells.

At division headquarters, tension mounted. Officers synchronized their watches, checked them, and rechecked them. Every few minutes someone ran outside to look at the weather – still raining and very dark. The illumination stopped on schedule, and five minutes later the smoke shells whooshed overhead. At exactly 5 A.M. a star shell burst over the front. The staff gasped. Would it tip off the whole raid? The Navy liaison officer dived for a phone and called the destroyers offshore. No further light showed. In the CP, they waited.

At the front, the assault companies

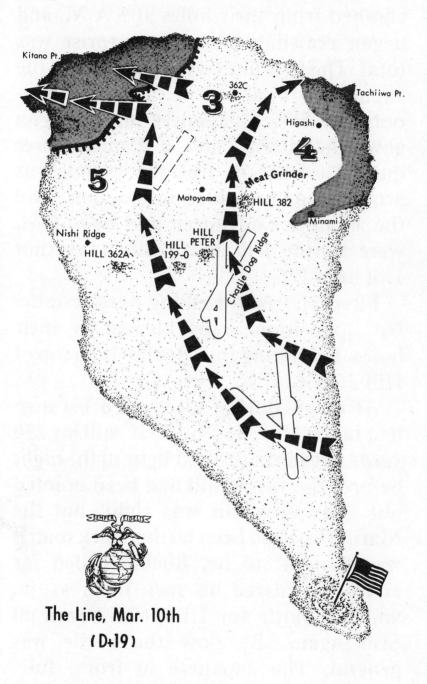

Kitano Pt.

362C

3

Tachiiwa Pt.

Higashi

4

Meat Grinder

5

Motoyama

HILL 382

Nishi Ridge

HILL 362A

HILL
199-0

HILL
PETER

Charlie Dog Ridge

Minami

SEMPER FIDELIS

The Line, Mar. 10th
(D+19)

climbed from their holes at 5 A.M. and began crawling forward. Surprise was total. The first lines were passed with the Japanese still asleep in caves and dugouts. At 5:35 a Japanese machine gun gave the alarm, and a flamethrower quickly seared it. But the enemy was aroused and stumbled into action. Still the assaulters advanced and by 6 A.M. were astride Hill 362C. But it was not Hill 362C!

First reports to Erskine were ecstatic. No opposition. Japs burned in their holes. Scattering fire. Boehm is on top of Hill 362C!

At dawn Boehm discovered his men had taken Hill 331. Hill 362C still lay 250 yards ahead. In the bad light of the night before, the wrong hill had been pointed out. The direction was right, but the Marine line had been farther back than it was thought to be. Boehm called for artillery, ordered his men to press on, and the battle for Hill 362C began all over again. By now the battle was general. The Japanese in front, fully awake, resisted hotly, and those by-passed earlier fought savagely in close combat.

To the right of Boehm, the other two battalions of the 9th had also achieved surprise. They drove straight ahead to meet Boehm's men as they came down from the left, and they made good progress. By dawn, Lieutenant Colonel Cushman's 2/9 and Major Glass's 1/9 had made 200 yards into the Japanese lines, but then the enemy sprang into life. This was Baron Nishi's 26th Tank Regiment, making its strongest stand. Its fire was devastating, and both battalions were cut off from the rear.

Erskine ordered the 21st to try to come in from the north, and on the south, Company G, 23rd Regiment, of the Fourth Division, moved in to help Glass. Toward afternoon it looked as if these two prongs might meet near Hill 362C and have Nishi in a pocket in front of Cushman's battalion. But it was not to be. Cushman's Companies E and F were fighting for their own lives.

Both were surrounded and unable to move in any direction. Tanks went in to try to extricate First Lieutenant Wilcie O'Bannon's Company F, but twice they were frustrated, the first time when the lead tank hit a mine in a narrow ravine, and the second time by broken ground. At nightfall, remnants of both companies were still pinned down.

On the south, one of Glass's companies captured a pillbox complex far out in front but then was cut off. The commander, Second Lieutenant John H. Leims, crawled out 400 yards to his men, dragging a telephone line, and brought the men back without loss. Then he found out that several wounded men had been left behind. That night he crawled out alone and carried one man back, then he went back and brought in another man.

Boehm's men fought on during the day, and by 2 P.M. Company K had captured Hill 362C, this time the correct hill and for good. What was left of Cushman's Companies E and F were rescued after thirty-six hours. Lieutenant O'Bannon had nineteen men remaining of forty-one, and Captain Maynard Schmidt came out with seven survivors from Company E. Baron Nishi still held what had now come to be known as Cushman's Pocket.

On the whole, it had been an excellent day. Erskine's gamble had paid off. Except for Cushman's Pocket, the last big obstacles toward the sea had been taken. It had been costly, but the gains were crucial.

On the other fronts, fighting was equally bitter but the gains less spectacular. In the center of the Fifth Division line, the 26th Regiment moved out at dawn, without artillery. The surprise was more valuable than the artillery, and after Tuesday's tremendous cannonading ammunition was short. The 26th made nearly 200 yards, capturing a strongpoint that had held up the advance the previous day, and found itself in front of a knoll, north of what had been Nishi village. The enemy fell strangely silent, and the Marines cautiously surrounded the hill. Demolitions men blasted one cave entrance closed, and machine gunners cut down Japanese who ran from a rear entrance. The hill still looked suspicious, but Marines ran to the top of it. Just then the whole hill shuddered and the top blew out with a roar heard all over the island. Men were thrown into the air, and those nearby were stunned by concussion. Dozens of Marines disappeared in the blast crater, and their comrades ran in to dig for them. Strong men vomited at the sight of charred bodies, and others walked from the area crying. The enemy had blown up his own command post, inflicting forty-three Marine casualties at the same time.

On the west coast, the 28th had little trouble, advancing 500 yards through rocky gorges, supported by destroyer fire up the canyons. Just before night there was a brief gas scare, the second in five days. This time, the gas alarm was sounded, and men put on their gas masks. In a short time it was discovered that the wind was driving sulphur fumes and gases from a burning Japanese ammunition dump down on the men, and the alert was canceled.

Before dawn Wednesday, the Japanese scored one of the few successful rocket hits of the battle. A huge projectile exploded at 5:02 A.M. near the command post of 2/23, at the northern end of the Fourth Division line. The battalion's communications chief was killed, and nearly every battalion officer was wounded, including Major Robert H. Davidson, the commanding officer; Major John J. Padley, the executive officer; Captain Edward J. Schofield, the operations officer; the battalion adjutant; and two clerks. Colonel Wensinger sent the regimental executive officer, Lieutenant Colonel Edward J. Dillon, to the front to steady the battalion. Davidson, badly shaken by the detonation, was back in command after four days, but Padley and Schofield saw no more service.

The Fourth Division found the enemy oddly quiet on certain sections of the front during both Wednesday and Thursday and began to prepare one of the few maneuvers Iwo Jima had allowed. The 23rd and 24th drove east, turning slowly south, forming a hammer to bring down on the anvil of the 25th, with the enemy between them. For the only time during the campaign, the 25th formed defensive lines, setting up mines and barbed wire, siting in machine guns, 37-mm. cannon and 60-mm. mortars, waiting for the Japanese to be driven down on them. In the pocket was Captain Inouye, with the last of the naval ground forces, and he had other ideas.

In the rear, the Army took over Iwo Jima. General Chaney became Island Commander, with responsibility for base development, air defense, and operation of the airfields. The Army's fighters began air cover for the Marines, and most of the warships sailed for Ulithi, to regroup for the Okinawa assault. Only the cruisers Salt Lake City and Tuscaloosa stayed on, with a few destroyers. The Army Garrison Group One arrived on Thursday and immediately began unloading. Six escort carriers left the same day, and the seaplane base was decommissioned. The 62nd Seabees rushed work on Airfield No. 2, and only at the front was there a war going on. They knew it there, and in the hospitals, where the casualties flowed in steadily, and in the Graves Registration Details.

On the hot hills above Yellow Beach 2, Captain Lewis Nutting struggled to keep up with his job. He was burial officer for the Fourth Division and the Corps. He had supervised burial at Saipan also and this, he vowed, would be "the most beautiful cemetery of all our campaigns."

"There will be a stone fence around the cemetery," he said, "and we hope to have all the grave markers up in three days."

The Captain pointed to Lieutenant

Walter Stonneberg. "He's been my helper this time, and I couldn't have gotten along without him," Nutting said. Stonneberg was sad, and not only because of the nature of his work. He was division bandmaster, and his band had been broken up for grave duty.

All day long, men carried litters to the field and placed them in neat rows. Two men passed along the rows, taking fingerprints, if the right index finger remained. Other men picked up one dog tag from each body, leaving the other for burial. If there were neither hands nor dog tags, and often there were not, the teams tried to establish identification by means of teeth, scars, tattoos, birthmarks, clothing stencils, jewelry, or uniform marks. Sometimes there was so little left that it was necessary to ascertain which section of the battlefield the body came from in order to determine to which unit the man had belonged.

When a row was ready, the bodies were wrapped in blankets or ponchos and placed in a trench. The bulldozer covered them with 6 feet of Iwo Jima sand, and a grader spread clay on top to keep it from blowing away. The sounds of battle off to the north were ignored. Since D plus 3, Captain Nutting's unit had suffered five casualties of its own. Even in the cemetery there was no security.

Late that afternoon a special plane arrived. The Red Cross in Honolulu had heard of the sulphur fumes, dust, and blowing volcanic ash on Iwo Jima and had sent out five thousand white gauze masks. The Marines refused to wear them but allowed as how "the Army boys will look cute in them."

General Schmidt's order for Thursday called upon the Marines to "capture the rest of the island." He did not mean that day, but so little of the island was left to the Japanese that intermediate phase or objective lines were no longer necessary. There were only the jumbles of rock ahead, and then the sea.

The 2nd Battalion, 27th, moved up the right side of the Fifth Division line, just north of the Third Division in the center. It was driving for the coast to the east of Kitano Point. Company E stalled almost at once. Jack Lummus, twenty-nine, of Ennie, Texas, ran out in front of his rifle platoon and was knocked flat by a grenade. After two days and nights of steady fighting, First Lieutenant Lummus was not to be stopped.

He arose, shook himself, and ran forward again, overrunning a gun emplacement and destroying it. Again a grenade downed him, this time shattering his shoulder. Lummus got up, charged and killed every man in a second enemy position, then turned and called his men. Company E began to roll, Lummus at the head, running from spidertrap to foxhole to cave, slashing at the Japanese.

Suddenly he was in the center of a powerful explosion, obscured by flying rock and dirt. As it cleared, his men saw him, rising as if in a hole. A land mine had blown off both his legs, the legs that had carried him to All-American football honors at Baylor University. They watched in horror as he stood on the bloody stumps, calling them on. Several men, crying now, ran to him and, for a moment, talked of shooting him to stop his agony.

But he was still shouting for them to move out, move out, and the platoon scrambled forward. Their tears turned to rage, they swept an incredible 300 yards over impossible ground, and at nightfall were on the ridge overlooking the sea. There was no question that the dirty, tired men, cursing and crying and fighting, had done it for Jack Lummus.

Lummus amazingly, lived on for a time. They carried him to a receiving tent at the Fifth Division hospital, and he smiled as they began to give him blood. He received eighteen pints in all, and in midafternoon he raised himself on one elbow.

"Doc," he said, "it looks like the New York Giants have lost a damn good end." The doctor, Lieutenant Evans, was astounded at the man's stamina. Late in the afternoon another surgeon, a fellow Texan, Lieutenant Howard "Stack" Stackhouse, Jr., came to see if anything could be done. Both he and Lummus knew further effort was useless, but Lummus was still smiling as he closed his eyes. He never opened them.

On another part of the front, Lieutenant Ginsburg was killed. He was the sixth commander the 2nd Platoon, Company B, 1/28 had had, and he had lasted three days. Corporal Mueller took over again, to wait for another officer to be found.

At the end of the day, Marines of the Fourth Division noticed unusual movement all across their lines. Captain Inouye had ordered all Navy men still able to fight to gather at his command post. He was obsessed with the idea that the Imperial flag must fly again from Suribachi, and he hoped to do it that night, March 8.

The eighth day of every month, was a

sacred anniversary of the attack on Pearl Harbor, and the Captain knew he would never see the eighth of April. It must be tonight.

By 11 P.M. nearly a thousand men had gathered, survivors from many Navy units. Many men had only bamboo spears, but some had grenades and rifles. There were a few machine guns, and some men strapped land mines across their chests, determined to blow up some Marines with themselves.

The band started south, not in a wild charge, but crawling slowly and quietly. One group got within 10 yards of 2/23's command post, where Lieutenant Colonel Dillon was still in command, before the alarm was given. Then the sailors lobbed grenades and charged, shrieking "Banzai!" In a moment there was chaos. The Marines threw up flares and star shells lighted the sky. Machine-gun fire, rifles, and mortars began to cut into them but still the Japanese came on. Some of them carried stretchers and shouted "Corpsman, corpsman" in fair

English. Finally the hordes faltered and broke, and no one knew where Captain Inouye was. He had last been seen running and shouting, his sword waving in the air.

Petty Officer Riichi Koyatsu, the Captain's orderly, looked at his watch; it was 3:30 A.M. He rolled into a bomb crater to tie his gaiters, and a shell blasted the spot where he had been. He was alone and undecided.

Then, far off, he heard the Captain shout "totsukegi ni mae-e" ("Everyone charge ahead"). There was yelling in the holes and rocks as the men responded, and then again the Captain's voice: Tsukkome!" ("Let's go!"), and a very short time later, "Banzai, banzai." It was Captain Inouye's voice again – the last time it was ever heard. He was five days short of his fiftieth birthday.

Koyatsu found some other men, and they all said, "What do we do now?" They knew the captain was dead, and they asked each other, "Do we still go to Suribachi?"

"To Suribachi or anywhere, we'll have to get the hell out of here," one said, and they began crawling east – away from Suribachi.

In the morning, the Marines counted 784 Japanese bodies in front of their lines. They had lost 90 men killed and 257 wounded, but the biggest Japanese attack on Iwo Jima had been turned back.

Not more than 200 sailors were left from the night's sortie, and at daybreak a lieutenant, once a Navy flyer, gathered them together. "You are now remnants," he said. "Navy discipline will continue. From now on, I am your commanding officer."

But their fighting was over. Each night the lieutenant sent out patrols of three to five men. They never returned. Others went into caves, and some died, of wounds, of sickness, or of thirst. Some drank urine and died.

The lieutenant lasted until April 29, the Emperor's birthday, when he told the others, "We will steal a B-29 and fly to the homeland. You others do as you please after we're gone." He left, accompanied by the chief Navy medical officer, an ensign, and a petty officer.

Koyatsu did not go. He stayed in the cave, except for night forays to the American garbage dump to get food. Early in June, Koyatsu and three others decided to try to escape on a raft, and they crawled to a cave on the beach. The next morning a corporal pulled them out of the cave at gunpoint. It was an Army corporal; the Marines were long gone.

On the night of Inouye's last charge, Admiral Toyoda again messaged Admiral Ichimaru, praising the brave acts of the Navy men and again begging them to hold out as long as possible. Ichimaru did not know that Inouye had already sacrificed the last of the Japanese Navy force on Iwo Jima.

By Friday, both sides were nearly exhausted, but the Japanese had suffered the most. On the Fourth

Division front it became clear that Captain Inouye's counterattack had spent a large part of the force in the east. Major General Senda was still in command, probably somewhere between Higashi and the sea. Turkey Knob had still not fallen, and other vicious pockets existed, but central direction of the eastern front was no longer evident.

Some units of the Fourth Division were so spent that reorganization was imperative. Colonel Jordan's 24th Regiment, which had landed about 3,000 men, had been decimated and had to be reformed. All that remained of the 1st Battalion were parts of two companies: A with 135 men, and B with 115. Jordan's executive officer, Lieutenant Colonel Austin R. Brunelli, took them over, relieving Major Paul S. Treitel. The 2nd Battalion had 300 men left in Companies F and G and was assigned to the 25th Regiment, to make up strength there. To mop up in the rear, the 4th Provisional Battalion was formed from support troops, under Lieutenant Colonel Melvin L. Krulewitch; for the next three days it swept up Japanese remnants behind Marine lines.

The Fourth Division made good gains at the north end of its line on Friday, and the next day swept forward 700 yards, nearly to the sea. In fact, patrols from 2/23 reached the beach at Tachiiwa Point on Saturday, and just to the south 3/24 scouted to within 100 yards of the sea. No enemy was found. In the center, 3/25 drove southeast and at 4 P.M. met 2/25 coming up from the south. Turkey Knob was at last surrounded and eliminated.

But honors for reaching the sea had gone to the Third Division the day before. On Friday afternoon, a 28-man patrol led by Lieutenant Paul M. Connally of Company A, 1/21 finally reached the coast. The men stopped for a moment on the high bluff, staring at the rolling gray water, then scrambled down the rocky cliff, past caves and pillboxes smashed by naval gunfire. There was no one around, and some of the men ran to the water, plunged their arms into it, and scooped it up to wash their filthy faces. A few took off their shoes and waded in to let the cool sea soothe their feet. In the entire company, which had landed with a strength of over 200 men, only three had come the whole way. But all had fought for this, and to Company A went the honor.

The patrol stayed on the shore nearly ten minutes, but suddenly mortars fired and two shells fell among the Marines. Seven were wounded, and the others carried them to a ledge halfway up the cliff. Connally called Lieutenant Colonel Smoak, and the regimental executive officer, aware that this was a high moment in Marine history, asked Connally if he could bring back a canteen of seawater as proof. The lieutenant said he could, and when the patrol came in he gave it to Smoak. Colonel Withers, the regimental commander, said the others might consider it a fake.

"Taste it," Smoak said, and Withers swigged from the canteen and spit it out. There was no doubt. He sent it off to General Erskine by personal messenger, with the notation: "For inspection, not consumption." The Third had reached the sea, and the enemy was split.

The Fifth Division had nearly had it, and between the front and Kitano Point lay the worst ground on Iwo Jima. Ridges and gorges cut the area, broken rock blocked out tanks and bulldozers, and caves and dugouts pocked the sides of every hill. At noon, General Rockey ordered his artillerymen to be ready on one-hour notice to send 10 percent of their number to the front.

Second Lieutenant Lester E. Hutchcroft and Second Lieutenant Ginsburg had started out together in the 27th Replacement Draft. Every time someone was killed at the top, Ginsburg moved up a notch and Hutchcroft followed him. Ginsburg got to the front March 5 at the head of the 2nd Platoon,

Company B, 1/28, and three days later was killed. Hutchcroft got to the front on March 9, taking over the 1st Platoon as its fifth commander. Two days later there was little left of the 2nd Platoon, and he took that one over too, from Corporal Mueller. The same day, Hutchcroft was killed. So depleted were the ranks now, that both platoons fell to privates first class.

On the same afternoon that Hutchcroft got to the front, Lieutenant Colonel Duryea of 1/27 went out to check his lines with Major Antonelli of the next battalion to the right, 2/27. They decided the main opposition lay to the north, instead of the east, and started to walk back. Duryea called to his runner, who was sitting on a rock, and the youngster replied "I'm coming, Colonel." He took one step and was blown to bits. He had set off the detonator of a 6-inch naval shell, buried in the ground to catch a tank.

A huge fragment of the shell tore off Duryea's left arm at the elbow and another smashed his left knee. Antonelli fell, blinded by sand. Duryea, still conscious, could not see his left leg, doubled under him, and thought he had lost it. Thinking an attack was under way, he shouted to others, "Come here, come here. Don't go away." He tried to roll over to get the pistol under his right hip, but could not.

A captain ran to get corpsmen, and they bundled Duryea and Tony Antonelli into stretchers. Duryea's left leg dangled off the side, and a bullet pierced it, breaking it. Duryea was out of the war, after four days as battalion commander, and so was Antonelli. The 27th made no gains all day, despite heavy fighting and the help of the Army's P-51's. The fighters, in action for the first time, strafed and bombed the gorges in precision attacks that made the Marines shout in admiration. The result was negligible.

The next morning, the rear-echelon men went into the line. A hundred artillerymen became riflemen in 3/28 (59 of them became casualties). Ninety-eight more went to 3/26 (58 casualties). Fifty-five men from the 11th Amphibious Tractor Battalion went to the front with 3/27, and 104 men from the 5th Motor Transport Battalion joined 1/28.

Admiral Turner broke up his command on Friday; the naval phase of the campaign was over. He sailed for Guam in the Eldorado, leaving Admiral Hill in the Auburn as senior naval officer with a small force. The Enterprise, last of the big carriers, departed at sundown; the Army now had air control.

Friday night made history in aerial warfare. Three hundred and thirty-four B-29's took off from the Marianas, taking nearly three hours to form up. Then they flew north, on the first great fire raid. Pathfinder planes marked the target shortly after midnight, and the B-29's followed in at low altitude, less than 2 miles, and strewed 1,665 tons of fire bombs on Tokyo. There was little opposition and fire sprang up every-where. Going home, the tail gunners could see the city burning for 150 miles.

In a brisk wind, nearly 16 square miles of the city were destroyed by morning and 84,000 persons had been killed. More than 265,000 buildings burned, and a million people were homeless. The holocaust exceeded any conflagration in the history of the Western World, including the burning of Rome by Nero in 64 A.D., the London fire of 1666, the burning of Moscow in 1812, the Chicago fire of 1871, and the San Francisco earthquake of 1906. It was the most destructive raid of the war, in Europe or Japan, with horrors beyond description.

Two damaged B-29's landed at Iwo Jima, and 14 others went down at sea but the crews of five were rescued. The Japanese were stunned, but at Iwo Jima the fight went on. Kuribayashi, knowing nothing of the great fire raid, reported to Chichi Jima that "our troops are still fighting bravely and holding their positions thoroughly." He admitted that the P-51 attacks against his headquarters had been "so fierce that I cannot express nor write here."

At the beachhead, a Navy landing craft drew alongside a transport, bringing out a badly wounded sergeant. Another small boat with a Navy captain aboard intercepted it, and the captain asked if he might have the casualty. Captain Charles C. Anderson carried his only son, Sergeant Charles C. Anderson, Jr., to his own vessel. The boy had lost both legs and one arm from a land mine, and he was dying.

"I'm feeling pretty good," he told his father. "I wonder how Mother will take all this." Then he died.

When a Navy chaplain called on Mrs. Anderson in Washington, she asked, "Is it my husband or my son?" The Chaplain said it was her son. "A force stronger than ours has taken charge," Mrs. Anderson said, "and our beloved son is with us on Earth no more." Then she dressed and went to work as a volunteer at Bethesda Naval Hospital.

By Saturday night the Third Division

held 800 yards of coast. The enemy had been split. General Kuribayashi clung to one square mile in the north of Iwo Jima; Major General Senda held small pockets in the southeast. The terrible two weeks was over.

The cost had been awesome. A total of 2,777 Marines had been killed or mortally wounded, 8,051 more had been wounded, and 1,102 lost to combat fatigue. In fourteen days of fighting there had been 12,000 casualties. When the flag went up on Suribachi, the battle had only begun. It was not yet over.

By the end of the third week, there were few newsmen left on Iwo Jima. They had gone off to join the forces getting ready for Okinawa, and the spotlight returned to Europe, where the Allies were sweeping into Germany. Lieutenant General George S. Patton's tanks sped through town after town, making 30 miles in one twelve-hour period. The 3rd Army was at the Rhine, 50 miles inside Germany, Coblenz and Bonn were on the point of surrender, and seven Red Armies were marching on Berlin. In the Pacific, the B-29's set fire to Nagoya, a city the size of Los Angeles. Coming back, seven cripples landed on Iwo Jima on Sunday, March 11, including "Dream Boat," which came in on two engines. The book said a B-29 wouldn't fly on two engines, but "Dream Boat" made it, patched up once more, and flew on to Guam. The newspapers barely mentioned it, or the fighting on Iwo Jima.

But there was fighting. The Third Division spent six days, Sunday through Friday, eliminating Cushman's Pocket. Crack men, such as the Third had been on D-Day, might have done it in a day or two. But the few regulars left were tired and without fire, and the replacements lacked experience. Artillery, half-tracks, and demolitions men banged away at the pocket, gradually squeezing it to 250 yards on a side. Even rocket sleds, especially built by the engineers to get into the rough country, fired at point-blank range. Their twenty tubes could deliver 640 pounds of TNT in a salvo, but after ten volleys, the Japanese fire came back as strong as ever. On Friday, 1/21 and 2/21 gave the pocket the coup de grace with flame throwing tanks. The pocket was overrun, but Baron Nishi was still inside.

His men could hear their comrades, now prisoners and working for the enemy, calling "Nishi-san dete koi" ("Mister Nishi, come out"). At almost the same hour, the Baroness Nishi and her youngest daughter arrived at the seaside resort of Chigasaki, south of Tokyo, to visit a sick relative. As they walked through the darkened town, the Baroness heard a radio saying, "All the garrison at Iwo Jima has fought to the death." She and the child walked to the sea, tears streaming down the Baroness' face, and they gazed over the ocean in the direction of Iwo Jima.

But the Baron was not yet dead. He stayed underground until 2 A.M. on March 19, when he went out with 60 men, all that remained of his unit, and headed for Ginmeisui, high on the east coast. In his three-tiered command post in the ground were 300 wounded men, with two days' food supply. "Nishi unit is to make an all-out charge to sure death," the Baron said in his last message to get through to Chichi Jima.

The circumstances of Colonel Nishi's death are not known, but most accounts agree on several things – that he killed himself, probably on March 22, and that he died with his Olympic whip in one hand and the hair from the mane of Uranus in his heart pocket. One account says that he committed hara-kiri on the northern cliffs, another that he fell before machine-gun fire near the second airfield and then put his revolver to his head, saying first to his aide, "Turn me toward the Imperial Palace."

The Baroness, still alive, has her own beliefs. She does not believe he committed hara-kiri, because he had often told her that the surest way was a shot in the ear. Nor does she like to think that he died under what is now the main runway of the airfield. She shrinks from the thought that his body is "daily and nightly run over by American bombers on Iwo." She likes, rather, to think that he died at the foot of the northern cliffs, and that ocean waves have scattered his remains.

During the same week, the Fourth Division overran the rest of the eastern sector, except for a circle of rock between Higashi and the sea. Major General Senda was in there, and a prisoner said he had about 300 men with him. Large rocket shells still came out of the circle. On Monday morning, General Cates held up his attack for two hours. He had a message prepared in Japanese, for broadcast to Senda by loudspeaker. The message praised Senda's defense, but said Iwo Jima "has been lost to you" and "you can gain nothing by further resistance." The message never got off; the gasoline generator for the amplifier refused to work. The attack was resumed and continued for four more days. The last major resistance in this sector ended on Friday, March 16. General Senda's body was never found. Prisoners said he had committed suicide on Wednesday. The six days of battle had cost the Fourth Division 833 casualties.

Chapter 5

By Sunday, March 11, General Kuribayashi estimated he had 1,500 men left. They had been pressed into a square mile of the worst ground on Iwo Jima, from Kita Village to Kitano Point, on the northwest coast. It was an area of broken and tumbled ravines running to the coast, and the most formidable of these, just southwest of Kitano Point, became known to the Marines as the Gorge, or Death Valley. It was here that the last stand would be made.

The Gorge, about 700 yards long and from 200 to 500 yards wide, was cut with smaller lateral canyons throughout its entire length, jumbled with rock, and lined with machine-gun, mortar and rifle positions. Some had very narrow fields of fire, but all were cleverly concealed, and the Japanese ammunition, smokeless and flashless, added a powerful advantage. It was nearly impossible to tell where the fire came from.

Colonel Liversedge's 28th Regiment, only a few men left from the assault on Suribachi, moved up the west coast with light opposition and by Wednesday held the last ridge overlooking the Gorge. There it was ordered to hold, while the rest of the Division fought up the center and from the east.

Colonel Wornham's 27th made good gains on the eastern end of the line during the week, forcing the fight with armored tanks and bulldozers and flame throwing tanks. The tanks were using as much as 10,000 gallons of flame oil per day now. But the attrition was terrible. On Monday, the 2nd Battalion, Major Antonelli's old outfit, now under Major Gerald F. Russell, was pinched out of the shrinking front and retired. It was so shattered it never fought again.

On Wednesday, the 1st Battalion lost its third commander in nine days.

Lieutenant Colonel Butler had been decapitated, Lieutenant Colonel Duryea had been maimed by a land mine, and now Major William Tumbelston's left arm was shattered by bullets in the wrist and forearm. The 27th lasted until Saturday but was then reorganized. Most of what was left became a special Composite Battalion of 470 men under Lieutenant Colonel Donn J. Robertson. He was the 27th's only original battalion commander left from D-Day.

The P-51's flew their last missions on Thursday, and the next day the Fifth Division artillery fired its last rounds. The forces were now too close for such support, and in many places there were more Japanese behind the Marines than in front of them. Nights became worse than the days, and there were no "friendlies." Anything that moved was fired at. Private Richard L. Shipton, nineteen, a BAR man in Company E, 2/28, watched three Japanese come from behind his lines, trying to get through his barbed wire back into their own lines. He tossed a grenade and saw arms and legs flying. He passed the watch to his foxhole mate, Private First Class Donald L. Feltmeyer, and fifteen minutes later a Japanese grenade fell in their hole. Feltmeyer was taken to the rear, blinded. The next day Shipton was shot in the stomach. There were no replacements.

Second Lieutenant Franklin W. Fouch took over the 1st Platoon, Company B, 1/28, on March 11, its seventh commander since D-Day. He was twenty-one and a product of the assembly line, the special Officer Candidate Schools that, back home, turned out hundreds of junior officers for the ranks. Fouch unloaded cargo at the beaches with the 27th Replacement Battalion – 54 second lieutenants and 1,200 enlisted men – until the losses at the front called them forward in groups.

Fouch went up in time for the battle on Hill 362A, was wounded in the back by a spent bullet, and refused evacuation. He lay over a sulphur hole at night, and the hot fumes seemed to help his wound. By the time he took over the 1st Platoon, many of the men he had gone through O.C.S. with were already dead – Al Garcia, Danny Ginsburg, Les Hutchcroft. Hyndman had gone out unconscious, with a critical wound, and Fouch inherited the platoon when Hutchcroft was killed. Three days later he inherited the 2nd Platoon too, its twelfth commander. He took this one over when Private Dale O. Cassell, Jr., was killed. The last regular commander had been Hutchcroft, and after that Private Cassell twice held command, before and after Gunnery Sergeant Julius C. Wittenberg, who was wounded and evacuated in one day.

The 2nd Platoon now comprised three men, two privates and Corporal Mueller. None of them had been in the original platoon. Those 45 men were dead or gone from the front, and of the replacements only these three remained.

Two days later, a bazooka shell fired from the rear fell short of the ridge and into a foxhole. The two privates were killed, and Corporal Mueller was badly shaken. Fouch took him into his foxhole and kept him there until dark, when he sent him to the rear. That was the end of the 2nd Platoon. Fouch stayed on the ridge and that night quelled a near mutiny. The men said they couldn't stand fire from both sides and were going to fall back. Fouch said snipers would get them on the way back, and anyway, they'd fought so hard for the ridge he wasn't going to give it up. Finally his last runner, Private Charles A. Arelt, a tall, slender, married man of twenty-seven, said, "I'll stay with you, Frank." "Thanks, Chuck," the Leiutenant said, and then the rest of the men gave in. They all stayed on the ridge. On both sides of them, up and down the ridge, other thin bands of tired men were holding the line.

On March 13, a patrol from the 26th Regiment came very near to Kuribayashi, peering into the cave in which he sat, near the eastern end of the Gorge. The General's orderly quickly blew out the candles and wrapped the General in a blanket. "Thank you," Kuribayashi said, and walked deeper into the cave. The Marines, one carrying a flamethrower, walked a little way into the cave, then turned and went out. The orderly sighed.

The next night, the 145th Infantry Regiment ceased to exist as a unit. General Kuribayashi asked Colonel Ikeda how long he thought the regimental colors would be safe.

"Maybe a day," Ikeda replied. Hundreds of men in the famed regiment had died; only six men were left to guard the flag.

Kuribayashi replied quietly: "Burn it. Do not let it fall into the hands of the enemy."

His last message from Colonel Ikeda said: "Here we burnt our brilliant regimental flag completely. Good-bye."

At 4 P.M. on Friday, March 16, Leading Private Yoshio Yamada of the 2nd Battalion, 145th Regiment, was captured east of Kitano by Third

Division troops. He said Colonel Ikeda was in a cave at his headquarters and offered to take a letter to him. General Erskine thought it was worth a try. He felt sure that Kuribayashi opposed surrender, but that he might agree if the proposal came through Ikeda.

The next morning Yamada and a second prisoner passed through the Marine lines near Kitano Point and began to make their way south toward Ikeda's headquarters. They carried a letter from General Erskine and a Marine walkie-talkie radio. During the morning they sent messages back to Erskine's headquarters, but then they stopped. The second man had stayed behind with the radio while Yamada went on. Yamada found the cave in which he thought Ikeda was hiding. He was very frightened and would not go in the cave himself. He gave Erskine's letter to Superior Private Yasuo Ueno, who was guarding the entrance, and Ueno in turn gave it to a private to take inside. In a half hour the private was back. He said he had given the letter to the Colonel, who had muttered something about "letters from prisoners of war" and about referring the matter to Kuribayashi.

Yamada waited a little while, but then terror overcame him and he fled back to where he had left his friend with the radio. They reported by radio that they were on the way in but they did not arrive. They became lost and finally walked through the Fifth Division lines. Intelligence officers were astounded at their story, and accepted it only after confirming it with Erskine's headquarters. No one will ever know if the letter got to Ikeda, but the surrender proposal was certainly never accepted.

That night General Kuribayashi sent his final message addressed to Imperial General Headquarters:

"The situation is now on the brink of the last. At midnight of the seventeenth I shall lead the final offensive, praying that our empire will eventually emerge victorious and secure. I am pleased to report that we have continued to fight well against the overwhelming material odds of the enemy, and all my officers and men deserve the highest commendation. I however humbly apologize to His Majesty that I have failed to live up to expectations and have to yield this key island to the enemy after having seen many of my officers and men killed.

"Unless this island is wrested back our country won't be secure. Even as a ghost, I wish to be a vanguard of future Japanese operations against this place. Bullets are gone and water exhausted. Now that we are ready for the final act, I am grateful to have been given this opportunity to respond to the gracious will of His Majesty. Permit me to say farewell.

"In conclusion, I take the liberty of adding the following clumsy poem:

Shells and bullets are gone, and we
    perish,
Remorseful of failure to fulfill assign-
    ments.

My body shall not decay in the field
Unless we are avenged;
I will be born seven more times again
To take up arms against the foe.

My only concern is
Our country in the future,
When weeds cover here."

The loss of Iwo Jima was announced to the Japanese nation that night. Premier Kuniaki Koiso spoke by radio, saying the defeat "is the most unfortunate thing in the whole war situation." He appealed to the people to show "a burning determination to defend the nation.

"There will be no unconditional surrender," he said. "So long as there is one Japanese living, we must fight to shatter the enemy's ambitions to pieces. We must not stop fighting until then."

On the same day the Imperial government promoted Kuribayashi to full general, Ichimaru to vice admiral, Inouye to rear admiral, and Nishi to full colonel. Chichi Jima messaged this news

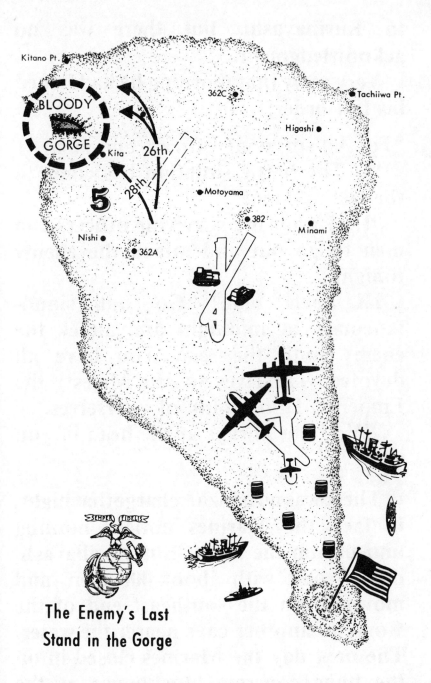

Kitano Pt.

362C

Tachiiwa Pt.

BLOODY GORGE

Higashi

Kita

26th

28th

5

Motoyama

382

Minami

Nishi

362A

SEMPER FIDELIS

The Enemy's Last
Stand in the Gorge

to Kuribayashi, but there was no acknowledgment.

Very early that morning he had issued his last order:

"To: All surviving officers and men:

"I. The battle situation has come to the last moment.

"II. I want my surviving officers and men to go out and attack the enemy tonight.

III. Each man! Go out simultaneously at midnight and attack the enemy until the last. You have all devoted yourselves to His Majesty the Emperor. Don't think of yourselves.

"IV. I am always at the head of you all."

There was no banzai charge that night; in fact, the Marines noticed nothing unusual on the front. But Kuribayashi did go out, with about 400 men, and moved from the southeast end of the Gorge to another cave nearer the water. The next day the Marines closed in on the huge concrete blockhouse at the head of the Gorge, the last one left on Iwo Jima, which apparently sat atop General Kuribayashi's former head-quarters. Tank dozers cut off some of the air vents, and the infantry smashed away at it for two days with 75's and 40-pound shaped charges. The blockhouse could not be reduced. Finally the engineers destroyed it with 8,500 pounds of explosives in five great explosions that shook the island.

Kuribayashi continued to report to Chichi Jima. On the twenty-first he said: "My officers and men are still fighting. The enemy front line is 200 or 300 meters from us and they are attacking by tank firing. They advised us to surrender by loudspeaker, but we only laughed at this childish trick and did not set ourselves against them."

This was the team of First Lieutenant John W. McLean, a Japanese language officer of the 28th Regiment. A prisoner pointed out the cave in which he believed the General was. McLean's party went down into the Gorge, waited while flame tanks hosed the area, and then called to the General to give himself up. There was no response.

There was a final message on March 23; it may have been from Kuribayashi. It said: "All officers and men of Chichi Jima, good-bye." The general's body was never found, nor were those of Admiral Ichimaru or Colonel Ikeda. The previous day the admiral's youngest daughter, Miyeko, nine, and other children made a special broadcast to Iwo Jima from the Japan Broadcasting Corporation studio in Tokyo. They told their fathers they were studying hard "and wish our fathers in Iwo will fight hard and protect our homeland."

The pocket in the Gorge was down to a square of 50 yards. On the 25th of March a pitiful band of Marines, some from the 26th and the 27th, and some from the 28th, including Second Lieutenant Fouch, came down over the pocket and that was all. The battle of Iwo Jima was over. Every junior officer

478

in Company B, including Fouch, had been wounded at least once. He now commanded what was left of three platoons, including the 3rd, which had been led for eight days by Private First Class G. C. Burk, Jr. This was not unusual; nearly every company in the division could tell the same story, even down to Private Burk. He had shrapnel in his belly and could not stand up straight, but he would not leave until the end. Burk was unusual in a way; he had landed on D-Day and gone all the way. Few men could say that.

One who fell in the last days was Private First Class Franklin R. Sousley, whom fate had placed next to Hayes in the Rosenthal picture. From Suribachi he had fought all the way north to Kitano, only to die in a ravine four days before his division retired, the battle over. The Indian had been right – Sousley was "gonna get it," and Hayes would not be there. The embittered Indian had played "Taps," and not alone for Sousley.

Behind them, Iwo Jima was being transformed. The Army's 15th Fighter Group began regular attacks against the Bonin Islands on Sunday, March 11. The first attack, by sixteen P-51's with General Moore along as an observer, dropped 8 tons of bombs on Chichi and Haha Jima. Thereafter there were daily attacks against the airfields and shipping in the Bonins.

The 31st Seabees finished the road up Suribachi on Monday, driving a 20-ton bulldozer to the top in triumph. Chief Warrant Officer Jack Purcell, bossing a 29-man gang, had done the job in six days. A port director was now in charge of unloading, and the Navy began laying nets around the anchorage. The Marines released their Army Dukw companies to the island commander, and the last of the escort carriers left. A transport sailed for Guam with fifty-eight prisoners of war, and bulldozers droned all day across Airfield No. 2, carving off the high ground in the center of the island, so recently wet with blood.

The Salt Lake City **and** Tuscaloosa finally departed on Monday, after many days of shelling, and on Tuesday, Kama and Kangoku Brocks were occupied. There were no Japanese on them. Eight more B-20's landed after burning 8 square miles of Osaka. Two more Seabee battalions, and the last of the Army garrison force arrived.

Up front, two more Fifth Division men won the Medal of Honor, but in the rear the Fourth Division began loading out. Clothing was now good in the rear; all you had to do was turn in your old stuff and draw new. The Fifth Division hospital was still getting 250 casualties a day, but that was a lot better than the 500 days. The Army Transport Command revealed that Iwo Jima casualties were arriving in Hawaii by air from the Marianas at the rate of 250 daily, and getting the best of care.

On Wednesday, March 14, the ceremony began promptly at 9:30 A.M., as ordered.

The sun on Suribachi, a few hundred yards to the south, was warm and strong, and the wind and the firing of artillery nearby sometimes made the words hard to hear. But everyone knew what this was; it was the official flag raising over Iwo Jima.

The uniform of the day for the color bearer, the color guard, and the guard of honor was clean dungarees, helmets, and arms. The generals were in whatever had come to hand – General Smith in sun helmet and a flight jacket. Standing in a line with him, on one side of the pole, were Admirals Turner and Hill, and Generals Schmidt, Erskine, Cates, and Rockey. Major General Chaney represented the Army.

In a line facing them were twenty-four enlisted men, the guard of honor, eight men from each division, under First Lieutenant Nathan R. Smith of Whitehaven, Pennsylvania. Their dungarees were clean, but badly worn.

Colonel Davis H. Stafford of Spokane, Washington, representing

VAC, stepped forward and began to read:

"I, Chester William Nimitz, Fleet Admiral, United States Navy, Commander in Chief of the United States Pacific Fleet and Pacific Ocean Areas, do hereby proclaim as follows:

"United States forces under my command have occupied this and other of the Volcano Islands. All powers of government of the Japanese Empire in these islands so occupied are hereby suspended. All powers of government are vested in me as military governor and will be exercised by subordinate commanders under my direction...."

As the reading went on, Private First Class Nello L. Biagini, twenty-eight, of Charleroi, Pennsylvania, looked beyond the Colonel, watching a tableau of two Marines carrying a third on a stretcher. As they arrived in front of a tent hospital, the bearers set down the litter and silently collapsed at either end of the poles – three men, spent.

And the reading went on:

"All persons will obey promptly all orders given under my authority. Offenses against the forces of occupation will be severely punished.

"Given under my hand at Iwo Jima this fourteenth day of March, 1945."

Corporal Jim Francheschini, twenty-two, of Charlestown, Indiana, brought his mind back to attention. He had been thinking of the cemetery down the road. As he had passed it, a burial service was in progress, and he was sad.

Private First Class Thomas J. Casale, twenty, of Herkimer, New York, walked to the pole, an 80-foot staff raised on the top of a Japanese bunker. With him went Private First Class Albert B. Bush, twenty-four, of Cleveland, Ohio, and Private First Class Anthony C. Yusty of Port Chester, New York – one to hold the flag, the other to attach it to the shrouds.

Field Musician First Class John E. Glynn, twenty-one, of New Orleans (he lived, ironically, on Humanity Street) was nervous and his mouth was dry. But the notes of Colors came from his bugle, and Casale began to raise the flag.

All present saluted, and the area fell silent. Men nearby stopped working, or walking, or speaking. Far to the north, there was a plume of black smoke in the sky, and off to the left a 105 cracked, firing north. The flag snapped to the top, and as it did, another flag came down, the one on top of Suribachi.

The ceremony was over, and there was little talk. The men just walked away, general and private. General Smith, his eyes wet, remarked to his aide: "This was the toughest yet."

At almost the same hour, in a cave far to the north, General Kuribayashi was listening to the voices of schoolchildren singing the "Song of Iwo Defense." It was a special broadcast from Tokyo for the Iwo Jima garrison, and it ended with prayers for victory by boys and girls from Kuribayashi's birthplace. He ordered a message of thanks sent to the people of Japan.

The next day, Airfield No. 2 was put in use. The runways were not paved or even finished, but they were usable, and some Seabee brass came up from Guam and rode up to the top of Suribachi on a bulldozer.

A 4,000-barrel tank farm for aviation gas was completed Friday, and Fifth Division carpenters began building crates to ship the division's equipment home. By that time, the division had lost 89 officers killed and 1,933 enlisted men, and its combat efficiency was rated at 30 percent.

More Japanese were surrendering or being captured every day. First Lieutenant Toru Nishiwaki and Second Lieutenant Masao Azuma walked out in front of Hill 362C on Friday, with their orderlies, and gave their swords to a couple of Third Division officers, Captain E. W. Foote and Lieutenant Lawrence C. Vincent of the 9th Regiment. Sergeant Juichi Saijo was finally able to surrender. Three shots whizzed by him before a Marine noncom yelled "Knock it off," and Saijo was safe. He had been wounded twice and was hungry and thirsty, and he had heard the propaganda appeals. He would have given up sooner, but did not like the order to disrobe. Now he had no choice. He knew something about the United States; his father had worked for a telephone company in Los Angeles for fifteen years. Saijo said there was nothing left of his outfit, 3rd Platoon, Machine Gun Company, 314th Independent Infantry Battalion. It had started out with four heavy machine guns, two 25-mm. Navy anti-aircraft guns, and 30 rifles.

In the afternoon, General Cates dedicated the Fourth Division Cemetery "to the memory of 1,806 of our loved comrades who have paid the supreme sacrifice." Off to the side, men were still putting the last coat of white on some of the crosses, and it was becoming a beautiful cemetery, as Captain Nutting had hoped. The Third Division Cemetery was alongside it, and on the other side of the airfield was the Fifth Division Cemetery, getting fuller every day.

"No words of mine can properly express the homage due these fallen heroes," General Cates went on, "but I can assure you and also their loved ones that we will carry their banner forward. They truly died that we might live, and we will not forget. May their souls rest in peace."

At 6 P.M. that day Iwo Jima was declared officially secure, the battle officially over after twenty-six days and nine hours. The Fifth Division had 134 casualties that day and faced ten more days of fighting.

That night, 307 B-29's dropped 2,355 tons of fire bombs on Kobe. They had to use the older thermite type, because all the newer and better oil fire bombs had been used up on other cities. But they caused havoc – 2,669 people killed, 11, 289 injured, 242,000 homeless, 66,000 houses destroyed in Japan's sixth largest city. Admiral Mitscher messaged General Le May: "We are proud to operate in the same area with a force which can do as much damage to the enemy as your force is consistently doing. May your targets always flame." Thirteen crippled B-29's landed at Iwo Jima, and the Seabees hardly looked up from their work. Le May said: "Iwo Jima is really making the job easier."

Admiral Nimitz issued a special press release to mark the end of the Iwo Jima campaign. He disclosed that the Marines had suffered 4,189 killed in action and a total of 19,938 casualties, making it the costliest battle in 168 years of Marine Corps history. He praised all arms of the service, particularly the Marines, and concluded with a phrase now famous in the Corps:

"Among the Americans who served on Iwo island, uncommon valor was a common virtue."

That night there was a wild celebration on Iwo Jima, but not because the campaign was officially over. A bored soldier (the Marines said it was an Army man) called over his walkie-talkie to a buddy nearby, "Germany has surrendered unconditionally." The frequency filtered into a truck where a Marine was copying news traffic from San Francisco, and in ten minutes the word was all over the island.

Firing broke out all over – rifles, flares, pyrotechnics of all kinds, even among the ships off the beach. Finally General Cates telephoned Harry Schmidt and said, "The only way you can stop this is a red alert." General Schmidt said he didn't have the authority, the Navy would have to do it.

Cates, a smile in his voice, said, "Surely there's something up there. You must be able to see at least one little plane."

Schmidt said no, so Cates gave the alarm. In two minutes the firing ceased. The Fifth Division hospital treated three casualties from "the German war," and there were certainly others. The bored soldier went to his commanding officer and said "Sir, I think I've done something wrong." At least that's the way the story goes.

General Holland Smith left Iwo Jima March 17. The campaign, his last, had been fully as hard as he had feared it would be. When he got to Pearl Harbor he said the loss of Iwo Jima had proved to the Japanese that "we can take any damn thing they've got.

"Watching the Marines cross that island reminded me of Pickett's charge at Gettysburg," the old warhorse said. "Mortar, artillery fire, and rockets fell among those troops, but they closed. In thirty-seven minutes after the first wave hit the beach we were on the southern end of the airfield. I say again, this was the toughest fight we have had so far.

"If there had been any question whether there would be a Marine Corps after the war, the battle of Iwo would assure there will always be a Marine Corps."

Secretary of War Henry L. Stimson

wrote to Secretary Forrestal: "My personal congratulations and the congratulations of the entire Army. The price has been heavy but the military value of Iwo Jima is inestimable. Its conquest has brought closer the day of our final victory in the Pacific."

The same day, Private First Class Shigeru Yoshida, twenty-two, finally surrendered. He had been terrified, because he had seen some Marines slash the ears from the bodies of his comrades, or pull their teeth with pliers, for the gold in them. Finally, he was exhausted from lack of food and water, and he walked out and gave up. Four other men came with him.

Some Fifth Division units began re-embarking on Sunday, March 18, and the next day the Fourth Division headquarters ashore closed. The Fourth Division sailed for Maui Monday, the 549th Night Fighter Squadron arrived, and the Fifth Division medical men spent the day tearing down their hospital. Leading Seaman Jinzo Horii surrendered at Kitano Point. He hadn't fought since D-Day, when his gun was smashed at Suribachi. The 147th Army Regiment arrived from New Caledonia, and the first Army truck, heavily loaded, was towed up Suribachi by bulldozers.

Major Lloyd E. Whitley, operations officer of the 531st Squadron was on his way to Airfield No. 2 by jeep with Captain William Benton to stand early alert. It was 4 A.M. on Monday morning, March 26, five weeks to the day from D-Day. Suddenly a Japanese ran across the road. Whitley stopped his jeep and fired his carbine.

At almost the same moment an outpost of Battery C, 506th Anti-Aircraft Battalion, challenged two Japanese walking south near the west coast, just above Airfield No. 2. In a short time there was general firing, and the last large battle of Iwo Jima was under way. Staff Sergeant Tom Hall of the 7th Air Force awoke in his tent. He had arrived only the day before and he was nervous. The crew chiefs and mechanics had told him of the strange noises on Iwo – muffled digging by Japanese trapped underneath them.

Hall heard gunfire and jerked upright. Someone near him said, "It's nothing. Probably just a couple of guards shooting each other. Happens every night." But the firing grew louder, and Hall recognized mortar fire and grenade bursts.

"██████, that's right in our area," someone shouted, and the tent was empty in a flash. At the end of the company street a man in bloody shorts was shouting, "The bastards! The dirty bastards! Hundreds of 'em." There were hundreds of them, and they were on a well-planned suicide raid. At least four Army outfits and the Fifth Division Pioneers were already overrun. Japanese were everywhere, coming out of holes in the ground, slashing tents, knifing sleeping airmen, throwing grenades. Many of the attackers had swords, others were armed with BAR's, M-1 rifles, Marine pistols, and even a bazooka.

In the darkness the fighting was confused and terrible. First Lieutenant Harry L. Martin of the 5th Pioneers organized a firing line in some foxholes near him and checked an onrush. He worked his way around forward to rescue some men and was wounded twice. Then he ran into a machine-gun pit, killed four Japanese with his pistol, and rallied his men to a charge, scattering the enemy. But the Japanese came back, wilder than ever, and overwhelmed Martin's position. He fell dead, the last Marine on Iwo Jima to win the Medal of Honor.

Two Seabees of the 90th Battalion were killed rushing into the fray, and the Japanese penetrated all the way to the Army's 38th Field Hospital, tearing out the telephone lines, slashing tents, and machine-gunning ambulances. Major Whitley, who had discovered the first moving enemy, was dead within a half hour, shot through the neck. Lieutenant Joe Coons, a fighter pilot, dived under a truck and emptied his .45 at a bunch of

Japanese. A bullet killed a pilot next to Coons. Another, running from his tent, grabbed a Japanese who was waving a sword and throttled him.

A Marine major came from somewhere, organized a skirmish line and began forcing the enemy back. Other Marines, aroused by the sounds of battle, joined him, and Army flame-thrower tanks came in.

Captain Robert J. Munro of the 5th Pioneers organized a fire line in the 21st Fighter Group area. His men were mostly Negroes who had never been in combat, but they fought now. Anybody with a weapon joined in – airmen, Seabees, Marines, Army medicos – and slowly the Japanese were driven back. When a detachment from the 147th Infantry arrived at 8 A.M., four hours after the alarm, the battle was over. Among the blood-spattered tents, 44 airmen were dead and 88 wounded. The 5th Pioneers lost 9 killed and 31 wounded. A total of 262 Japanese were killed, and 18 were taken alive. Rumors went around that Kuribayashi had led the raid, but his body was not among the dead.

The last high Japanese officer reported alive was Admiral Ichimaru. After the war a one-legged man named Iwamoto called on the admiral's widow. He said he was a survivor of Iwo Jima and was with the admiral on March 27 when he made a last charge with twenty men. Iwamoto said he had been hit by a shell and lost consciousness, and that when he came to he was a prisoner. He said he and other prisoners were threatened and cajoled to tell where the high officers were, but not a man would tell. Mrs. Ichimaru pictures her husband, sick, thin, and wasted – hobbling into final battle with cane or crutches, clutching his sword to the last. The sword, if taken as a souvenir, will show the name Tadahiro, a famed swordmaker, on the hilt.

On the same day as the Japanese raid, the last units of the Fifth Division came down from the hills. They stopped at the division cemetery and then went aboard ships. One hundred and seventy-seven men were left in the 2nd Battalion, 28th Regiment, which had taken Suribachi. It had gone into battle reinforced to 1,400 men and had received 288 replacements during the campaign. Of the 177 left, one-third had been wounded. On the other side of the line, Jumpin' Joe Chambers' battalion, which had seized the Quarry on D-Day, left the island with 150 men. The other 750 of the original 900 men were dead, missing, or wounded.

When Private Johnny Lane got to the beach for the last time, he again saw Minor Dalton, a Negro from Pennsylvania. They had first met on a transport, in the early days of the fighting, when both were doing mess duty and waiting for the 30th Replacement draft to be called in. It seemed another world ago now, and Minor Dalton said:

"How did you make out, little fella?"

"I'm alive," Lane replied.

Dalton said he had been working on

the beach, from the first day to the last. All that time, he said, the body of a Japanese soldier had lain nearby, half-buried in the sand.

"He didn't bother me, I didn't bother him, but the Army dug him up," Dalton said. He seemed, somehow, sad that the little brown man had been taken away.

Private Lane said good-bye and climbed into a boat to be taken out to a transport. It was over.

By early April, 7,000 Seabees were at work on Iwo Jima. Working ten-hour shifts, seven days a week, they were moving 3 million yards of earth, leveling the Motoyama central plateau for a giant aerodrome. The central airfield had a main runway 10,000 feet long, the longest in the Pacific, and Airfield No. 1's main runway was 6,400 feet. Gone were Hill 382, and Charlie-Dog Ridge, and the beaches were hardly recognizable. Housing, tank farms, breakwaters, and finger piers went in. Twenty miles of roads, runways, and hardstands were paved. Rock-crushers and hot asphalt plants, drilling rigs and pumping stations appeared; trucks and bulldozers buried the island in smoke and dust, mashed it down, rolled it out and paved it. Iwo Jima was becoming what the Marines had been told it would be, a great, solid-rock airfield.

The sand, first bound with blood, was now bound with sea-water, asphalt, and sweat. The cost, once reckoned in lives, was totaled in terms of square yards of paving, tons of rock crushed, loads of asphalt delivered. But no one forgot the real cost.

"This," said the Seabee boss, Captain Johnson, "is the most expensive piece of real estate the United States has ever purchased. We paid 550 lives and 2,500 wounded for every square mile of this rock. Pretty expensive."

Land-based fighters from Iwo Jima accompanied the B-29's to Japan on April 7, for the first time. Nearly every day the island rescued crippled bombers. On June 7, 102 B-29's landed on Iwo

Jima, and on July 24, 186 of the giant planes came in to the island. By the end of the war, 2,400 B-29's with 27,000 crewmen had used the Iwo Jima airfields. Not all of these men would have been lost had the island not been in American hands, but Admiral King's final report said that lives saved "exceeded lives lost in the capture of the island itself."

Two months after D-Day, E. B. Hadfield visited Iwo Jima and wrote for the Mid-Pacifican:

"April 17, and spring is coming to Iwo Jima too. The desolate rock has not blossomed into a riot of color, but here and there heavy spring rains are bringing out sparse grass, buds on broken trees, even a few flowers.

"In the heavy volcanic ash extending from Mt. Suribachi half way up the island, big clumps of coarse, shining Johnson grass have already pushed ten inches out of the black, shifting grit where the Marines struggled for footing.

"In some shady spots a small plant

with heart-shaped leaves similar to the violet is displaying its scentless blossoms and a low shrub is covered with delicate pink and rose leaves.

"One solitary hibiscus stands full of startling bright red blossoms in the middle of what once was the Japanese hospital in Higashi village.

"But not all is spring. Up a draw over a ridge from Higashi, where yesterday four Japs were killed, 16 more surrendered, and still others are holed up, the giant limbs of the remaining trees are a hideous mockery of the season.

"Great blue flies cling to those broken limbs, so numerous and so close they almost touch. They don't hover or buzz. They just cling. Brushing a limb barely starts them. They just cling, surfeited.

"The dead limbs and the lethargic flies resemble great sprigs of evil, black pussywillow. Rising among the grim rocks of the canyon, the whole scene is one huge, grotesque parody of a Japanese flower arrangement."

Later in April the American soldiers

finally discovered the 2nd Mixed Brigade Field Hospital, nearly 100 feet underground in the eastern part of the island. A language officer appealed to the Japanese to come out. After a long discussion, a senior medical officer, Major Masaru Inaoka, called for a vote. The ballot turned out sixty-nine for surrender, 3 opposed. Of the three nays, Corporal Kyutaro Kojima immediately committed suicide. The others came out, including two more medical officers, Captain Iwao Noguchi and Lieutenant Hideo Ota. Captain Noguchi, beset by remorse that he had lived while so many had died, later emigrated to Brazil, unable to accept life in Japan.

On the last day of the month, Private Lane, now in Hawaii, wrote to his mother:

"Just a few lines to let you and Pop know the Christmas package arrived last night. Although it had been in the mail since November the package was in excellent condition. Everything was swell and none of it is left now, except the chocolate powder and the bouillon."

The Fourth Division insignia at the top of the letter had been changed. On the fourth side of the square a new name had been added to Roi-Namur, Saipan, Tinian. It was Iwo Jima.

The war ended, and now it was ten days before Christmas, 1945. There was a cold wind and a hint of snow when the train pulled into the station. Tony Stein was coming home. Doug Jacobson, who had also won the Medal of Honor at Iwo Jima, was with the body. All flags in North Dayton, Ohio, were at half-staff as the casket was drawn through the streets on an ammunition trailer.

Tony's wife, Joan, was there, and his mother, Rose, and many friends. Tony had gone to Kiser High School, and he'd done a lot of things – pin boy, softball, caddying, a little boxing in the Golden Gloves, a hitch at CCC Camp. He knew a lot of people, and they liked him. His hair was curly, and his eyes a very strong gray, but pleasant. Joan had last seen him in July, 1944, when she had left him in California after a three-day honeymoon. He had been going back, for a second time, to join the new Fifth Division, and he was not too unhappy. He liked combat.

They took the casket to Our Lady of Rosary Church, and there was a solemn high requiem mass. Then he was buried in Calvary Cemetery, the end of a journey. His mother knew all these things about him, and she was not surprised. "Tony always had to be doing things, hard things," she said. "That's why he just had to be in the Marines. He wanted to see if he could do it."

He could.

The publishers hope that this book has given you enjoyable reading. Large Print Books are specially designed to be as easy to see and hold as possible. If you wish a complete list of our books, please ask at your local library or write directly to: John Curley & Associates, Inc. P.O. Box 37, South Yarmouth Massachusetts, 02664